Tharon Ann

From Orphan, to Actress, to Mother, to Seeker

by Jennifer Brookins

© 2014 Willow Grove Press
Princeton, New Jersey

ISBN-13: 978-0692239964
ISBN-10: 0692239960

All rights reserved.

Title page photograph: Doug Brookins
Back page photograph: Doug Brookins
Cover Design by: Web Design by Trisha

Includes bibliographical references.

Dedicated to

Doug Brookins

Table of Contents

Note to the Reader i

Prologue 1

Part I: The Early Years

Anyone know where my folks are?	9
Mama – black as the ace of spades	10
I'm just a little girl from Little Rock	19
My Okie grandparents and them Cherokee Indians	46
Class of 55 – Little Rock Central High School	49
I'm mad at God, Thelma, Sam or whatever your name is	53

Part II: Show Biz Here I Come!

Hollywood, junkies and strip joints	57
Sex is an hors d'oeuvre in Hollywood	63
I love Lucy but what ever happened to Lucille Ball?	68
Ronald Reagan and me	71
Give my regards to Broadway	76
My big Broadway break	80
Marilyn Monroe and Arthur what's his name	86
Performing in Germany	89
Lovie'n me, hooting it up in Manhattan	92
Andy Warhol	95
Larry Rivers	98
Performing at the Spoleto Arts Festival in Italy	104
Nice meeting you Mr. Sperm Donor	107
I'm off to Spain – a movie for him, a niño for me	111
Saying goodbye isn't easy	117

Part III: A New Beginning

I'm back in East LA	125
Looking for Mary	138
Meeting an American mystic	141
It's the Sperm Donor check out time	152
Bye Bye Sperm Donor	154
Driving across country with two kids and one in the oven	157
Mommy! Our suitcase flew off the car again!	164
Welcome to the Garden State	168
Pull off the road, I'm having a baby!	174
Miracles do happen	178
I'm back in Manhattan where I belong	180
Manhattan epiphany	183
Standing on our own two feet	186
Miracles delivering newspapers	191
Meditating on a cake of ice	194
Please pass the fucking butter!	197
A precedent setting case	202
Boot camp	205
Moving on up	211
The best way to get praise is to die!	213

Part IV: My New Life

Remembering you	219
Laughter is the Best Recipe	226
Letting go	230
The Anurag Sagar (Ocean of Love)	236
Meeting Baba Ji	239
Born Anew	245
Will you marry me?	249
Come to India	254

Epilogue

Note to the Reader

How coincidental that the meaning of Tharon with an "A" as a boy's name, is a variant of Theron from the classical Greek meaning hunter, and that my own life would take on a hunt of its own. I was born in the Bible belt where our Baptist blankets told more yarns than the *Arkansas Gazette*. Most of us didn't know the first name of the Vice President, but we could reel off last week's line up at the Grand Old Opry. For someone like me born with the word "why" on my forehead, nothing made sense. Growing up as I did in the segregated south, I couldn't reconcile the racial bigotry I saw in churches with the teachings of Jesus. My personal journey began on the back row of a white church in Little Rock, Arkansas; the last two roped off for blacks only.

In 1955, I left my southern beginnings to chase dreams or at the very least, get my foot in the Hollywood door. Too naïve to be discouraged when it repeatedly slammed in my face, I never stopped trying. Always the square peg trying to fit in a round hole with another hurdle to overcome, another failure to cope with, I eventually did break into television and film, but not without the struggles that accompany success. My desire to be a respected actress eventually led me to New York where I won the World Theatre Award for best actress in the 1964 Obie award winning off Broadway play, *The Dutchman* by LeRoi Jones. Yet through it all, I continued to search for something to give my life purpose, but that answer always eluded me. I threw myself into all the pleasures the world had to offer which left me feeling like the only enlightenment I would ever experience was not eating ice cream too fast and getting brain freeze.

In 1971, personal circumstances forced me to give up my career to raise our children as a single mother. Leaving show business far behind, the kids and I began a new life by driving across America in my old Chevy, our large suitcase tied to the top, little money, and clueless as to what the future offered. During those years I became a seeker. I wanted to know the truth for me. That is all. My journey never included judging others or their beliefs. I wasn't looking to save the whales, only myself.

Years later when I was in the kitchen practicing the fine art of recycling leftovers, a close friend walked in, leaned into my skillet, and nonchalantly offered the suggestion that I write a book about my life. I hardly looked up as the mere thought of it was too ludicrous to acknowledge. In a salty tone I replied, "Before dinner or after?" Writing a book was never on my bucket list but after weeks of nudging, I began to write the first chapter that quickly resulted in a wastebasket filled with crumpled pages. Then came the great epiphany, that I should write about my own incredulous life rather than figments of my imagination. Armed with enthusiastic resolve, I was good to go. "It's a no brainer," I told myself, "I can knock this out in three months."

Did I say three months? Talk about your writer's block. In the beginning it was uphill all the way; the voice in the first chapter was aloof, stilted and detached. Worse still, I hit roadblocks every step of the way by omitting most of my childhood, remembering very little of my career as an actress and even less about my life in general. I had forgotten it. Imagine. In fact, I wondered where it had gone since I couldn't remember it. The first draft was only twenty pages – hardly enough for a book. I felt like the oldest woman with the worst case of memory loss still alive on earth.

Four years later, after many awe inspiring trips to India this book has arrived alive and kicking as *Tharon Ann*. It is written in first person just as it happened, when every forgotten life sequence began to slowly unfold in the writing of it. In addition, each phase of my life carries with it four distinct voices with different tones and vocabularies: first, as a spunky child speaking a colloquial southern dialect who experiences both the pain of being orphaned along with the joyous perspectives of childhood, then as a witty, ambitious young actress climbing the show business ladder to success. Just as my career began to fall in place, the events of my personal life so drastically changed, I was forced to relinquish everything I had worked so long to attain in order to raise my family. The third voice reflects the humor as well as the struggles of a single mom trying to raise three sons, which segues into the fourth, richest part of my life. It speaks to meeting a mystic friend, along with the highs and lows of finding resolution.

No matter the struggles I have always seen the comedy of errors, the incongruity of me klutzing through life in an upside down world. Laughter, mostly about myself, has taught me never to give up. Thank God for that beautiful sixth sense – a sense of humor.

Note: With some exceptions, I have changed the names of most people I've met through life's journey simply for the sake of privacy.

Tharon Ann

From Orphan, to Actress, to Mother, to Seeker

Prologue:
Time douches the bloom off a cheating rose

I've gone from a scrappy kid wondering when I'd get to China digging a hole in the backyard with a spoon, to being a Hollywood starlet, then to Broadway and the highlife, to the present. I'm a very pregnant crazy lady with two little kids and ten hours out from a long, hot cross country drive across America in my old Chevy. I can't sleep for all the memories running through my head. If there was ever a time for a mind boggling quote from Dylan or a sobering passage from *Moby Dick*, that rambling classic with a point I never quite grabbed by the tail – this is it. Oh, and just in case I forget to mention it, with so much going on and all, my future looks like zip, and what really happened to J.D. Salinger?

The big day is here. Insomnia is driving my mind nuclear reliving every piece of minutia from my birth to the present. It's 3:00 a.m. and I can't sleep. I've cried so much, I'm alarmed at the amount of snot one person can lie in without being glued to the pillow. How did it all come to this? Seems like only yesterday, I was a rising Broadway actress with successes under my belt. I can still hear the knock on my dressing room door, the stage manager giving me the last call, "Showtime Jennifer! It's a packed house tonight." As usual, I'm so terrified before going on, I can't remember the first line. But the moment I step onstage, my jitters long gone, I vanish into character and I'm fine. It's make believe time. The thrill of playing before a live audience is better than dope.

I'll be driving straight through the Mojave Desert from LA to New Jersey, no doubt my three year old kicking the back of my seat all the way asking, "Are we there yet? Mommy, I have to go." If

Romie kicks hard enough, with my luck I'll go into labor and have this baby next to a cactus. I can't sleep for stressing over the future – no husband, no money, no job, bills to pay and three kids to raise. How will I do it? All these years I've supported myself as an actress. What am I supposed to do – squat on the sidewalk and sell pencils out of a shoebox? My choice is either fall back into my old, destructive ways or wrap myself around a future I know nothing of. Being clueless at thirty is a bitch.

Why cry over the "Sperm Donor?" He makes love like shoveling spaghetti with both hands. Lots of women have husbands who cheat. You could monitor how often they drop their pants by putting a metronome up their ass. They don't fall apart like me. The ones I know marry wealthy men, and find it convenient to ignore their over active libidos. They compensate by shopping on Rodeo Drive until they pass out, then to spring shows in Paris, then to Milan, having affairs along the way, and thanking God for revolving credit. For some men, the more submissive the wife and mother, the less appealing she is as a woman; the sexual attraction and challenge no longer exists. Like a hound chasing a fox: hound chases fox, hound catches fox, hound kills fox, hound hunts for another fox. The Sperm Donor is never home. I doubt he even knows how fast the kids are growing.

I closed our joint bank account today. What I took is barely enough for this trip, the hospital bill and rent for a small apartment once we arrive in New Jersey. That's *if* we make it to New Jersey. Just saying those two words makes me run for Imodium, and what's wrong with me? I always make the same mistake – jump first, and look afterwards.

I'm home late tonight. I worked overtime on a *Gunsmoke*. Thanks to Arness it took forever to hear, "It's a wrap!" This house looks like a tornado just passed through, popcorn all over the floor, the kids eating Wheaties out of a box, and our latest addition, my husband's five year old from a previous marriage racing from room to room wearing a Batman cape, his school uniform still not washed for tomorrow. The Sperm Donor is sprawled out on the couch watching *Mod Squad*, oblivious of the circus going on in front of him. Working all day, then coming home to a nightmare like this would push anyone over the edge. Some things never change. I shift to high,

Prologue

make dinner, wash and iron Willie's uniform for tomorrow, and do a quick tidy-up. Afterwards, I bathe the boys and tuck them in for the night, knowing full well they won't go to sleep unless I read to them. I sit on the edge of the bed, and begin the next chapter of *Wind In the Willows.* They love the Badger.

I still have ten pages of new dialogue to memorize for tomorrow, get five hours of sleep, be at the studio at 6:00 a.m. in makeup, and pray to God I don't have bags down to the floor. I can't keep up this pace. If I don't step back from my career our homelife will be in worse shape than now. There's not enough room for two careers in this family. Let him have it. It's what he wants.

Something is wrong.

How long does it take to answer a simple question, and what's wrong with me that I can't confront him? The two of us stand in this small kitchen that looks out over the mountain, his back facing me as he pours himself a second cup of coffee when I finally say, "You leave mornings, and don't come home until dawn."

Moments of silence pass. He continues to sip his coffee and stare down at the floor before he finally turns around, his dark eyes focused into mine and replies matter-of-factly, "I don't love you anymore. I'm done."

My response is frozen in silence that so reverberates in my ears that I'm deafened to its clamor. My breath pushes me to smart-ass, flippant silent retorts, "You're done? What about me and the kids? Are we done too? When you leave the house each morning, I make you a brown-bag lunch with fresh banana bread sandwiches, the crusts cut off the way you like. My paycheck goes to you after every job. I've all but given up my career for you. We have two children, another on the way, and now you say you're done?" I listen to my unspoken thoughts coming through this mealy-mouthed person I hardly recognize. I'm unable to speak because there are no words left to come right out and say, "How many hours can one man spend at the Actor's Studio? I know damn well what you're doing and who you're doing it with."

The Sperm Donor wastes no time describing his passionate feelings for her, and the futility of living one more second trapped in a loveless marriage. He talks to me like I'm not in the room, and explains in great detail how good it is to finally let it all out, that he's not the type man to live in shadows. I can't catch my breath ... I'll stop breathing if he doesn't shut up. Still unable to speak, I grab both kids by their hands and run along the narrow, weathered path alongside Aunt Lowee's house, a brick missing here and there, the smell of Eucalyptus guiding me like a silent friend to the top of the mountain that overlooks dark clouds of gray smog hovering over East Los Angeles. I can't stop crying for the uncertainty of our future, for having wasted so much of my life, for the baby growing inside me, and for Willie, his five year old son who just came to live with us and misses his grandparents.

Several weeks ago, he mumbled something about a new project he was working on with some actress at the Actor's Studio West. When I asked about her, he casually mentioned a name I immediately recognized. The exact same feelings of rage and jealousy welled up in me again, precisely the same as I had experienced twelve years ago. As soon as I heard her name, I knew I'd lost him ... and remembered the first time I saw her face.

Twelve years earlier in Hollywood, long before I moved to New York and met the Sperm Donor, a friend gave me an article he'd cut out of the newspaper about a beautiful actress who worked in Elvis Presley films, as well as B-movies. It showed her photograph along with details of a large sum of money she inherited. It wasn't the money. It was the recognition of her face that filled me with jealousy, feelings out of proportion to the situation. So many times I've asked myself why I reacted like that to someone I didn't know. She looked like every other starlet in Hollywood, as opposed to me who was somewhat offbeat compared to the Barbie Doll look of the sixties. I threw the paper back and snapped, "This has nothing to do with me." Ironically, as quickly as those feelings of anger entered my psyche, that's how fast they left. That incident still puzzles me. Perhaps my reaction was a premonition of events to come – although I'm not into crystal gazers, psychics, telemarkers hawking spirituality, fake gurus and all the other scams to support their mansions. What difference does it make now?

I'm beginning to sound like those women in supermarket tabloids next to the check-out. If it's a long wait, I'll take one off the rack and give it a quick look. If I read about one more female who attempts suicide over a failed marriage, I'll pull the plug on myself. I can't stand whiners yet much as I hate to admit it, that's what I've become.

"Yeah you are, so shut up!"

Prologue

"I'm not. Am I?"
"Does a bear pee in the woods?
"What kind of man abandons a pregnant wife and two kids?"
"The one you married stupid, now shut the hell up!"
"How will we live? I have no money."
"Stop watching *As the World Turns.*"

It's as though two people live inside me. One like sand in an hour glass, moment by moment drained of self-worth, crawling through each day begging to be punished for everything I've ever done in my life. But the other more predominant one is a hard-edged, spirited fighter who laughs her way out of every impossible predicament.

Dammit, I may cry, I may bitch but I won't fall under the train. There's got to be more to life than getting married and having babies – even a career. I remember having a close friendship with a powerful presence as a child, but somewhere along the way I lost it and I don't know why. I'm fighting for my life, for that lost girl I only vaguely remember; one buried so deep, I fear she may never be resurrected. I fight not to fall into the depths of a mental abyss so intense, I might never recover; the ugly face of ambition rides me like a horse frothing at the mouth. Three lives depend upon rising from this quagmire of self-loathing to reinvent the person I began life with. I still talk to a God I can't see, and I still can't shut up. I know there is something powerful in me, something outside myself, otherwise how could I have survived the past thirty years?

Where's my damn tissue? Blowing my nose is the only constant in my life. I always feel secure in one good blow on anything outside of my Hermès, God forbid.

Dear God, Dorothy, Sam or whatever your name is,

May I shake your hand for giving us Oil of Olay and Kleenex, or do you prefer Puffs? Store brand? And the big winner hands down is ... ta dah: Puffs!

Sincerely lost in East LA
P.S: Need sleep fast

Part I

The Early Years

Anyone know where my folks are?

I am here, Mother. Over here. Lay your hand on me ... here. Can you feel me now?

Father thinks it's a good day for a drive in the mountains to help a farmer who just telephoned, begging him to come see what ails his sick pig. Afterwards just the three of them, Uncle Willie and Uncle Zack will stop for a barbecue and a beer. No one says what the others think, that sometimes it's good to get out of the house on a little outing with just each other. My two uncles are here for the sole purpose of keeping my father company. Suddenly without warning, a drunk truck driver runs my father's car off an Ozark Mountain. He is killed instantly. His name was Tharon Albert; he lived for thirty one years. Uncle Willie says his engraved gold pocket watch stopped when he died. I don't know what happened to it – lost I guess, along with other memorabilia with meaning only to those left behind. This tragedy occurred three months before my birth. Mother's name is Haldane.

I'm born into this world on September 22, 1937, three months after my father died in a car accident. They say he was a County Agent, one of the first to teach farmers in this backwoods area how to best use their land by switching to conservation plowing, and crop rotation. A small town nearby was named for him. I don't know much more than that. Not long after someone, and I can't remember his face, or even the color of his shirt, drives us to a house where my mother's sister lives on West Tenth Street in Little Rock with her husband. Her name is Lowee.

Mama – black as the ace of spades
My perspectives: ages 4 - 12

Haldane is antsy to get back to work, away from me I reckon. She got to find someone to look after me. Today, when Aunt Lowee in Hudson's Market payin the bill for all the food we gots on credit, she spots an envelope with a name'n address scribbled on the back. It's tacked on Mr. Hudson's bulletin board near his cash register. Must be some neighborhood woman lookin for work. Aunt Lowee jots down the address, then starts walkin round the corner, past rows of houses where colored folks live, some sittin outdoors on the porch steps. Poor Aunt Lowee. She walkin so fast the heel on her shoe falls off again – don't matter none cuz ever one round here goes barefoot in the summer. Aunt Lowee don't want to meet her with one shoe on'n one shoe off. She wants to make a nice first how d'you do.

The woman lives on a street for colored folks only, in a little house with a victory garden in the front yard. Ever row of tomatoes, okra, corn'n collard greens, gots pretty red, white'n blue streamers showin her support for the soldier boys in the war. Soons she opens up the door, Aunt Lowee, still standin outdoors, beads'a sweat rollin down her face from the summer heat, tells the woman all bout me, tells her what Haldane wants. Flies buzzin round so the colored woman careful to keep the door shut so's not to let flies in the house. She already swatted one that still gots fly mess smushed all over the screen door.

The colored woman tells Aunt Lowee, the white woman she been workin for, passed last week. She not sure what she passed from, she just passed'n that's why she put the note on Mr. Hudson's bulletin board. She invites Aunt Lowee to please come indoors for a glass of ice cold lemonade, but Aunt Lowee say no thank you. She politely explains how important it is for her to get home lickety split'n her sayin, that even though she sure would love to have some lemonade, it's more important to get home. She caint hardly wait to tell Haldane bout this colored woman.

When Aunt Lowee gets back home, hot, perspirin'n barefoot, Haldane already here. When she tells her bout the woman, Haldane don't waste time none. She goes to see her this very day. She hires her'n on the way home, she probly jumps right outta her lace drawers runnin up the hill jus thinkin of finally gettin out of the house away from me.

Haldane left home early this mornin cuz it's her first day at work. Aunt Lowee gonna show the colored woman to me. I hear knockin on the back door. Aunt Lowee invitin her to come in to have a glass of fresh lemonade'n sayin for her to sit at the kitchen table'n take a load off. All the while Aunt Lowee talkin'n squeezin lemons, I'm lookin inside this colored woman, so I don't hear none what she sayin. It's real hot outdoors. Lemonade tastes good after the long walk uphill from Hudson's market to our place. But she more interested in the chigger bites on my legs, than sittin down at the table drinkin lemonade. She takin one long look at me. I'm sizin her up too. She gots titties big as watermelons'n skin so black, it glows in the dark. I can see my face in her cheeks, if I get close up. She gots a pocketbook with all kinda things. I'm want'n to turn it upside down'n see what in it. That what I'm gonna do. I wish they'd drink more lemonade so I can take a look. If I had a pocketbook, I'd put my rocks in it. I like her blue dress'n white apron. Oh'n the feather in her hat, I feel like sneezin on it, ah choo, it makin my nose tickle. It fly away when I sneeze. I love feathers ... so do Aunt Lowee; she collects pigeon feathers from outdoors'n sticks'um in Grapette soda bottles; that how she decorates the kitchen window sill.

The big colored woman walks over'n lifts me up in her arms. She kiss me with her big juicy lips – they smellin jus like garden strawberries. When she do this, I trace her face with my finger; I can see me in her black shiny cheeks'n press mine next to hers to find out what colored folks skin feel like. It very soft; oh, you cheek smells good, jus like peaches, like a real Mama. No, don't wanna get down ... don't put me down. I wrap my legs tight round her waist so she caint put me down. She does anyways after givin me a swat on my behind. I don't know her name. I'll call her Mama. She gonna teach me cuz that what a Mama does. She won't let Haldane hurt me no more.

Tharon Ann

Mama gots her hands full, due to my affection for doin the opposite to what my mother says – like gettin in her jewelry box'n paintin bunnies on her linens with her red fingernail polish. I love to run'n weave, run'n weave ... in'n out rows of fluffy sheets hangin in the fresh air, ever sheet holdin on to the next by one little clothespin. I smell sunshine in the pillow case when I lay my head down at night. Sheets is my best friend, la la la la la ... sheets is my best friend ... la la la la la sheets is whisperin in my ears to draw pictures on'um ....la la la la la ... if I get in trouble ... it they fault for lettin me play with'um ... la la la la la.

I try hard to get her attention. Only time Haldane talks to me is when I'm bad. Today she walks through the front door from work, same time I'm headin for her jewelry box. Mother sees me'n faster'n you can say jack rabbit, she headin my way. She slap me hard on my hand. It hurts. I can tell by her face, Mama don't like the way she treats me, but what can a Mama do? Haldane turns away, but I got my mind set on openin the box'n, once again, she slap my hand harder still. This gonna go on til she kills me if Mama don't do somethin. She pick me up in her arms real quick like'n turns to Haldane sayin, "Dat nuff Miss Haldane – dat nuff!" If Mama hadn't did that, she might'a beat me to death, cuz I make my mother real mad, but I not never givin up ... not never. Mama say, "Chile, if you doesn't behave you little bad self, you Mama gonna tie you leg to dat bed post!" Sometimes she do – but I wiggle out.

When evenin rolls round'n Southern katydids chirp all together, the wind caint help itself'n blows sweet honeysuckle through the bedroom window, that's when I always climb on her lap. My head finds a restin place on her big, fluffy bosoms, a signal to rock me in her arms. Ever single night Mama sing Mister Chuck Willis song til I'm tuckered out. I try'n sing like Miss Bessie Smith, same as Mama teach me. I wish my skin purty like hers.

See see Rider,
See what you done done,
Made me love you,
Now yo Mama gone

When Mama go food shoppin, I come with her on accounta me'n her always together. Soons we board the bus, the driver looks at me sayin, "Baby girl, you gots to sit in front'a the bus with them other white folks. That nigger woman you with gotta go to the back of the bus with the rest of them niggers." I pay him no mind, instead I run to the back'a the bus'n sit on Mama's lap for the whole ride, matchin stares with whites who is shootin ugly looks at me for sittin in the colored section. If I was black like Mama, none'a this would happen. It all my fault.

Can you hear me Mister God? Is they two heavens – Jim Crow heaven for colored folks'n a different one for whites?

When me'n Mama is ridin on the bus one day, I look across the aisle to see a woman wearin a nurse uniform sittin by the window. She wearin a blue cape with shiny medals'n a hat like the kind soldier boys wear in the movies. The man sittin beside her keeps pattin her mouth, so she don't make a mess. Look to me like she gots spit runnin down her chin. I don't know what to make of it. Durin the bus ride, folks turnin they heads ever which way starin'n laughin ever time the man pats her mouth. I guess he gots enough of them bus people cuz all of a sudden the man stands up'n turns round. He explainin to the bus people, the woman sittin in the seat next to him worked for the Red Cross durin the war, that she was in a Japanese concentration camp'n they cut her tongue out. He tells the bus people he pats her mouth so dribbles don't get on her uniform. He's tryin real hard to protect her from gettin her feelins hurt, but they hurt anyways. When he stops talkin, he pulls the cord to let the driver know they wantin to get off. Ever one is real quiet when the man helps the woman to the front of the bus; they lookin straight ahead, not lookin to the left or to the right, not sayin nothin when they get off. No one looks'um in the eye. The bus people keep starin at'um through the window, some lookin down at they laps in shame. I dream bout that nurse. I pray Jesus give her a new tongue.

Mister God, how come you let them cut out her tongue? I don't want to be nothin like the bus people.

I love goin to church with Mama, but I caint figure out in my head why, if she thirsty, she got to use a different water fountain. She caint go to the white church, she caint go inside the cafeteria, she caint come in the front door to our house. Separate schools, separate churchs – separate ever thing for folks like Mama. They even Jim Crow in white families that's poor as dirt daubers, where colored folks take care of they children. If they trust someone enough to take care of they kids, why don't they trust'um to drink from the same water fountain? This don't make sense to me. It jus don't.

Any color'a folks is welcome in Mama's church. We have fun dancin in the aisle when they sing, *What a Friend I Gots in Jesus*. Mama say I'm the only white ever come here. She teachin me how to clap my hands'n sing gospel songs, keepin time while we clap'n sing together. They times I get carried away when me'n Tessie dance in the aisle with the grown ups. Mama laughs til tears roll down her face'n her best Sunday hat falls off. Mama jus laugh and say,

"Chile, best you don be singin'n hoppin round like dat in dem white folk's church cuz iffn you does, dey be callin you lil nappy head girl. I'm givin Tessie'a wupin for teachin you be talkin like a colored girl."

I'm feelin right at home with Tessie, her bein one of Mama's grandkids'n all. We best friends'n always play together. Right from the start, we love each other, not mindful of black'n white. Mama say we be lovey dovey cuz Lord made both'a us outta piss'n vinegar. One Sunday, her'n me gets into it over which ones turn it is to be swingin inside the sixteen-wheeler tire hangin on the Oak tree behind Mama's church by a long rope. Tessie start shoutin at me like I don't gots ears, "You cheatin little nigger, it's my turn!" I'm not bout to let that girl get away with this when she know in her cheater's heart it my turn.

I flip right back at her screamin at the top of my lungs, "No, you cheatin little nigger! My turn!"

Ever one within ten miles hearin us scream "nigger!" "nigger!" "nigger!" back'n forth til Mama'n the other church women come runnin out from choir practice to give us both a lickin. Me'n her still mad as hops'n don't look at each other. They sit us down then all together, like the Hallelujah Chorus with an "amen" throwd in, they says how "nigger" a very bad word. Mama say if she catch us sayin it again, she gonna stand us in the corner for ten years. She say folks who says that word don't deserve a best friend. Mama make us face a tree for an hour with both hands behind our backs, cuz we both so bad sayin "nigger." I swear. After five minutes or so, she start to feel sorry for us. Mama say time up.

Me'n Tessie already forgot why we argued in the first place. We laugh'n hug each other as Mama lifts us up in her big arms'n carries us back to the oak tree, where she crams our tail ends back into the sixteen-wheeler tire. We take each others hand'n swing back'n forth holdin onto the tire'n each other for what seem like forever. I take my

Cherokee Indian arrowhead outta my coveralls, the one my grandpa gave me for good luck'n I give it to Tessie so she always be rememberin me – forever like. She takes a wad of gum outta her mouth'n gives it to me to finish chewin so I can still taste the juicy fruit. All the while, Mama jus standin there laughin with her hands on her big hips. I notice for the first time how white her teeth is. I say, "Mama, how come you got pearly whites?"

Mama say, "If you black as me, you teeth be pearly white too. But the main reason dey like dis, is cuz you Mama don't picks round her food like you does. I thank the Lord'n eats'n dat's why I gots pearly whites'n you doesn't!"

Another thing bout Mama is she uses ever occasion, ever question, ever answer, ever birth'n someone's funeral to drive home the smallest point. With these final words outta her mouth, she turn round'n heads back to church, her big tail end swingin from one side to the other like someone beatin on a tub fulla fat back. But the minute she outta sight, Tessie laughs'n whispers in my ear, "You still a little nigger'n Jesus knows I'm right!"

I laugh'n whisper back in her ear, "You a little nigger too – Jesus told me so last night."

Not one to leave well enough alone, Tessie say, "Tharon Ann, what wrong with you hair – why you got them long pigtails when you ain't a pig. How come you hair not like mine? They chicken fat in the kitchen – let's do each other's hair then we be the same."

That girl already planned this out'n I didn't have sense enough to know it. If Tessie want to have her way, she always be sayin like she recitin the Golden Rule, "Tharon Ann, ain't no grass growin under my feet!" Shoot fire. I wonder where that girl heard that.

I shoot right back at her, "Some people best get outta bed real early to pull wool over my eyes!" But what her and me agree on is once the deeds done, we both gonna look the same. I whisper, "If Mama hear us say "nigger" again, we in big trouble. Let's talk pig latin." But Tessie don't like nothin with pig in it; she won't talk it with me cuz she don't like the way pigs oink. She say we gotta go with her idea'n say "nigger" backwards – then no one gonna know. So "little nigger" becomes "elttil reggin." That what we start callin each other – "reggin" for short.

"When I howl like a coon dog, it mean Mama close by'n you gots to hide the evidence quick. I be the lookout." Then we argue over which ones the best howler. I'm of the opinion Tessie was born grabbin hold'a life like some folks wish they could touch a star. She gots no fear. She say me'n her together is a question mark. At first I don't get it, then she explains that I'm the question part at the top'n she the dot. I gots questions bout ever thing but Tessie just is. Even though the two of us bicker over the littlest thing, we still in perfect harmony, if that don't sound like the craziest thing ever. After thinkin about it – it sure does. We both in agreement that messin with Mama is dangerous business.

In five minutes, Tessie come runnin outta the church kitchen like a streak'a lightnin. Real quick, we hide behind a tree in the woods. I smear chicken fat on her hair to calm it down. She unbraids my pigtails, cuts'um off, then rubs chicken fat on what hairs I gots left. She frizzes it up, fore she pulls a bottle black Shinola boot polish outta her coveralls'n empties it all over me. It takes a while to rub it in, but afterward we real fulla ourselves. Me and Tessie know for sure, we the same now – like real sisters. Me'n her of the opinion we the two purtiest little cheatin "reggins" in town.

Mama callin to know where we are. She got her hands on her hips, which is not a good sign cuz she headin our way. We step out from behind the tree grinnin like chessy cats. When Mama gets herself a good look at us, we think she havin a stroke cuz she down on the ground from laughin so hard. She laughs'n laughs'n laughs. Mama laughin so hard she caint hardly stand back up on her feet. Pastor Roy Big John'n two other big men from choir practice, come runnin in our direction like they gotta put out a fire somewheres, but when they see Mama lyin on the ground they start laughin too. They says without a forklift, only Jesus can pull up a woman who gots titties bigger'n a elephant's tail end. Everbody laughin so hard, tears runnin down they faces. Other church folks come out'n gets caught up in it too. Look to me, like they all bout to pass out on the ground. All in all, Tessie'n me a big hit.

But now, Mama gots a problem. Haldane gonna fire her if she bring me home lookin like this. She think fast. We go back to Mama's house; she put us in a washtub where shoe polish come off easy, but gettin chicken fat outta our hair hurts terrible. Tessie's mama work two hours tryin to clean us up. Problem is what to do with my frizzed up short hair. Me'n her gonna keep one chopped-off pigtail apiece, for good luck charms. All of a sudden I'm scared. I caint lose her – not never.

"Mama, I'll tell Haldane I gots bubblegum stuck in my hair'n I cut it all out when you went to the bathroom. I gonna say you already whipped me good so she don't need to do it agin. Never you mind Mama, one whippin enough!"

Haldane happy these days. When she smiles, I got to wonder what for. I tell Mama over'n over how much I love her til the day I die, that I won't never forget her even if I move to China with the starvin children. Whenever I ask what heaven's like, all she ever say is, "Chile you ask too many questions. Mama jus don't know the answer – it jus the way it is'n iffen you don't shut dat little mouth, it gonna fall right off!"

Mama sure love Jesus. She gots a friendship with him that don't need questions'n answers. I'm always askin things like, "Mama, you ever talk to him in person like me'n you talkin right now? What's his last name? Can I meet him fore I go to heaven?"

She go headfirst past my questions'n say Jesus be like the sun, him lovin everbody. Mama say, "Chile, Jesus de Lord'n we his little Jesus sunbeams. Sometimes cloud come in between, but after a spell they be goin away, then we be seein for ourself how he been lookin after us all the time. Amen! Praise Jesus!" Anytime the subject come up bout Jesus, she ends that sentence with, "Amen! Praise Jesus!" So, me'n Tessie start sayin "Amen! Praise Jesus" after ever sentence too. Mama give us a lickin for bein smart alecky'n says, "You two best stop on accounta Jesus got no use for chilren made outta piss'n vinegar. Amen! Praise Jesus!"

One night Haldane comes home from work'n tells everbody she gots another husband, that we got to pack up, cuz we movin to N'arleans. She says, "Tharon Ann, that colored woman caint come with us, so you can get that out of your little head!"

That jus how she says it, jus shootin it out like "please pass the potatoes," like it was nothin, like the way I feel bout Mama mean nothin too. I love her same as whites love they white mamas. I cry myself to sleep jus thinkin'a leavin her'n bein left alone with Haldane. Last night I dreamt her singin the jaybird song to me.

Poor little jaybird don't you cry
Mama don't believe in saying goodbye
Poor little jaybird, my oh my
Mama gonna sing you dis lullaby

Tharon Ann

Poor little jaybird gots no wings
Mama don't care none about these things
Poor little jaybird wantin to fly
O little baby, you making me cry

Poor little jaybird, can't you see,
Mama gonna buy you a wishing tree
Now little jaybird flying so high
Flapping you wings in the deep blue sky

Mama little jaybird can't you see
Me and you sleepin in a wishing tree
Me and you sleepin in a wishing tree
Me and you sleepin in a wishing tree

The Early Years

I'm just a little girl from Little Rock

My new daddy is nice I guess. He gots a mole on his face right next to his big nose'n he wears a real high wave in front, which looks goofy'n I'm not sure I like his hair. We live in a town called N'arleans on a street that's spelt: "B-o-r-d-e-a-u-x." I'm learnin French from readin street signs.

Mister God, you recollect me writin you a letter'n stuffin it in a bottle in the Gulp of Mexico?

Ever Sunday, Haldane dresses me up in a white pinafore'n shiny black leather Mary Jane shoes; I hate'um with all my heart'n soul. We go to the French Quarter for donuts'n they do not call'um by that name. They donuts is spelt: "b-e-i-g-n-e-t-s," cuz they French, with yummy sugar on top. I can eat three beignets, one right after the other. I also get one cup of chicory coffee. Haldane never comes with us. She sleeps a lot. It's OK in her book for my daddy to show me off cuz then she don't have to be with me.

Mister God, did the mailman give you my letter yet? You figurin on writin me back? When you figurin on mailin it?

Last night, we got another practice air raid with sirens goin off'n all cuz of the war. Daddy says N'arleans is close to the Gulp'a Mexico'n that why they gots air raids. When the sirens go off, it mean turn off the lights'n hit the floor. Air raids is happenin all the time plus we got to use coupons for food, sugar'n other stuff. Oh'n we caint waste paper'n that goes double for toilet paper. Rainy afternoons I sit at the bay window watchin people. Haldane gots a girlfriend named Darlene. My favorite thing is visitin her house with Mother. Soons I go through the front door, I make believe I'm not me no more, like I'm seein everythin through her eyes. I know how much she love flowers. She gots little purple ones in the kitchen window sill'n talks to'um like they was her babies, like little pigeons cooin. When I shut my eyes, I can smell the summer lilacs she planted out back beside the porch steps. Last week her old dog Suzie had puppies under them steps. I wish I could hold a little puppy. I'd give anythin if Haldane would get me one, but she not gonna do it. The lilacs burstin out perfume like they know it's me smellin'um, like they love me cuz they know how much I love them.

Mother'n Darlene like each other a whole bunch. They laugh'n tell each other secrets'n split a Nehi Orange drink like girlfriends do. I wish my mother'd be like that with me.

"Put a record on the victrola," Haldane says, "You got "Rum'n Coca Cola?" Let's dance." She throw her hands up in the air like she got no cares in the world, laughin'n shoutin to Darlene, "I love this song!"

They start dancin to the Andrews Sisters. I listen'n begin swayin too. I love dancin to Darlene's music.

The best part'a now is sittin on the front steps, watchin people go by, tryin to figure out what's on they mind. I can tell by how they move, by the look on they face, what they think. I don't talk bout this cuz Haldane gonna say I'm crazy. All the shy folks in the world get they feelins hurt. I'm shy. Things don't work out so good when I'm jus me cuz of bein tongue-tied'n all plus stutterin a lot. When I stutter, I forget things. I don't know why. I jus do.

N'arleans is a lonesome place cuz I miss Mama'n Tessie so much. Ever night I cry myself to sleep jus thinkin bout'um. My paper-dolls, the ones I cut outta Haldane's old Sears Roebuck catalogs, keep me company.

Mister God, whatta you eat? Do folks eat collard greens in heaven? Ya'll gots Sears Roebuck up there?

Grandpa used Sears Roebuck catalogs for his outhouse in Oklahoma, where my family lived with the Cherokees. Once my grandpa said I was part Cherokee, but now he says he don't feel like talkin bout it. Don't that jus beat ever thing, him sayin that now, jus when I'm thinkin to be one? Anyways, when I'm done playin, I put my paper-dolls to bed in my grandpa's old cigar box. I can smell his chewin tobacco. I tried it once by puttin a jar on the floor'n pretended it was his brass spittoon. I stood there awhile, concentratin hard before I hurled my wad straight at it. Instead it went crazy-like, down my legs, all over the floor on my new store-bought lace up shoes Haldane makes me wear to school. I hate'um with all my heart. Grandpa says it's a mortal sin to waste fine chewin tobacco. Once, when I lit up his cigar'n took a few puffs, my throat hurt somethin fierce when I tried makin smoke circles. I won't be doin that no more.

Haldane never plays with me. The other day she comes in, looks over my shoulder'n actin jus like she was a ghost or somethin'n says, "Whooo, whooo, whooo, Tharon Ann live in her own little world, don't you T.A.? I never know what goin on in that little head of yours or who you really are ... whooo, whooo, whooo." You know, talkin like a ghost.

Why you figure she says she don't know who I am. If she's my mother, then why don't she know who I am? I don't preciate her sayin I'm little, two times in a row. I'm seven years old. I have a liberry card'n I can read'n write. When she talks like that, I feel like runnin away.

We always movin; first N'arleans, now Banton Ruge where they gots air raids too – you know, lights off'n hit the floor. I want this war to be over. I hate Hitler. When we go to the movies, they play newsreels showin how many soldiers is dead'n, how many planes got shot down. Our next door neighbor lost three soldier boys cuz'a Hitler.

Mister God, do the devil gots horn'n a tail? If I was you I'd shoot him dead.

If I ever meet up with Hitler, I'll pull his tail off for what he's doin to the soldier boys. They are very brave. I cry durin the newsreels, when they show all the coffins comin back home.

Mister God, how come you let all our planes get shot down? Why don't you jus put your arms up'n catch um' when they fallin to the ground?

We stayed in Banton Ruge for awhile. Sometimes I feel like all I do is move. I reckon we'll keep on goin til we fall off the earth. Today, we movin again to Louieville, Kentucky where they gots race horses. I love them a lot. Last month we drove to where famous ones go when they gets old – like big Man-O-War and Whirlaway. When they run, they don't hear nothin cept the sound of wind in they ears, the track under they hooves. Race horses run cuz they gots the blues. Racin what makes'um forget they troubles.

People say horses caint talk. They sure wrong on that score. Horses talk in code tween theyselves through the snort sounds they blow out they noses. When they ears go flat back, it means they good'n mad at somebody. At the start gate, they size each other up, braggin bout how many, an this is how it spelt: f-u-r-l-o-n-g-s, it gonna win by, bout how one coat is grander than the other coats, bout how strong they are, bout how it don't bother them none if they jockey put on one hunerd pounds. They don't care nothin bout him bein fat'n all.

Race horses born to win. That's how they live out they life'n don't never think'a retirin, they only think'a winnin. They don't worry none bout they legs bein fragile'n all. They gonna run even if it takes they last breath – they'll cash it in to win, even if it kills'um. They heart full to overflowin with the joy of runnin round that track. After the last race, when that old heart bout to explode – even then, that horse don't know it's time for pasture, shut far away from the cheerin crowds, away from the sound'a wind under they hooves, away from the stampin'a feet at the start gate. Once they runnin days is over, they'd sooner be dead than live in the place where visitor folks come, listenin bout the last great race. Man-O-War gots a little red bantam hen'n a billy goat in his room to keep him company. Tourists talk bout this too, cuz they got nothin else to say. They talk so loud, he hears'um sayin how lonesome he is. That why Man-O-War gots the reputation for bitin. He gots ears'n he don't preciate folks remindin him how he was the fastest horse alive.

If I don't come indoors when Haldane calls me to dinner, she pulls a switch off a tree'n whips my legs til I got welts on'um. After that, she sends me to bed without supper. When my daddy gets home, he comes in my room'n pulls my pants down'n whips me with his belt. I swear, once is enough.

Sometimes Haldane almost nice, like today when she gives me a big box of Fleer bubblegum. I'm always askin her to blow big bubbles like I do, so they'll pop all over her face same as me – like we playin together. Haldane says if I don't stop askin her to do that, I'll make her brain explode. I'm thinkin she jus teasin. It's real nice for her to chew bubblegum with me – like girlfriends do, like her'n Darlene. Maybe now we can be friends too,

This mornin, Haldane burnt the toast when she was makin scrambled eggs. When I point out how black it is, she say toast supposed to look like that'n, she burnt it jus for me on accounta it's her secret recipe for makin a "bird nest." She looks me straight in the eye'n says, "Tharon Ann, promise not to tell anyone?"

"Mommy, it's our secret." I think it's nice Haldane did somethin special for me, like havin a "bird nest" for breakfast. It wudn't take much for me to love her a whole bunch.

Mister God, you ever chew Fleer bubblegum? I'd sure like to see you do that. Oh, I almost forgot the most important thing. Haldane says I can have a bike with a basket when I get to be nine years old. Is this good news or what? I prayed for one so thanks a bunch.

Somethin's wrong. He yellin,"Tharon Ann! Come in here now!"

I'm sleepin. Daddy hollers my name out again, "Tharon Ann! Now!" I jump outta bed'n run to the bedroom. Haldane sittin straight up in bed, her face white as a ghost'n cryin like she's hurt ... what's wrong with my mommy? Daddy yells at me to run two blocks down the street for Nelly, her best friend. Daddy screams at me again, "Tharon ... now! Go now!"

Snow comin down ... I'm barefoot with jus my jammies on ... runnin fast as I can. I caint hardly see cuz snow comin down so hard. I'm cold ... forgot to put on my coat ... freezin cold ... caint feel my toes ... gots snowflakes inside my eyelashes ... Mommy, please don't cry ... don't cry.

Soons I get to Nelly's house, she takes off my wet jammies, dries me off'n hands me her pink fuzzy robe to put on. I'm shiverin half to death. Nelly says to crawl in bed with her husband. She in a hurry to go help my mother'n says to me again, "Go ahead Tharon Ann, crawl in bed with him so he can keep you warm," then she leaves. Nelly's husband touches me. I caint remember his name or what he looks like. I caint remember how I got to school the next day. I caint remember what I'm wearin. I caint remember nothin at all.

Mister God, I was callin for you but you didn't come. You mad at me or somethin?

After school, I caint hardly make up my mind whether to run away, whether to run home, or whether to take my time gettin there. I feel fuzzy like. What's wrong with my mother? I threw up my lunch in school today'n teacher sent me to the nurse office. I'm embarrassed over somethin, but I caint remember what it is. I caint feel my legs, like they went somewhere, like I'm walkin with no legs at all. When I get closer to my house, I start to feel scared cuz there's a white ambulance leavin our driveway. Mother is in the ambulance, but I don't know why.

When my daddy comes home from work, straight away he says we goin to the hospital. I don't want to go, cuz I hate hospitals. We go inside her room. Mother very white'n her eyes is closed shut'n she's hooked up to a bunch of tubes ... they gots doctors all over. I whisper in her ear, "Mommy, please get better, I won't ever make you blow big bubbles again. I promise."

She opens her eyes'n jus stares at me like I'm a stranger. Her hand is ice cold when she touches my cheek'n says, "Tharon Ann, be a good little girl."

That's the last thing she ever says. She holds onto my fingers for the longest time without sayin a word before she turns away from me. I press against the hospital bed'n stretch myself far as I can to see her better, but she didn't wait for me. She already closed her eyes shut'n died. Daddy havin a hard time pryin my hand outta hers. He says it's time for us to leave. Mother is dead on accounta her brain blowin up'n all. She'd still be here if I was a good girl'n hadn't begged her to make big bubbles. It's all my fault'n I'm sorry I did this to my mommy. I'm sorry I'm a bad girl. I hate bubblegum. I won't ever chew it again.

Mister God, please forgive me for killin my mother. How come you didn't make me a good girl? Why don't you answer me? I don't want to burn in hell fire.

I'm back in Little Rock with Aunt Lowee. Daddy'n me are here for Haldane's funeral, but I'm not goin. I already made up my mind to it. I'm not lookin at my mother dead in a coffin, since it was me who put her there.

Mister God, can you please fix it so I don't have to see her dead and me not knowin where she went.

I'm runnin up to the garage where theys an old fishin blanket in the pickup truck that don't work. He caint make me go to her funeral if I hide. Aunt Lowee begs my daddy to let me stay here, but he snaps back at her real ugly like sayin, "Lowee, shut up and mind your own business!"

Daddy not like he used to be, pullin me out of the pickup while I'm beggin him not to make me go. He's draggin me to the back seat of his car, me tryin hard to pull away, but him usin both arms to shove me in the back seat. I kick him hard as I can. I shouldn't have done it, but I'm not sorry cuz he hurt my arm'n told me to shut up. He used to be my daddy, but no more. On the way to the funeral home, he tells me to shut up again. Whenever I try'n talk to him, all he ever says is, "Shut up." I'm so scared, I wet my panties. I'm ashamed'a myself cuz big girls don't do that. Good I got a coat on, now people caint see what I did.

I never saw a dead person before. Ever one round here knows what I did, that I'll be locked up in jail cuz good girls don't kill folks. I'm thinkin maybe I'll run away'n go live in the woods with bears. Everbody starin at me'n my daddy as we walk up to the open coffin with her in it. I wish I was dead, him squeezin my hand so tight it hurts'n him sayin over'n over, that I should look down at my mother in the coffin'n kiss her on the cheek. I shut my eyes'n jus keep on walkin. Haldane always said if I made her blow big bubbles, her brain would explode. I should've died instead'a her.

After the funeral, my daddy says he's drivin back to Louieville to pack up our stuff. He says I got to go, whether I like it'r not. His sister Rose comin to help close up the house. I don't like her cuz she's mean. I try talkin to him, but he don't believe somethin terrible happened to me at Nelly's house. All he says is for me to shut up, that I make up stories jus to get attention, him thinkin I'm bad to the bone.

Mister God, how come you didn't make me a good girl?

Here we are back in Louieville. I hate this place a whole bunch on accounta ever night I gots terrible nightmares. Last night I dreamt grasshoppers climbed in bed with me'n spit chewin tobacco all over my legs'n my pigtails. I used to like grasshoppers, but after last night I never will again. Daddy says the only good thing bout it bein 1945'n all, is the wars over'n no more rations, no more air raids'n no more funerals. When folks hear bout the war bein over, they horns start tootin'n all kinda dancin goin on in the streets. But some folks not happy, them with poor soldier boys in coffins. I caint hardly stand thinkin bout them comin home dead.

While they inside packin up, I ride my bike outdoors with my Magic Skin doll asleep in the basket. I only come indoors when it's time to clean up before supper, cuz of her bein so mean'n all. Tonight, when my blue jeans'n shirt is piled in a corner, Aunt Rose comes in the bathroom without even knockin. She look at me sittin in the tub naked as a jaybird, then at the pile'a dirty clothes in the corner'n says, "You really are a dirty little girl." I don't rightly know what to make'a her, cept she looks like a man'n smells like a bear.

Where'um I gonna live? Last night I heard him say theys no room in his future for a stepdaughter. Aunt Rose told him, that since

I'm an orphan, he oughta put me in a state orphanage cuz I'm not blood kin. What's he mean sayin he gonna let my real family duke it out? Now, I got no Mama'n no Daddy either. I got no one.

Mister God, we can run off together if you want, but the deal is you gots to talk to me. You strike me as awful quiet. It's OK sometime, but not all the time.

I don't like not knowin where I'm gonna live, me bein nine years old'n all. Ever since Haldane died, I'm not his little girl anymore'n that's the gospel truth'n, I wouldn't say it if it wasn't. He don't even look at me half the time. Soon's he finishes packin up here in Louieville, we drivin back to Little Rock where he's droppin me off at Aunt Lowee's place. I don't much like him anymore, but I don't hate him neither.

Mister God, can you keep a secret? Cross your heart'n hope to die, stick a needle in your eye if you tell? On the way back to Little Rock, we stayed in a motel room where I pinched a Gideon Bible. I read the good parts'n tried to match'um up to the same parts in the Bible Haldane gave me when I learnt to read. I'm very confused. Those two Bibles don't sound nothin alike. Grandpa says it's cuz translators gots different ideas. I think you best straighten this out, cuz folks might go off the deep end not knowin what to believe. I'm feelin guilty bout stealin that Gideon Bible on accounta maybe best to send it back. I'll keep it, but only if it's OK with you.

Somebody in my head – like someone knows what I'm thinkin. I look up to see Tessie sittin on the limb of an old tree, like the one behind Mama's church where we used to get into so much trouble. She looks the same'n hollers down, "Hey little nigger." It's Tessie.

When my daddy dropped me off in Little Rock, the first thing I did was go lookin for Mama. When I heard Tessie died, I wanted to be dead too.

I holler back, "Tessie ... that you? Where you at? I been lookin for you. Ever time I ask bout you, people say best not talk about it. I know somethin terrible happened." Flashing her best toothy grin, she looks directly into my eyes'n says, "You mouth not workin? Call me by my name, you cheatin little nigger; come on girl, jump on this limb jus like we used to."

I know what she wanna hear. I look at myself'n I'm five years old again with pigtails, faded denim coveralls'n my favorite red tee shirt I wore when we climbed trees together. I holler up at Tessie'n start scalin the tree, "Hey you cheatin little reggin! Move over, cuz I'm comin up to put chicken fat on you hair!" We sit together for the longest time – jus holdin hands, feelin good bein together again. I say, "Where we at?"

She say, "We in heaven."

I laugh'n fire back like I used to, "I'm glad to hear it cuz you so bad, I'd be scared you livin with the devil."

We both laugh and Tessie shoots out, "Amen! Praise Jesus!" All I hear for the longest time is laughin, us sittin together like old times, holdin hands'n laughin ... then silence. Most folks is afraid of bein quiet, but not me'n Tessie. We like sittin together'n listenin to the wind'n knowin we always gonna be together.

After the longest time I say, "Tessie ... you ever meet up with God?" Tessie wastes no time answerin, "Sure, we best friends."

I'm glad to hear this cuz I never met anyone who ever saw him in person, who ever talked to God'n him answerin questions. I press on, "What color is he?"

She thinks for a minute'n laughs sayin, "One side'a God face black as boot polish, the other side be white like flour,"... she laughs'n flips her legs back'n forth up in the air like she always did, before crossin'um. Tessie nudges me on the shoe, sayin, "He look like all the diamonds in the world. So do all the chilren where he live. I gots to look'n talk like this cuz you so dumb, you don't gots sense to know the real me like I is in heaven, where theys no black'n white – they jus love."

I cover my face'n cry. "I got no one. I don't like it here. Ask him if me'n you can be together again."

Her black eyes are set in mine. She wants to say more, but holds back. Finally she speaks in a firm voice, "No, Tharon Ann – you got to go back, cuz you got lots to do before meetin up with him. He already know what you want. When you meet him, there won't be no more questions, cuz he gonna answer ever one jus by lookin at you. God ain't like nothin you hear bout in church ... you'll see ... one day, you gonna know for yourself." The last thing she says is, "Listen girl, you be here soon nuff. Now get on with the business of livin."

I wake up ... it was jus a dream ... Oh, Tessie...

Goin to school here in Little Rock is OK, but my teacher is coo coo. Today she says we got to memorize a horrible poem bout a tree with titties called, "Trees." They shoulda named it, "Titties," instead of beatin round the bush like that. Teacher says everbody in my class got to read it out loud front of the whole class tomorrow. I'll jus die if I have to.

My little cousin Sue listens to the stupid poem while I practice sayin it, "I think that I shall never see, a poem lovely as a tree." The minute I say that word "breasts" both me'n her start laughin so hard our stomach hurts. Ever one round here calls'um titties.

The next day in school, everbody got to stand up front'n recite "Trees." Ever single person in my class cracks up when we take turns sayin that awful word "breast" out loud. Teacher says she's plumb fed up with folks who gots such an ignorant way of thinkin. Well, why'd she make us recite a stupid poem like this? Teacher should'a made us read good stuff, some of my grandpa's poems would'a been fine. Mr. Robert Frost better'n readin bout trees with titties. I swear. I probly got to go to summer school.

Aunt Lowee workin the midnight shift as a nurse cuz Uncle Zack a bad drunk. I know for a fact she joined the Christian Scientists cuz it's cheaper'n goin to a doctor. Whenever she works the night shift, my job is takin care of Uncle Zack'n Sue. I got to see to it, he sticks to his guns'n don't drink on the wagon. Aunt Lowee says if he does slip outta the house, my job is to follow him to the bar'n jus sit there'n do my homework, til he runs outta money'n wobbles home. I got to make sure he don't pass out in his puke on our front yard'n embarrass Aunt Lowee. If he wants to pass out on his own grass, it's none'a they beeswax. What do I care what neighbors say bout me – bunch'a nosey roseys! Yesterday Sue locked herself in the bathroom when I says in a funny voice with clown teeth, "Buck up ol' buttercup!" I was jus tryin to make her laugh. I swear.

Eatin fire'd be easier'n goin through the DTs with Uncle Zack. Over'n over I call his AA friend, a guy named Wood Carter. He's probly all liquored up'n that's why he don't answer the telephone. When Uncle Zack is sober, all he ever does is talk bout Wood like he's the second comin. It's Wood Carter this'n Wood Carter that. I swear, I've heard bout enough of Wood Carter as I can tolerate, 'specially since he never picks up the telephone. It'd be easier talkin to a bump on a log than talkin to Wood Carter. I'd sooner call our two party lines for help, cuz they'd be easier to reach than him. Where are folks when you need'um?

Aunt Lowee hides our lunch money in an empty Farina box but Uncle Zack knows all our hidin places, includin the laundry basket. I got to get up early fore he steals our lunch money to go buy muscatel. Aunt Lowee says we poor as Job's turkey cuz'a him gettin liquored up all the time. He gets real mad at me for not tellin where I hid his Jack Daniels'n starts chasing me round the table with a butcher knife. I know all his tricks'n jus keep runnin round'n round the kitchen table til he passes out. Sue gets scared'n locks herself in the broom closet. I won't let him hurt her cuz I got a gun'n know how to use it.

Me'n Otis got a real BB gun for Christmas, but he still caint hit the broadside of a barn. I know how to use mine cuz I target practice in the back near the incinerator. Sue gets scared when she hears ol' black Sam walkin'n tappin his cane on the sidewalk front'a our house. That girl scared of her own shadow. Blind Sam won't hurt no body. Ever day him'n his old seein eye dog walks to the school for folks who got no eyes, a couple blocks up the street. Jus coloreds go there – not whites. I don't know why that is. When I ask Blind Sam what old dog's name is, he jus laughs'n says it got no name ... jus "dog." Me'n him have a good laugh over this. Wonder how he keeps from bumpin into things?

Mister God, What did ol' Blind Sam do to get hisself born blind. How come some folks born with eyes'n some don't got none. You think that's fair?

Uncle Zack'n Leroy go fishin ever Saturday on Rebsamen Lake. Uncle Zack don't drive on accounta he got drunk'n ran into a telephone pole with his old Ford pickup. Now it don't work'n he don't have money to fix it. They go in Leroy's pickup. Leroy is Uncle Zack's best friend, but he still got to come in through the back door. He caint go no further'n the back porch cuz he's a nigra man.

I caint hardly figure out what makes white people tick. Now that Aunt Lowee joined the Christian Scientists, I tell her Mary Baker Eddy told me she wants Leroy to come in through the front door, cuz Leroy is a Christian Scientist too. I make a big point'a sayin Jesus told me so. Aunt Lowee says Leroy gots to come through the back door'n she don't believe Mrs. Eddy said that. She says I oughtn't lie bout Mrs. Eddy'n Jesus. Even if Leroy is a Christian Scientist, he still caint come indoors through the front livin room. "It's jus how things are," she says'n, "You oughtn't question ever thing on accounta you like Leroy." She likes him too, but not enough to have the neighbors gossip when they see a nigra man come in our front door.

Mister God, is that your first name or your last name? Do you gots a nick name? I do. Aunt Lowee calls me T.Annie, sometimes T.A.'n sometimes Nanny, which I do not like one bit. When boys hear her callin me to come indoors, they say, "Nanny like Banany, your mama's callin you." I swear! Next time they call me that, I'm beatin tar out of um. I won't if you say not to, but I hope you don't, cuz I really want to.

I like Leroy lots cuz he gots a pickup that works ever time he turns it on. Another reason is, once when Sue was terrible sick with ashma, Leroy drove me around Little Rock just to find a funny book she wanted. He's a real good friend. But the main reason I like him is he told Uncle Zack to take me'n Sue fishin when they go this Saturday. On the way, we get to sit in the back of his pickup. After awhile, Leroy drives off the main street onto a dirt road in the woods, where we stop at a little shack. I keep askin Uncle Zack what it is. He calls it the magic house. I know that's a crock when I see him come out with a big jug, which tells me Leroy'n him gots a still for makin homemade shine, on accounta this a dry county.

We all get in the fishin boat but after ten minutes, me'n Sue tell Uncle Zack we gotta go - bad. Now, he gotta row all the way back'n he's fired up mad. Afterward, we get back in the boat again. Fishin is borin. Actually, it's very horrible. I'd sooner watch a bucket'a paint dry, than ever go to Rebsamen Lake fishin again. Uncle Zack'n Leroy make us swear on the Bible we won't tell Aunt Lowee bout them two makin bootleg liquor. I can keep a secret. Anyways, who cares? Shine tastes very yucky, like drinkin rubbin alcohol. I tell Uncle Zack I'll swear on a Bible, but only if he takes me'n Sue to the Mile Long Hot Dog House and gets us one. Me'n her can split a Coke. He says it's a deal but he gots to borrow money from Leroy to pay for it.

Today, Uncle Zack'n Leroy comin back earlier'n usual. They tell a big lie to Aunt Lowee that me'n Sue, "Damn near talked the fish to death'n," that's why they didn't catch nothin – cept one or two. Aunt Lowee real mad'n says his brains is fried from the sun'n stinkin'a Jack Daniels'n fish. It's a big mess.

I don't like the part of killin the fish'n choppin off they fish heads, slicin'um open, scalin'um. I keep thinkin that fishes caint do nothin to hurt us, so why we hurtin them? Uncle Zack pulls a fish out from the bucket. He throws it down on a slab, while it's still alive'n starin right up at him'n flippin all over the place. I'm thinkin it must be horrible, bein borned a fish with no legs to run away. If they gets caught, what they supposed to do when they got no legs to run? They got no arms to grab the knife outta Leroy's hand. I'm glad I'm not borned a fish, on accounta they don't breathe good outta water. The fishes in the bucket look real pitiful how they gaspin for air. I never saw nothin killed before.

I eat fish but I never think bout how they die, bout what it would feel like havin a hook in my mouth, like a razor blade rippin it wide open. It gotta hurt bad. Leroy takes a knife off his belt'n while Uncle Zack holds the fish down, he chops it's poor head right off. Jus like that. The fish is starin up at Leroy'n Uncle Zack, right up to when it dies, probly prayin for Jesus to save it's life while it's head bein chopped off. I'm wonderin if God listens to prayers of his creatures, like this fish still starin with it's eyes wide open. I caint hardly stand lookin at it. Leroy then slices the fish's tummy wide open, with blood squirtin ever which way'n him gettin it all over his shirt'n hands. After he's done, Uncle Zack reaches inside the fish's body'n pulls out her eggs. He tells Aunt Lowee, that he gots real caviar jus for her like they got in Paris, France.

Aunt Lowee flushed that caviar right down the toilet.

Once a year we visit Sue's grandma who jus happens to be Uncle Zack's mama. She's not my blood kin'n praise Jesus for that, cuz she's tighter than a tick. She lives way out in the country close to where Cajuns live, where they gots funny accents you caint hardly understand, same as Uncle Zack. Anyways my point bein, I don't know what to think bout Sue's grandma saying, we can only have three squares'a toilet paper each when me'n her gotta go. I swear, never in the history'a my whole life did I ever hear'a anythin like that. Aunt Lowee says, she squeezes a dollar so tight it makes the eagle poop. My grandpa once told me uncommon situations, like the one we got here with this toilet paper business, call for words outside the ordinary. I'm thinkin to start cursin. Not big ones, jus little swears, like damn'n dammit to hell. Theys a few more I might take under conderation too, but not out loud where folks can hear'um.

Sue's grandma gots a big farm with chickens, bantam roosters, horses, cows'n a real Brahma bull. Uncle Winston says they use him for havin kids. He gots a bunch of wifes'n that's why he's mean as hops. Uncle Winston makes my heart beat real fast, cuz he's so handsome with his dark red hair, and green eyes makin me feel like sunshine all over. He look jus like Sir Lampsirlot. When I grow up I'm gonna marry him if Little Margie don't get him first.

Ever Saturday night, she waits til he goes to town for drinkin'n arm wrestlin. She waits outside the bar til he comes out three sheets to the wind, wobblin all over the place. Little Margie uses her big, fat arms to pick him up once he passes out. She struts down the sidewalk with poor Uncle Winston hangin over her shoulder like a gunny sack. She wants ever one in town to see her throwin him in the back'a her pink Ford pickup, jus so she can say they got engaged. After that, she drives to her farm with poor Uncle Winston, him probly not wakin up til the next day'n, not even knowin what country he's in. I reckon she makes him breakfast, but I wouldn't want her sittin on me.

Sue's grandma says Little Margie gots affection for pink. She says if it's pink then, sure nuff, Little Margie want to wear it, drive it or drink it. She wears her pink halter top so tight them big titties jiggle all over the place when she coughs'n her hackin like that from smokin too many Cuban cigars. She wears tight pink shorts to show off her big tail end hangin out ever which way. She says Little Margie scares folks into votin for her when it's election time in this neck of the woods. Ever one round here is democrat to the bone, but Sue's grandma don't like Little Margie on accounta she always lookin at Uncle Winston'n throwin her big titties round like theys headlights to the promised land. I swear! I won't be surprised if he don't wake up one Sunday mornin to find a ring on his finger.

Anyways, today Uncle Winston's drivin his mama into town to get herself some Grapette soda pops. She's so stingy, her sayin ten times that if me'n Sue is good girls while she in town, we can split a Grapette soon she gets back. I figure that's bout four swigs each, probly not worth the effort. Anyways, jus as she's gettin in the pickup she turns round'n one more time, says for us not to go near the right pasture where her investment is: that would be her prize Brahma bull. Once again, repeatin herself in a high, grandma voice, "Don't ya'll two forget, that bull over yonder's real mean."

And jus when I think she's gone'f good, don'cha know she rollin the window down, her forgettin that it's broke'n always gets stuck halfway down, but her bein of a mind to repeat herself one more time, stretches her mouth up to the top part'a the window'n hollerin out at us like we was monkeys hangin from a tree somewheres, "Don't ya'll forget none, that Brahma bull yonder cost me a whole lot'a my money. He gonna hurt ya'll two real bad, y'hear?"

The Early Years

Sue's grandma jus gave me the idea to outrun her investment. I sweet talk Sue into gettin on the back of her grandma's horse called "Old Ned." She agrees to come along, cuz she don't know what else to do with herself. Me and her ride Old Ned through the barnyard, with all them chickens cluckin, they feathers flyin round like crazy'n me jumpin off Old Ned to open'n shut the gate so we can take off. I spot her investment right off the bat. I swear, it's like he been waitin for me. But I stop Ned a ways back, cuz Sue's gettin scared'n startin to cry. I'm scared too on accounta I never saw a meaner look in anyone's eye. I'm in big trouble cuz I know what he's up to'n, I gotta get outta here. I turn Ned round'n race him back so fast, Sue nearly slides off his tail end. I can feel the bull breathin down my back, his nostrils makin sounds like he wants to dig his horns in Ned's stomach. I jump off to open the gate, then I jump back on Ned'n take off. Theys no time to shut the gate'n lock the bull outta the barnyard, cuz he right behind me spittin out hell fire'n little Sue cryin like a sissy baby'n sayin ever five seconds,

"Tharon Ann, I got to pee!" and me screamin at the top of my lungs,

"Hell fire Sue, then pee for goodness sake!" And her doin jus that, cuz we caint stop for nothin'n – now, me havin hot tinkle all over me, on accounta Sue almost sittin on my back from her bein scared'n all. I swear. Soons we get to the house, we jump off faster'n you could shake a stick'n, nearly knock each others brains out runnin into Sue's grandma's kitchen. Faster'n lightin, we bolt the door shut. Oh, shoot! One of her drinkin cups jus fell off the shelf ... glad it's not broke cuz she'd never stop talkin bout it. My heart racin so fast, I got to pull up my shirt to see if it's still there. I swear, it bout to jump outta my body. I'm wonderin do bulls jump through kitchen windows, or breakdown doors? That bull in the barnyard's knockin everthin down'n them chickens scared half to death'n runnin ever which way. Times like this call for fresh buttermilk. We sit down'n have ourselves a big glass each til we both got white mustaches. I wipe off little Sue's mouth so her grandma don't know we been into it. I got so much on my mind, I almost forget to holler at Sue to go take off her underwear'n put on a pair of her grandma's underpants, "Sue, throw away the evidence!"

When Sue's grandma gets back, she throws a hissy fit the minute she steps outta the pickup'n sees the gate wide open. When she spots her prize Brahma bull in the barnyard, she drops her Grapette soda pop, spillin it all over her Sunday dress, wavin her hands crazy'n callin out to Jesus for help. I'm thinkin she'd do a whole lot better to call on Uncle Winston, cuz he's here'n I caint see Jesus. Uncle Winston had a time gettin the bull back in the right pasture. He's so brave. It jus makes me love him all the more.

I'm not allowed outta the house for awhile, but it was worth it cuz I love excitement.

I'm thinkin of ridin bulls when I grow up – you know, like in the rodeo.

Ever night me and Sue listen to *Inner Sanctum* on the radio, same time we polish our shoes for school the next day. I'm so scared when the creaky door comes on, I lock myself in the bathroom til it's over. It's thrillin but scary.

It's excitin havin our own television set – course Uncle Zack won it in a poker game, but who cares. When he's kinda halfway drunk, he says in his Louisiana accent, "Lowee, bring m'smoke jacket'n Joan Crawford, cuz we wantin to watch, *I love Lucy*."

Joan Crawford is Aunt Lowee's pet red hen don'cha know. Aunt Lowee helps him put on his fancy smoke jacket his sister gave him for his birthday, afterward she sits Joan Crawford on his shoulder who straight away starts droppin chicken mess all over his fancy jacket, the couch too. Aunt Lowee mumbles under her breath, that she already late for work'n don't have time to fool with chicken mess. But she don't say nothin, cuz Uncle Zack is in a half-drunk, half-sober kinda mood. But the minute she out the front door, me'n Sue gonna play beauty parlor.

First off, we put Uncle Zack's hair up in pink rollers, then lipstick'n rouge. After that, we take the rollers out ever so careful, mindful not to yank his hair'n wake him up when we tie ribbons in'um. Me'n Sue laugh so hard our stomach hurts. Another reason me'n her happy is cuz he's home. In a little while, I'll put Uncle Zack to bed, but first I gotta take Joan Crawford back to her pen.

Don'cha know someone jus stole Joan Crawford right outta her pen in our back yard! Poor Aunt Lowee havin herself a hissy fit from grievin over that hen bein cooked for Sunday dinner. Joan Crawford lays one egg ever mornin jus for her'n that's the gospel truth'n, I wouldn't say it if it wasn't. I'm drawin a picture that's a honest to God likeness'a Joan Crawford to nail on telephone poles'n trees from where we live, all the way to the bottom of the hill by Hudson's Market. The sign reads, "I gonna give you a one dollar cash reward if you tell me who kidnapped Joan Crawford, my red hen who answers to that name," plus our telephone number, which gots two party lines in use most'a the time.

Me and Aunt Lowee decide to go on a search'n seejure for her red hen, but first we got to stop at the grocery store since it's round where we goin. Aunt Lowee says I got to look pitiful'n cough on my shirt sleeve when I go indoors to ask Mr. Hudson if he'll give us more credit. It's a real hot summer day; my feet hurt like all get-out from me goin barefoot all the time. This pavement is hotter'n fire from black tar spread on it yesterday. I swear, right out of nowheres her voice starts tremblin as she whispers in my ear, "Tharon Ann, ya'll hear that? Do you? Sweet Jesus, that's my baby, Joan Crawford, inside that washtub yonder!" Then she starts'a runnin like a woman with her hair on fire.

Oh, no! She headed into somebody's backyard. She's almost knockin they fence down tryin to climb over it. She's gettin her white underpanties all knotted up on the wire. If someone walks down the hill, they gonna see her big tail end stuck on that wire fence; oh, please, please get her unstuck. Thank you Jesus. Now she's over the fence. She's runnin over to the washtub, on accounta she hears Joan Crawford hen cluckin her brains out. I holler, "Aunt Lowee! What you doin?"

She lifts up the washtub to find Joan Crawford hen just sittin there cluckin away like she been waitin her whole life to be rescued.

"Aunt Lowee! You best get outta there fore someone calls the cops!" But Aunt Lowee caint stop kissin Joan Crawford, so I yell out again, "Aunt Lowee! I'm worried someone gonna come outta that house'n see me'n you trespassin on they private property'n call the cops on us. Aunt Lowee! Me'n you goin straight to jail! Jump back over that fence! Jump! Aunt Lowee, Jump!" But she so crazy-happy findin Joan Crawford, that she caint stop for nothin, jus kissin'n a'cuddlin that chicken in her arms. Then, jus like she sprouted angel wings, Aunt Lowee leapfrogs over that busted fence, red feathers flyin ever which'a way'n, Aunt Lowee holdin Joan so tight – I swear I'm scared her eyes bout to pop right out.

We runnin so fast up hill Aunt Lowee trips on one of her shoes that keeps fallin off, but we keep right on runnin, me and her not stoppin even one minute to pick it up. Aunt Lowee hollerin, that she don't give a tinkers damn bout that shoe, it's worth losin on accounta gettin her baby back'n all. Anyways, she gets our shoes from the markdown barrel at Kroger's for a dollar.

I caint go to Hudson's Market today on accounta all the commotion. We don't got much to eat in the house so Aunt Lowee wants me to go out back'n pick polk sallet to go with biscuits'n pan gravy she's bout to make.

Mister God, you ever hear'a this joke? How come the chicken crossed the road? This here's the answer: that chicken crossed the road, on accounta he had to get hisself to the other side. I don't think it's all that funny either, but I figure you must get so lonesome that you'd laugh at jus bout anythin.

Whenever the party line not talkin its head off, I call his folks who live here in Little Rock. Even though I know he's moved on, I still want to see him, cuz he was my daddy. Whenever I call, his mama always promises to make him come see me. Times when I think he's comin, I wait all day, jus sittin on the front steps til it gets dark'n mosquitoes start bitin my legs …waiting, just waitin for him to come, but he don't ever come'n I don't think I'll ever see him again. Love is like that. Bein in love with somebody don't mean somebody loves me back. People caint help how they feel, jus like I caint help lovin them. Love sorta like the ocean. It surges onto the shore whether it's in the mood for it or not. After'a while when it gets pitch black, Aunt Lowee calls me indoors. I guess that's how it is. People together for a while, then we all alone by ourself. I'm always lonesome, even with folks around. The best time to sit on the front porch is when the sun goes down'n fireflies start lightin up the night. They got nothin to do cept twirl round waitin for they tail lanterns to turn on. I swear, they gots to be thousands of'um out tonight – all happy together in they firefly world. Maybe I'm waitin to be lit up so I can be like that.

Ever now and then, sittin here on this ivy covered porch, I'm full up with so much happiness, I could bust wide open. It jus lasts a little while. I caint see God. He never really talks to me, but times like this, I feel he's right here, so close I can almost reach out'n touch him … like he's me. In the same way I hear the ocean talk when I put a seashell up to my ear, in the same way I want to hear God's heartbeat, in the exact same way. He don't care what I call him so longs I love him. I wish Jesus would turn hisself into one of my Magic Skin dolls. I'd jus squeeze the bejesus outta him if he'd do that.

Mister God, I'll give you my jacks'n baseball cap if you want. I got nuthin else to give on accounta I got no job – but then you already got that information.

It's awful hot in Alma'n nuthin much to do. I'd rather stay with Aunt Lowee in Little Rock all summer long but cuz of this court custody deal, I gotta visit my real father's family whenever a holiday rolls round. Most of the time, I stay with Grandmother'n Grandfather Jack Henry in Alma, sometimes with Aunt Lucille'n Uncle Dale'n too much time with my cousin Otis. I like my real father's family, but not the kinda love that makes me wanna squeeze the bejesus outta someone. You know, jus squeeze'um til they eyes pop right outta they head. That's how I loved my Mama.

The only thing I like bout Aunt Lucille is Uncle Dale's victrola'n his records. She used to sing out-front in the church choir. Lord only knows she tells ever one often enough'n Lord knows she caint sing a lick, even if she tried. Otis says she gots a bad ear on accounta her piano not bein tuned since the flood.

Whenever they go shoppin for groceries, they invite me to come along. I answer in a good manners way, "No thank you – ya'll jus go on without me. I'm stayin here to read the Bible, if that's OK with ya'll."

Aunt Lucille smiles when I talk polite like that. Then she tells me ten times not to open the door to strangers, that I'll be murdered if I open the front door, that little children are shot dead all the time when they open the front door to strangers, right after they been told not to. The minute I see the two of them pullin out the driveway in the Studebaker, I run to the victrola'n put on Uncle Dale's big band music. I'm marryin Tommy Dorsey when I grow up.

I caint figure out Uncle Dale. One minute he's one way'n the next minute he jus shootin it out. You'd think all he'd want to talk bout is Tommy Dorsey, since he gots all his records, but oh no – it's always bout his big ol' Studebaker'n how much he likes linen'n how much finer it is than seersucker. It's unmanly for him to talk like that. Aunt Lucille is nutty as a fruitcake. I caint say I'm crazy bout her, but I don't like seein her feelins hurt. The other day she was jus foolin round with Uncle Dale'n says, "Dale, last week when I was grocery shoppin, the checkout boy offered to help out round the house. He says he'd be real happy doin odd jobs here. What ya'll think bout that Dale?"

He jus shoots right back at her, forgettin all bout Tommy Dorsey, forgettin his manners'n, forgettin them goin out this afternoon in his green Studebaker. He jus stands in the doorway with a big chessy cat grin on his face, like the words bout to come outta his mouth are worth listenin to, like he bout to say the grandest remark ever made in the history of all mankind, "Well, Lucille," then he stops, like he waitin for trumpets to come outta his mouth before makin his big announcement,

"I'm real happy someone finds you attractive."

I swear, it was just like Uncle Dale put a bullet right through my heart, that's how sad it made her'n me both. Maybe she wouldn't be so silly if there was someone to talk to. Like I said, I'm not all that crazy bout her, but I don't see a need for him to talk like that when she was jus foolin round. I don't like the meanness in him, even if he does like Tommy Dorsey.

I'm worried bout my old dog Laddie. You recollect me tellin you bout him chasin cars'n all? Do you Mister God? Right before I left to visit my relatives, Laddie got his tail broke when he was hit chasin cars again. I hear him cryin at night on accounta his poor tail hurts somethin fierce. Will you tell it not to hurt?

Ever time I visit Aunt Lucille, that would be my real father's sister, she near trips on herself callin the society editor to come out'n take pictures of me havin tea with horrible Karalynn Eldred. Aunt Lucille'n Uncle Dale play canasta ever Wednesday night with Dr. Eldred'n his wife, May Ella, who live down the street. The only reason they fiddle round with this stuff is to get on the society page. Karalynn says she loathes nick names. She says "loathe" like it's the grandest word in Webster's Dictionary, like someone jus paid her a dollar to say it. Today, when I walk through her front door, I politely say, "Mornin Miss Kate."

She shoots back at me'n says, "Tharon Ann, I don't preciate you callin me Kate. Abbreviating my name is vulgar." It's time I call the witch's hand.

I shoot back, "And I don't appreciate your egregious attitude ever time I come visit either. Mr. William Shakespeare wrote a play'n the main girl is called Kate. Did you know that Miss Kate Eldred?" I'm not tellin her it's *Taming of the Shrew,* on accounta she never reads anythin cept funny books. She says likin to read books makes me look weird. Well at least I know what that word means, not like some snooty people with they nose so high in the air, that if it rains they'll drown!

When people see me readin they always say, "My my, there she is with her nose stuck in a book ... how well-read you are for your age." Why do they say, your age? I figure I'm well-read for any age. Grandpa Leo taught me bout the adventures in readin. I love books. Folks aren't happy unless they shoot somethin smart outta they mouth, specially when someone isn't as dumb as them. I swear.

I'm invited to a bunking party at horrible Kate's house down the street. I told Aunt Lucille that I don't like sleepin overnight at a stranger's house'n I'm not goin cuz, all they gonna talk bout is titties, paint'n toenails'n boyfriends. Whenever Kate talks bout boys, her left eye twitches. At first, I thought she was goin blind til I figured out, she was boy-crazy. Anyways, Aunt Lucille says I got to go whether I want to or not.

This is the worst night I ever spent on earth. Theys six girls exactly like horrible Kate'n, all they do is talk my brains out bout boys'n brassieres. When they ask me what size I wear, I hike my t-shirt up over my head'n yell out, "Look at these babies! Mosquito bites don't need'um!" I'm thinkin folks say titties when they already wear brassieres, but when they don't – they jus come right out'n say bosoms.

One girl says they got creams to make titties sprout like corn stalks. I already know bout this from an ad I saw in the back of a funny book, that says if a person rubs titty cream on they chest ever night, in no time, that person will grow big ones. I'm thinking it'd be a whole lot easier to jus cut pictures'a titties outta Aunt Lucille's magazine'n glue'um to my chest. But then I'd miss the bonus part, a real good exercise that comes in the mail with the cream. After rubbin it on my chest, I'm supposed to stand in front of a long mirror, stretch out my hands to the side'n, bend my arms back'n forth to my chest, repeatin ten times, "I must, I must, I must develop my bust," or somethin like that. Anyways, the company who makes this stuff wants one dollar'n fifty cents plus stamps. I can sure see me askin Aunt Lowee for that kind'a money, jus so I can grow titties. Ha! Ha! Ha! Ha!

I'm thinkin to build myself a treehouse when I go back home to Little Rock. I'm gonna sit up there all day til school starts, drinkin lemonade'n shootin peas outta my sling shot at boys when they pass by. Grandpa Leo says I cud probly wup'um all if I got a mind to do it. That's good to know in case one of them tries to pull somethin.

Mister God, please make Kate Eldred's titties grow so big she gots to be pushed through the door. I know I oughtn't to, but I hate her guts.

The big deal'a the day in Alma is lunchtime. You'd think it was the partin of the Red Sea the way everbody rushes round, maids runnin here'n there sayin over'n over again – like they don't got nothin else to say,

"Hurry up, Doctor gettin out of his car, hurry up, Doctor gettin out of his car" – like folks didn't hear it the first time, like he was the second comin. The dinin room table is covered with my grandmother's lace table cloth'n set with crystal glasses, the kind that makes a ding when I flick it with my baby finger'n, maids hoppin round like the Queen of England at the front door. Grandmother gots the habit of repeatin everythin she thinks is important. I hear her tellin one of the maids, "Carrie, ya'll use the fine china, Carrie, now ya'll use the fine china. Doctor likes that pattern, he sure does."

I never hear her call my grandfather by his first name, even his last name for that matter. No, it's always the Doctor this, and the Doctor that. Anyway, my grandmother says Carrie oughta bring her girl to work, so me'n her can play in the backyard. Her name is Billy Jo. We get along good. I caint hardly wait.

Some days, I'm bored even before I wake up. I know right off today will be a borin day. No matter what I do, I'll be bored to death. I tell Billy Jo how I feel'n she reckons that she's bored lots'a times too. Today, we both so bored we could spit. We play jacks, we play with dolls, we play hide'n seek in my grandfather's barn'n, then we go adventure huntin for snakes in the rose garden. Nothin to do after that, cept stare at each other. Theys nothin to do in Alma, cept wonder what to do.

I get the idea to ride "Ol' Horse." I don't rightly know if he belongs to my grandfather but he's always in the field behind the barn ever since I can remember, so I figure he must be his. Anyways, me and Billy Jo decide to get on Ol' Horse'n have ourselves a ride. I wanna saddle up but I caint find one, so we make up our minds to ride bareback through downtown Alma which is bout one street long. Billie Jo scared on accounta she never been on a horse. She's so scared, that when I try to help her on, she almost rolls over to the other side'a Ol' Horse, on top her head. I start yankin on her leg closest to me, so she can sit herself straight up. Instead, while I'm yankin, she's rollin backwards'n knocks both'a us on the ground. Now she even more scared. I'm tryin with all my might to calm her down sayin, "It's OK Billy Jo, you best wait here while I go find us a stepladder."

We finally get back on top Ol' Horse, me, regular'n her the stepladder way. I tell her to put her arms round my waist'n hang on for dear life. I say, "Giddy up" to Ol' Horse'n he starts runnin faster'n he ever did in his whole life. Me'n her gallop all through Alma, past where my grandfather sees sick people, past the movie house, past the hardware store, past the dime store'n, past the feed store. Billy Jo not scared anymore, cuz she figures she's not gonna die. It's real hot. Me'n her dyin'a thirst. Jus thinkin'a ice cold lemonade makin my mouth water. Billy Jo sticks her tongue out to show me, her mouth dry too. We decide to go back to the house, but I know once we get off Ol' Horse, she might not be able to get back on again without a stepladder. We can almost taste the ice cold lemonade'n decide to go straight back. Soons we ride up to the house, I see everbody runnin out the front door, crazy-like. Even the fat on my grandmother's body is hollerin for me to get off the horse, "Get off Ol' Horse!" she screams, "Right now little missy! I mean business, now get yourself off that horse right now, Tharon Ann!"

When she's mad, all the fat on her body jumps up in the air the minute she opens her mouth. If she's standin in the sun, a bucket'a sweat rolls'n drips off her forehead like fat back'n a fryin pan. She starts hollerin at the top of her lungs, that it was OK to play with Billy Jo in the backyard, but now everbody in Alma callin to say her granddaughter ridin Ol' Horse with a nigger girl! I hate the way she shoots out this word. I hate her! I hate her stupid ways!

We run indoors through the back kitchen, cuz black folks not allowed to come in through front doors. I tell her to meet me in the backyard'n I'll bring out two ice cold glasses'a lemonade'n my Magic Skin dolls, cuz they make me feel better when bad things happen. I can tell by the look on her face she been cryin. Words hurt more than whippins. Probly her mama'n everbody in the house hopped all over her. I feel like knockin' um all on the head for treat'n Billie Jo like that. We sit down under a shade tree sippin lemonade her mama made for us. I tell her all bout me'n Tessie, but she gots her feelins hurt so bad she caint hear nothin I'm sayin. After today, I know my grandmother won't let Billie Jo come play with me again. I hate her for bein mean to my friend. I won't forget this. Not ever.

Mister God, you white or colored? I caint rightly understand why you let Billie Joe get her feelins hurt. Why did you?

Grandfather Jack Henry made up his mind, I need somewhere to put my "over abundance" of energy. He says the only thing that works for someone like me, is a hard day's work to cure my balanced hormone – the one causin me to get in trouble night'n day. I overheard him talkin bout all this to Aunt Lucille last night on the telephone. He's makin my hormone sound serious. I swear.

This is the first day workin in my grandfather's doctor office. He sits me down in a room no bigger'n a broom closet'n gives me a white doctor gown'n green rubber gloves. He tells me over'n over what an important job I have'n, I'm to be mindful never to spill the green slimy stuff I'm supposed to pour inside the long tubes. I feel very important workin here, seein folks come in sick'n goin out happy. But some is poor as Job's turkey, on accounta they mountain folks who got no money. They don't like charity, so my grandfather lets'um pay from what they grow in the field. Grandfather says it's called barterin.

On my second day at work, I get done puttin the green stuff into the long tubes earlier than yesterday. I don't know what to do with myself, so I start lookin for my grandfather'n go into his office ... but he's not here. Then I notice a door at the end of the hall with a red light blinkin. I'm thinkin that light must be some type SOS he's usin to send me a secret code tellin where he is. Everbody knows a red blinkin light means "come on in." I open the door to one of the most horrible sights I ever witnessed on earth. One of my grandfather's sick people is lyin on his big belly on the operatin table. He's a big man, probly weighin a thousand pounds or more, with his big tail end stuck high in the air. I'm speechless. Grandfather Jack Henry is puttin the tube of green gooey stuff, which I personally made all by myself yesterday, into his big tail end. I'm not much interested in his parts, but I do feel a certain pride seein my work put to good use. Standin here like this, takin it all in, I'm startin to feel real proud'a myself, like I've done somethin important, same as Columbus musta felt standin all alone when he discovered America. No one knows I'm here til I say in a cheerie voice, "Hi Grandfather."

Grandfather's sick person looks at me with a funny look on his face'n starts blinkin his eyes like a chicken peckin grain, when he sees me standin in the doorway admirin his tail end up in the air. He gots an expression on his face I've seen before like, "Oh, Sweet Jesus, what's next'n," him hollerin at the top of his lungs, "What in Sam Hill's that kid doin in your operatin room Doc? God-a-mighty, ain't even a feller's ass sacred?"

I caint figure out why my grandfather isn't happy to see me. So I slam the door shut'n run home fast as I can. I tell Otis what happened'n he nearly blew his cork, "Shoot a monkey Tharon Ann," he hollers at me, "You makin a mountain outta a mole hill. That green stuff is what doctors use for people sufferin from humanoids!"

Whew, that's a relief. I thought maybe it was poison from the way they was actin, like I killed him or somethin. I swear. I'm just sorry this type information had to come outta his mouth. You know, from God's mouth to Otis Henry. It wouldn't take much for him to get a big head.

Mister God, sure hope they more to do in heaven than here in Alma. Will you send me a genie lamp for my birthday? Could you please make sure it works first.

If I die'n don't know where I am but I see a sign on the road sayin, "Welcome to Alma, Arkansas," I'll know for sure, I have not gone to heaven.

Mister God, please don't send folks to Alma if they like to have fun.

Summer's draggin on forever. They got nothin to do here but talk. Folks talk bout the weather like that's all they is to talk bout on the face of the earth. My feets at least ten inches bigger from goin barefoot all the time. Alma's so little, if you spit, they hardly a place for it to land. Main Street gots a hardware store, a whole bunch'a other stores plus a movie house that plays Westerns for a month. It sits one hunerd or so, including the popcorn guy who owns it. At least that's what Otis says. He saves one seat for hisself to watch Gene Autrey over'n over. Otis says this guy also owns a place where they take dead people when they die, but I don't know if it's true comin from him. You know, from God's mouth to Otis Henry. But the big deal is, Jim Bob's Traveling Roller Rink, that's in a big tent on the outskirts'a Alma, bout four blocks down to the end of town.

Hillbillies from the Ozarks, that drunker'n Cooty Brown on homemade shine, go there for a spin or two.

I make my grandparents nervous cuz they caint figure out what to do with me when I come visit. I don't know what to do with them either. Lucky for me, someone told my grandmother bout the roller rink in town. She passed this information on to my grandfather'n before I know it, he says to my grandmother, "Get one for Tharon Ann. Y'listenin Mother? Get that pass today, y'hear me!"

Doncha know that very day, they get me a summer pass to, Jim Bob's Traveling Roller Rink. They reckon I'll skate the devil out of me. Billy Jo's mama, says that's my grandmother's exact words. From God's mouth to my grandmother. I swear.

I'm so excited bout goin to the roller rink that I caint hardly sleep. They bought me new skates on accounta my grandmother got her head set on me gettin foot'n mouth disease wearin skates other folks had on. I'm not tellin Otis cuz he'd ruin it for sure blabbin his mouth to Aunt Lucille'n there you'd have it! She'd blah, blah, blah to my grandparents not to let me go. On the big day when I walk up to the ticket taker to show my summer pass, he looks me square in the eyes, "Little lady," he says, "This here's the first time ya'll skated?"

"No sir," I answer polite like'n cross my fingers, "I been roller skatin my whole life." Southern folks like it when kids talk polite like this. Finally, after him givin me the once over like I'm a gangster or somethin, he lets me go indoors.

Standin here like this, my whole life is passin before me. What I'm lookin at leaves me breathless. The skaters is flyin round like little angels with golden wings, skatin thru the air like ever kinda bird'n paradise, like beautiful angels flyin round heaven. I caint hardly breath cuz I never saw anythin so grand. I always been wantin to watch a ballet, but toe dancin caint be better than roller skatin. Even though folks is older'n, even though they not many kids here my age – still, everbody is real nice. They treat me like family.

Summer's blisterin hot in Alma which is fine with me cuz, like I said, weather bout all folks got to talk about. Mountain women is different. They figure sweatin slows'um down'n that's why they skate half-naked. Skinny tops'n shorts is OK by me. We make friends right off the bat. Estelle my best girlfriend cuz she keeps her eye out for me, "Tharon Ann, watch out for that drunk! He bout to mow you down honey-baby!" She says mountain people drink home-made shine fore they skate'n, they gonna knock down anybody who gets in their way. They real polite'n say "sorry" right after your brains'n guts spilt all over the floor on accounta that's how they are. Estelle reckons the deal is for me to skate fast'n, use my elbows'n, get Sam Hill outta the way ... if I'm lookin to see daylight.

At the end of each week, my grandmother asks me the same question over n'over, "What you'n your little friends doin at that skatin place?"

I always answer the same way, "Nuthin much, it's a whole lot like the 4-H Club."

And her answer to me is the same as yesterdays, "I do declare Tharon Ann. Well now, ya'll ought never forget to keep your legs crossed," and adding for emphasis, "Always keep your legs crossed, y'hear."

"Yes Mam, I'm keepin'um crossed."

Mister God, don't get depressed or nothin like that, but I'm thinkin I might not be goin to heaven if they don't got a roller rink up there.

Tharon Ann

My Okie grandparents and them Cherokee Indians

I could jus squeeze the bejesus outta my Okie grandparents cuz that's how much I love'um. They sent money in the mail for Aunt Lowee to buy train tickets for us to come visit'um in California where they nothin but movie stars'n oranges growin on trees. A long train ride is the type adventure I always dreamed of. Me'n Sue are havin so much fun eatin in the dinin car once a day, we caint hardly stand it. I can jus imagine me sittin there all gussied up fancy-like, smokin a pipe'n strikin up conversations with black porters bout world affairs. Rest of the time, we ride in the sit-up chairs, eatin cheese'n crackers – apples too'n peanut butter Aunt Lowee keeps in a shoppin bag, cept for suppertime when we dress up in our Sunday outfits to go eat in the dinin car. I love trains so much I'm gonna buy me one when I grow up.

Grandpa lives in a big magic house with hidin places for me'n Sue to play in. Overlookin the front walkway, he got hisself a day dreamin room with windows to look out at the mountains'n for watchin sunsets'n playin gin rummy'n keepin a lookout for who's comin to visit. Ever night he explains how things was in Oklahoma back in the good ol' days when it was wild'n wooly'n how he moved his family to Ada to build a post office for Cherokees so they could get mail. He says outside'a them, they wasn't'nothin for miles on end, cept a handful'a Okies round about. Grandpa gonna teach me to talk Cherokee if I make good grades in school. He says they don't like white people none'n that's why he learned to talk Indian.

Grandpa says I make him crazy askin so many questions'n all, but I like knowin how folks lived back then. He built hisself a log cabin back'a the store. Some nights I dream bout that little creek behind my grandpa's log cabin'n the water mill Grammy used for

The Early Years

grindin corn for the Cherokees; wish I was there, specially in the evenin with my grandpa spinnin yarns bout Ned Christy, the famous Cherokee bandit. I cry when he says they caught up with Ned'n killed him. What's wrong with white folks? Grandpa says kids back then made they own fun playin in the woods'n chewin rabbit tobacco growin wild. After sayin that, he looks at me'n laughs'n says I better not look for it, cuz it's nikotine. The Cherokees was always invitin him'n the family to the all day stomp-dances'n barbecues.

Most'a the time, Grammy busies herself in the kitchen when my grandpa spins yarns – I reckon she heard'um all. But today, she comes in, sits herself on the bed'n starts tellin me how Cherokee women taught her how to find herbs in the woods for when the kids was sick. Grammy says, the closest neighbor was a Cherokee family answerin to the name of "Hummingbird" who lived in a one-room log cabin with a dirt floor. They little girl Lucy was blind ever since she was born. On Christmas day, my grandpa took the family big baskets'a food'n a doll for Lucy. Yesterday, he gave me a pretty store-bought doll with long black hair'n brown skin. I sleep with her ever single night'n named her "Lucy."

When I asked my grandpa how he went from livin on a Cherokee reservation to now, he says he moved out west with all them other hell raisin Oakies'n that's how he ended up in East Los Angeles. The Mexicans reminded him of the Cherokees, that'n the property bein so cheap'n all. Grandpa says, he believes in the American dream, that if folks not afraid to put in a hard day's work, they can be anythin they wanna be. He uses his sister, my great Aunt Alice as a for instance. She lives alone in the log cabin her granddaddy built high up in the Ozark Mountains. Grandpa says Alice never married'n to hear him tell it, it's lucky for mankind she didn't. She grows her own food, goes huntin for possum, makes her own shine, chops kindlin for cold winters'n can kill a rat three yards away with one spit-chaw'a tobacco. Whenever the G-Men Revenuers is brave enough to travel on foot the long ways up the mountain to her log cabin, she pulls out the welcome mat'n … right here is where my grandpa stops talkin so I can finish the sentence. I pick up where he left off, and say with determination, "She plugs they ass fulla buckshot!" When Grammy hears me say that word "ass" she bout to have a kanipshun fit. Grandpa jumps in real fast'n explains that I only said it cuz I heard him sayin it. Anyways, he convinced Grammy we both meant it in the donkey way.

When Alice run outta supplies, she rides her ol' horse bareback through thick backwoods to the nearest town where she's well known in these parts. Mountain folks protect they own, specially where Revenuers is concerned. Grandpa reckons Alice been makin shine for neighbors too. He says she could get a government check cuz'a her old age'n all, but she downright burrs up ever time he tries to talk bout it. She turns down anythin smackin'a charity. Aunt Alice don't believe in state aid'n she's quick to say so. Grandpa says she's stubborn as a jackass, and not to get her riled up on accounta she got a bad temper'n a gun. He paid good money for a radio, but she won't use it cuz theys no electric. One day when me'n him playin gin rummy'n spinnin yarns, he looks up at me'n says, "You jus like Alice. Both'a you made outta piss'n vinegar!" Grammy don't preciate him usin swears to describe me, but I take it good like a compliment.

Grandpa's a home grown democrat'n union to the core, but certain subjects make him real mad'n that's when he uses words Grammy don't like. He found hisself a way'a gettin round sayin swears in front'a her. He says, "Government's a bunch of SOBs, that would be sons of bitches. They oughta stay outta folks GD, that would be goddamn, business!" Grandpa says he's convinced swearins'n art form'n, "Damnation to hell fire, I'm not about to stop!" That is, til Grammy walks into the room.

When he was young, my grandpa belonged to a literary society but nothin ever came of the short stories he wrote, explainin he had too many mouths to feed to be fiddlin round spinnin yarns. I cry when he reads Mr. Robert Frost out loud cuz I know in my heart it's his way'a sayin he's leavin soon. I caint hardly stand thinkin bout it.

> *The woods are lovely dark and deep*
> *But I have promises to keep*
> *And miles to go before I sleep*
> *And miles to go before I sleep*

Class of 55 – Little Rock Central High School

I have a particular affection for my hometown of Little Rock, Arkansas outside of segregation being so much like a bee to honey, and people around here hardly ever talking about it. Unless that is, I brought a negro friend home for dinner, worse still if I brought one to dinner through the front door; just when it can't get any worse, my family actually thinks it's the acceptable way of Southern living. Whenever I bring up the subject all I get is, "Tharon Ann, I have no idea what ya'll talking about, we treat nigras good." This town is a livewire of racial tension that sits right beneath the surface of our lives.

Most of the time my uncle is too drunk to know what color he is, much less the color of anyone else. Whites worry about colored students being integrated into Little Rock public schools that have always been for whites only. But whatta' you know, I'm actually graduating from Little Rock Central High School, Class of 1955. It's one of the largest, most beautiful segregated public high schools in the nation. I love sitting outdoors, having lunch with my friends on the grassy knoll – though Lord help the colored person who sits down beside us. None of this makes any sense to me. I'll never forget how Mama and Tessie were treated.

Every now and then for no reason at all, a feeling of anger wells up inside me … it comes and goes.

I don't know what gets into me sometimes. Like on the first day of high school when I walk up the long front steps; hard to believe by the time I'm inside my mind is already set on being popular. If you ask me when it all started, why wanting to be popular is like a phobia – beats me, just crazy I guess. All I know is, I want everyone to like me. This determination wins me the prize of all prizes. Whoo! Whoo! I am a Little Rock Central High School cheerleader with all the pom poms to go with it. I love my cheerleader friends, especially Maureen. We go to church together, but I don't invite anyone over on account of Uncle Zack, but what else is new around here?

I'm sixteen and no longer a bucktooth gangly tomboy but a curvy teenager – and what is wrong with that I ask you, really what's wrong with it? High school is about the "haves" and the "have nots." The "haves" don't wear hand-me-downs, they don't walk to school when it rains, they drive their own car, and they always have spending money. They live in nice houses on the right side of town. When anyone in a "have" family gets engaged, it makes page one in the society section. The only time a "have not" gets in the Arkansas Gazette is when someone gets hit by a car driven by one. When school starts, the "have" girls wear pretty clothes they pick out themselves at Pfeifer's, the nicest department store in Little Rock. A "have" girl is easy to spot, and so is a "have not." Being popular is the only way around it. I'm voted "Best Personality" in the *Class of 1955 Yearbook*, a prize I've earned from smiling so much my jaws ache. I'm starting to get bored. Things always look better when I don't have them, but once I get them, I'm like, "Is this it? Is this all there is?" It's crazy.

A month or so after my seventeenth birthday, and quite by accident, I discover one of the favorite sports of some white boys around here, is a little hometown venting of spleens known as "coon conking." As many boys that can pile into a car drive to the colored section, better known as "niggertown." When they spot a colored person standing on a street corner or a bus stop, they pull a long pole out from the backseat of the car, and hit as many on the head as the pole can reach before driving back to brag about it. I don't recognize any of their names but after hearing about all this, my desire to be popular falls away like old snakeskin. I wonder if this is what wanting something so bad does to people. I don't belong, not here – not anywhere.

I've made some new friends. There's Miles with a cowlick in front where his hairline begins, and writes poetry about how miserable he is. Even when it's hot, he wouldn't be caught dead walking down the hall without wearing his long black cape. There's Billy who walks like a girl, and says he's a dancer, Gwen who glides down the hall like she forgot to take off her toe shoes. I love to say her name: Gwen-n-n-n-n-n-n with an N; Gwen-n-n-n-n-n. I'm crazy in love with the way she dresses – different from the rest of us who wear poodle skirts and white bucks. She pulls her hair back into a bun covered with a knitted snood like ballet dancers wear. She has a nonchalant attitude towards everything. Gwen feels good about herself – unlike me, who wants to be loved by everyone on earth.

My favorite friend in the universe is Illah Rae who writes poetry and lets me read it. I'm not sure what type job her mama has, but there's just the two of them living in a one bedroom house. I like spending the night because her next-door neighbor is a graveyard. When the sun begins to set, we walk through the graves and read the inscriptions on every headstone. Illah Rae says she hears ghosts moaning at night everytime she opens her bedroom window. That's about the same time we start to hear ghosts shuffling about in the trees. Soon as it gets pitch dark, and we've scared ourselves half to death, we scream and run all the way back to Illah Rae's house to write poems about dead people.

She reminds me of the world of poetry and books my grandpa exposed me to, and managed to shove under my cheerleader pom poms for a while. In turn, I try to help her feel better about herself. All the time I say, "Illah Rae, you're the next damn Emily Dickinson. You never get out of the house cept to school, and you're always writing about how much you suffer. You got to read, 'I felt a Funeral, in my Brain,' and then you tell me, I mean it Illah Rae, you just tell me you didn't write that poem!"

She reads it over and over. Now she's hooked on Emily Dickenson. Illah Rae says forever. She makes good grades, unlike me who barely squeaks by. Plane geometry and algebra look like Chinese, and I still count on my fingers. What's worse than me failing home economics and having to repeat it in summer school? Who fails damn home economics? I can't figure myself out. Truth is, school is boring. My home life is such, that going to college has never been a subject for discussion. I have responsibilities other kids don't have.

Aunt Lowee says I'm a dreamer, that my feet aren't planted in this world. Some people sure have room to talk. Yesterday she sent me to Hudson's Market with enough money for a loaf of Wonder Bread. Just as I was walking out the door, she hollered so loud the whole neighborhood knew what she wanted, "Tharon Ann, bring me back a *Photoplay Movie Magazine* y'hear." She knew full well I didn't have enough money for both. Mr. Hudson won't give us any more credit. I tell Illah Rae all this so she'll know her life isn't so bad. I may be popular, but am I stupid or what to fail home economics?

I say, "Illah Rae, you're smart but look at me: I can hardly spell c-a-t."

Aunt Lowee never takes me to task. All she ever says is, "Pass Tharon Ann, Sweet Jesus just pass." She's too tired from working the nightshift to read my report cards.

I'm mad at God, Thelma, Sam, or whatever your name is

"Strange Fruit"
by Abel Meeropel
Recorded in 1939 by Billie Holiday

Southern trees bearing a strange fruit
Blood on the leaves and blood at the root
Black bodies swinging in the southern breeze
Strange fruit hanging from the poplar trees

The climate in Little Rock gets worse by the day. Christian preachers don't let colored people in their churches, and the few that do make them sit in roped off sections in the back where no one can see them. If God knows everything, then he knows how fed up I am right now. He could have stopped all this hate between whites and coloreds. He didn't. He could have stopped our soldiers from being killed in the war. He didn't. So I made a deal with him: if he doesn't bother me, then I won't pester him anymore. It's not right to call myself a Christian when I'm mad at him half the time.

All my life I've tried to love Jesus same as Mama did, but I don't and I'm not proud of myself for it. I feel so let down these days wondering why someone like him isn't around here now. If God gave people a teacher back then, why can't he give me one now? But when I say things like that, people look at me with that "shut up" look on their face, then comes ten quotes from the New Testament. Why should I believe them when they can't give me one good reason for claiming Christian whites are better than Christian negroes. If Jesus wasn't a racist, why are they? I have serious questions no one can answer outside of the usual stock answer, "Little lady, just read your Bible every day, have faith, and everything will work out." Well, maybe that answer is enough for some people but not for me.

And another thing, how come every question I ask always ends with them saying I'm sitting in judgment. Is wanting to know the truth same as judging others? I'd like to believe they know what they're talking about, but when I heard some preacher cheated on his wife at the drive-in last Saturday, and him with his hand in some girl's blouse, his tongue halfway to Memphis down her throat, and breaking the same ten commandments he preaches on Sundays, I thought to myself, "What's the Gospel done for him?" I know all Christians aren't like this but it's enough to turn me off.

I ask the same question over and over: what's the point in bringing someone to Jesus and getting them baptized, when you don't let coloreds in your church? Another time, I asked the same minister why God bothered to make me in the first place. I asked him where I lived before I was born, where I'll go when I die, and what kind of God makes war? He just looked at me like I didn't have my head screwed on tight. I should have asked him what he does on Saturday nights. I'm fed up asking questions no one can answer, like where my grandpa went when he died, like who decides what's to be born an animal, or a blade of grass, or a human being. Another thing, where do my thoughts go when I die? Where'd my old dog Laddie go when he got hit by a car and died? We buried him out back. I can't stop wondering about things like this. The Christian Science people are sincere, but they can't answer my questions either. I only go to church because it makes Aunt Lowee happy.

I passed. No one in my family is coming to see me graduate outside of Aunt Lowee and Sue. I'm moving to Los Angeles, California to live with my aunt and uncle who've already got my whole life planned out, beginning with U.C.L.A. Where will I smoke without them knowing it? Grammy still lives in the old house up the street. I don't have a thinker for school. I have other dreams. Haldane always said I live in my own world.

Today I leave Little Rock for good. It's like every other day, no band playing, no one calling to say goodbye, no one coming over to see me off – just Aunt Lowee. Uncle Zack is sleeping one off in the bedroom; Sue just locked herself in the bathroom. She's mad at me for leaving.

Part II

Show Biz Here I Come!

Hollywood, junkies and strip joints

I got a job waiting on tables in Hollywood. Finally. Top of that, I rented a room in a boarding house off Sunset Blvd. I'll have fun making dinner on a hot plate. At least I'm in Hollywood and, hooray hooray, finally moving out of my aunt's house. I've tried hard to get along with them, but honestly I can't stay here another minute. It's my life and I want to be free to live it. Being here is like choking to death because of my uncle's temper. This morning when my aunt told him I was bent on moving out, all he said was, "Good, she can leave today for all I care. I know what she's up to!"

And what might that be I wonder? Well, whatever it is … it's a mystery to me. I've never had a real boyfriend – you know the kind you do "that" with. Aunt Lowee never talked about "that" with me. Not ever.

My aunt never misses a chance to tell me what a disappointment I am, that I ruined my life when I dropped out of college. I swear, she acts like if I don't get in U.C.L.A., I'll go straight to hell. Anyway, that's her dream not mine. I'm going to be an actress.

I'm head over heels in love for the first time in my life – with his Cherokee good looks, soft blue eyes, and long black hair in contrast to his fair skin. He has a gentle way about everything he does, the way he lifts my hair, kisses the back of my neck, then whispers my name. I'm not even twenty, and loving so new to me. I'm also in love with a career I don't have yet.

Now for the reality check. I spend most of my fairytale marriage traveling back and forth on a bus to Chino State Prison whenever he's busted for drugs. Each time I visit, I get body searched for weapons and dope. Prison has a stench about it that follows me until I get home and soak in the tub for an hour – even then I smell it. It's the odor of hell that eeks out the pores of everyone locked up in there.

Prison is where he cleans up from smack but soon as he's released, Billy's back on the street again hustling for drugs.

When we got married, I was too naïve to know what I was getting into. It didn't take long to discover it was heroin that gave him the illusion of being someone he wasn't. Maybe buried underneath layers of dope is the person he could have been. I smoke pot but I'm too vain to have track-marks up my legs and arms like him. All my friends dabble with drugs, but I know enough to stay away from the hard stuff. I'd go so far out I'd never come back.

It's easy to understand how he became a druggie. At sixteen and still in high school, he was already playing in jazz clubs around Manhattan, and gaining a reputation for being one of the best jazz drummers around. One day the telephone rang, and the voice on the other end of the line asked for Billy. Naturally his mother thought it was for her husband as they have the same first name. She explained to the caller that he was doing studio work, and she would give him the message soon as he got home. The caller was the great jazz musician Charlie Parker who had no interest in the father; he wanted his son. Billy dropped out of high school to join Charlie Parker's famous band. He thought it was the greatest moment in his life, not realizing it was the beginning of the end.

I sometimes wonder how he felt playing with the greatest jazz musicians who ever lived – strung-out on heroine. He was the only white boy in Charlie Parker's band. At sixteen he switched from pot to smack, the perfect way to ward off stress and blend in. Today, Billy is just another strung out musician. Why doesn't God flag the events of our lives that will destroy it?

Lots of jazz musicians work in clubs like The Hot Kitty Cat, a well known strip house on Sunset Blvd. Billy is one of them, and talks the owner into hiring me as a waitress. I'm nervous about working in a place like this but what choice do I have? We're broke. Lucky for me someone just quit. I'm hired on the spot. The owner orders me to wear stiletto heels, black mesh hose, devil red lipstick, a bustier, and the type shorts that make men want to pinch my ass before I have a chance to knock the bejesus out of them. These horny old men think I'm for sale. I hate working here, but who pays the rent if I don't? Billy shoots our paychecks anywhere he can find a healthy vein in his arms or legs. Today the electric was shut off. Great!

Show Biz Here I Come!

Several days pass before I finally get the hang of this place. For me to get a tip depends on how well I play the game. I'm a fast learner when it comes to playing games without being touched. The dressing rooms are located backstage where the bartenders make drinks; these strippers never shut their doors. I can't help but notice what they do in front of bartenders, waitresses, or anyone else unlucky enough to work in this X rated hellhole. I don't have the temperament for this crowd. The Hot Kitty Cat, one of the most popular night spots in Hollywood, is packed every night with famous, as well as infamous male actors, producers, directors, and rich old men trying to grab a cheap thrill. Some try to get it on with waitresses by sticking a large bill down their boobs. If one of them tries that on me, I'll knock him to hell and back. I can't stand much more of this stinking place.

Tonight, as I'm going through my usual drill of wading through smoke and tables so close together, I'm amazed at the balancing act I've learned carrying oversized trays of drinks to bald horned toads. I bend over to serve a large group of white-haired fossiled men, when one grabs a handful. I'm so angry I purposely drop a tray of drinks hard as I can on his bald head, as glasses of booze crash down, scattering in the most unlikely places, staining their Rodeo Drive suits and ties. Strains of, "What the hell you bitch!" and "Someone get this bitch out of here!" are headed straight to the owner's ear. I don't care. Good! Do me a favor! Fire me! I've had enough of this hellhole to last me a lifetime!

All my pent up anger shoots back, "Kiss my ass you sons of bitches! I'm calling your wife! I'm telling her where you are and what you're doing! I'm out of here ... and kiss my ass again!"

Heads are turning. People are beginning to enjoy this little side show rather than the strippers. Here she comes. The owner heads my way. I turn to her and shout, "Keep my paycheck! Go buy yourself a new face!" Then I take off my high heels and throw them as far as I can back into the crowded smoke-filled room. So long hell. I'm out of here!

Every day I plead with Billy to let me help him clean up. I can't unless he agrees to the hell days of withdrawals. If a ten year old girl could live through DTs with an alcoholic, then shouldn't I be able to help him? I want to. I'm naive enough to think I can, but then again didn't I learn my lesson with Uncle Zack? I try and make myself believe a part of him wants to be free of a habit that destroys everything it touches, me in particular. A part of me dreads this ordeal. All my eyes see anymore is the dark side of life. I know more than any non-junky should, much less see: how to score, how to shoot up, and how to avoid narcos. Last night I dreamed I was both the warden and prisoner locked up in a cell. I searched everywhere, but couldn't find the key to escape.

Billy's sick. We drive to a small bungalow on Fountain Avenue in Hollywood where he scores from two mean, skinny lesbians ... the nasty bitches. We go inside. Three junkies I don't recognize are making jokes about two young narcotic cops who sent them to Chino twice but now work the Hollywood scene. These guys are blond, good looking narcos who resemble the Crosby boys. A middle aged, gaunt-faced man walks over to the junkies, and motions them to follow him to the back room. I always wait upfront, never where the deals go down in back; if this place gets busted I'll go down with everyone else. I stand here feeling very uncomfortable, not knowing what to do or what not to do. I look over, and wonder if it's my imagination that a girl wearing blue silk pajamas hiked up to her kneecaps, is sprawled out on a couch by the window. I walk to that side of the room to find a young girl with long auburn hair, maybe my age – maybe younger, with fresh track-marks on her arms and legs. Another woman walks over and whispers in my ear, the girl on the couch is the daughter of a famous movie star. When I ask what's wrong with her, she nonchalantly replies, "She just shot up," and abruptly turns and walks back, anxious she'll miss her turn to score. No sooner do I sit down beside her than she reaches out for my hand, her fingers cold and lifeless. Someone volunteers she's about to enjoy a large inheritance on her eighteenth birthday. She is a hard-core junky, young, beautiful, strung-out, just biding time for death to come. I doubt she'll ever see eighteen.

I'm almost out the door when the telephone rings. I answer. It's Billy. I know from his voice that he hurts and can't score, like someone in the bottom of a well. He begins to cry, "Tharon ...Tharon honey, I'm sorry ... I can't take it anymore ... I can't." He begs me to help him clean up. I make him tell me where he is ... to just wait there ... that I'll throw some things in a bag and pick him up; we'll drive to Malibu, lock ourselves in a motel room and just do it. Outside of going back to Chino it's the only way.

I say, "Wait ... don't hang up ... wait ... Billy, just wait ... I'll pick you up in thirty minutes ... it'll be alright ... don't cry ... it'll be alright baby, I'm leaving now."

There he is. An immediate wave of sadness runs through me to see him like this, standing on the corner in front of Barney's Beanery. He was my first love, handsome, talented and so gentle. Now look – gaunt, thin with track-marks on his arms and legs. He mumbles hello, and hardly looks at me as he gets in the car. I drive to a motel in Malibu. He tells me in advance, that no matter what he says I'm not to let him out of the room. He tells me to hide the car keys as well as the key to our room. There are no words to describe what it's like trying to hold on to someone going through heroine withdrawals ... someone who isn't there.

By day three, I'm sick from exhaustion, he's sick from hurting, and freaking the hell out. He threatens to kill me if I don't give him money and my car keys. With his hands around my throat, he screams in my ear, "Gimme the keys, or I swear to God I'll choke you to death Tharon! Gimme me the goddamn keys or I'll kill you right here ... you're a dead bitch," as he tightens the hold on my neck.

He'll kill me if I don't do something. I give him my purse. He throws it on the bed, and takes all the money ... twenty five dollars. I unlock the motel door, and tell him the car keys are under the mat on the driver's side. They aren't. He'll sell my car for a fix if he gets his hands on them. He grabs the money and shoves me aside. As he runs to the car, I quickly lock the door. He'll be back when he can't find the keys. I'm so scared I can hardly breath. Oh my God he's back, banging on the door, threatening to kill me again. "Get out of here Billy! I called the police. They're on the way."

This will be a long night. My back propped up against the wall, I sit on the floor and wait for the sun to come up; I need to make sure he's gone. Billy's looking to score. After that he'll be OK, until the next time he thoughtlessly shoots up again.

I'm just starting out in Hollywood, not having much luck even getting a walk-on. I try not to get discouraged, but it's hard when I need to take acting classes. We're always broke. There's no money for anything. Because of heroin, we barely make ends meet; the telephone was just turned off. It's only a matter of time before he gets busted again. I hate these strung-out freaks coming here. Every morning he wakes up sick, rifles through my purse for money then leaves to score … can't live in junky hell anymore … nothing but darkness here. I'm pregnant. Billy's gone. He's never coming home.

After a nervous breakdown followed by a miscarriage, I file for divorce. Who knows where he is – maybe dead from an overdose or bad needles … don't know … I'm so messed up … no good to anyone. How many times do I reinvent myself to survive … how many? I can't get any lower than I am now. When is it my turn?

Sex is an hors d'oeuvre in Hollywood

Every day I run back and forth to the Chinese Grauman Theatre, working crazy odd hours with breaks in between shows. Oh, the life of an usherette. Ha! At least I have a job, and one step closer to my goal. I have to start somewhere. I'll never let anyone push me in the dirt again. Never.

It's so cool living at the Hollywood Studio Club. It feels like a luxury hotel, but it's more like a sorority house for starlets and other show folk like me floating around trying to get their foot in a door – any door. Lots of contract players from major studios live here. There's so much to say about this town – the seedy underbelly of ambition, the many times I've been in a car when suddenly his arm slides down, and confuses my leg for the gearshift. Sex is an hors d'oeuvre in Hollywood, a precursor to fast-tracking goals, a route I won't take – thank you very much.

After dinner I decide to sit in the lobby and work on a scene from *This Property is Condemned,* a one act play by Tennessee Williams, for acting class tomorrow. My room is so small, the lobby is the only place to read and study; the other residents do the same. It's also where guests come to visit. No one is allowed upstairs with the exception of those who live here.

I'm sitting here with my nose in a script when I'm hit on by one of Howard Hughes, or so he says, talent scouts – like seriously, who can believe anyone in this town. He is a tall, nondescript man who tries to strike up a conversation about how hard it is to get parts in Hollywood if you don't know the right people. The man says he's waiting for someone who lives here that was just put under contract to Howard Hughes, along with his pitch that he is setting her up in a new apartment. In addition, he pays all her expenses and pushes her career. He asks me the question, "What do you think of that?"

Without looking up, I reply in my old Southern accent, "Sounds good to me." Those words are the ammunition for his big finale.

He continues to explain that when Hughes calls for this girl, she must be available for him. He makes it sound like such a great opportunity, that if I'm interested he can make it happen for me too. This guy is the usual Hollywood wall snot. I'm insulted by his offer. In my softest Southern ladylike voice, I look directly into his eyes and without blinking an eyelash, smile sweetly and ask, "Would you kindly take that offer and shove it up your ass?"

He's shocked by my reply, but I continue to focus my glassy stare on his very nervous face. I have no idea what he is about to say; I take the lead once again and continue our one-sided conversation, "If you so much as look at me again, I'll have you arrested for pimping." I'm angry because I know I'm better than this. Perfect timing. The girl he's been waiting for enters the room. He quickly turns from me. She's happy to see him. Smiling, he takes her hand and they leave. I know her. She is Elizabeth Taylor gorgeous.

A week or so later I notice that same girl in the dining room. She catches my eye and motions me to come join her for dinner. After we exchange the usual chitchat, I begin to describe my brief encounter with the so-called Howard Hughes guy she went out with. To my surprise, she's genuinely happy I have an opportunity to get ahead in this town. Still thinking she's putting me on, I laugh and begin to share my exact words to "pimpman," that I have no interest in being any man's whore-girl. Horrified, she abruptly gets up and leaves the room in a huff. She never speaks to me again. Well go damn figure Hollywood.

I share a room the size of a shoebox with a goofy dancer, Betsy Fillmore, at the Hollywood Studio Club. She has the one single bed in the room. Mine is on the sleeping porch at the end of the hall, number fifteen to be exact, where the Miss Universe contestants dream of becoming queen of the world during runoffs. She reminds me of a slightly off-centered Christmas tree angel. Each morning on the way to ballet class, she walks through the Hollywood Farm Market to test sausage samples for breakfast. Betsy's leaving soon to go back home and marry her high school sweetheart. I'm glad. She would never survive Hollywood; way too sweet for this town … reminds me of back home. I'll miss her when she's gone.

Show Biz Here I Come!

I know what I want. When push comes to shove, I'm a survivor. Otherwise, how did I live through the first two years in Hollywood trying to break into television, trying to get an agent, trying to get anything. Agents always tell me the same thing, "Little lady, you're no hot house orchid. You got no headlights, and a voice like Minnie Pearl. Take your cute little ass back to Little Rock and marry the milk man, but whatever you do – get out of show business. You're in way over your head. You'll never make it."

Actually, I do have an agent of sorts who calls herself, "Mrs. Virginia, agent for the stars." She represents midgets, talking dogs, parrots, jugglers, a ventriloquist, a spider monkey she stole from a street vendor and me. One day, she calls to say that such and such is casting a great role, "Dahling, you're perfect for the part. It will put you on top dahling. Now you must be there on time dahling."

I suspect Mrs. Virginia is a man in drag. I could be wrong, but I don't think so. She has a deep, show biz voice sprinkled with "dahling this" and "dahling that" in every conversation. Whenever she opens her mouth, I envision hot prune juice running down the side of her face.

When I arrive at the casting office, Mrs. Virginia's entire circus act is in the lobby, flying and swinging in all their glory. Are we here for the same part? It could happen. This is Hollywood. I take her into my confidence, cough a few times on my sleeve and explain that I'm dying of tuberculosis, adding in my sweetest voice, "I haven't the heart to waste your precious time."

I may be new to the Hollywood scene but I've come a long way from this type mass cattle call, and half-assed agents who book clowns and monkeys for car shows in shopping malls. It's easy to be eaten alive in this town.

Being a starlet has the same value as a cheerleader in a nursing home. My dream is to be a real actress on Broadway. Last week, someone from the Actor's Studio told me Hollywood actors aren't respected on or off Broadway. Well that's great, but I need to pay the rent. I have to begin somewhere.

At last, my foot is finally in the Hollywood door doing bit parts on television shows like *Alfred Hitchcock Presents*, *Father Knows Best, Dobie Gillis, Suspicion* etc. If you blink you'll miss me, but it's something. Warner Brothers grinds out shows, one hit after the other. Sitcoms sweep the nation week after week. One of the most popular is *77 Sunset Strip* starring Ephrem Zimbalist Jr. and Roger Smith, along with Edd Byrnes and Connie Stevens. Overnight, Edd has become a household name after his hit record, "Kookie, Kookie Lend me your Comb." Teeny boppers go wild for this song. When Edd's contract is up for renewal, his agent holds out for more money. Where Jack Warner is concerned actors are dispensable, no matter their popularity. Edd wants more money than Jack Warner thinks he's worth, and fires him. That's the end of his rising star, his agent's big commission, and another hard lesson to learn in this town. The pendulum swings both ways. A headliner today stands in the unemployment line tomorrow.

My agent just called to say I got the job I auditioned for months ago … so excited I can hardly breathe. I'll be part of a summer repertory company in Connecticut as well as a proud, card-carrying member of Actor's Equity, and the union dues that go with it. He tells me to buy a plane ticket and be there in two weeks. Whoo! Whoo!

Summer stock isn't what I expected. I hardly have time to unpack! On the upside, it's an opportunity to learn the techniques of performing on stage with well known character actors like Dora Merande, a great comedian in her late seventies. She makes it her life's ambition to stand in the wings each night and critique my every performance – comedy in particular. Dora is like a badger hunting prey, her long nose always checking me out, her buzzard-like eyes, small, squinty blue dots that at first glance seem cold, unyielding and lacking in humor. On the other hand, her odd-shaped nose has made a grateful friend out of me. If I look at it long enough, it begins to assume a life all its own.

Dora feels it's less painful to teach me her lifelong bag of comedy trade secrets, than to have me step on her laugh lines every night for the rest of the summer. She's tutoring me in all the tricks of comedy, how to come in when a laugh peaks, how *not* to step on a laugh line, how to do a double take in a natural way, how to take a slap, how to give a slap, how to take a fall without breaking every bone in my body, how not to upstage another actor, and how *to* upstage another actor. In short, she has become my mentor in comedy, and likes me despite herself. I adore her, and hang on every word she says. Lucky for me, because directors in summer stock have little time for anything outside of blocking scenes and preventing the actors from killing each other. We rehearse next week's play from early morning until late afternoon. Afterward we go home, wash up, and grab a bite before returning to perform the play of the week for packed houses six days a week. Monday is dark. This is hard, grueling work, not at all what I thought it would be, but I'm not complaining. Where else could I learn the technique of performing on stage, as opposed to television and film – two different mediums. I'm lucky they hired me; at least that's what Dora says. Ha!

During the day, I rehearse for next week's lead role of the sexy waitress Cherie in *Bus Stop*. In the evening I play twelve year old Ann Frank in *The Diary of Ann Frank*. When Bus Stop is in performance, we begin rehearsals for *Separate Tables*. I've learned so much from this strenuous schedule. The disciplined give and take of ensemble acting isn't for sissies. Not a week passes, I'm not taken to task by the older, seasoned cast members. I hope to have more confidence in myself by summer's end. Saying goodbye to Dora won't be easy. Seems like that's all I ever do.

I love Lucy, but what ever happened to Lucille Ball?

I'm back in Hollywood with practical experience under my belt. Working with seasoned character actors this past summer has given me new confidence. I'm beginning to get parts in little theatres around Hollywood, a good showcase for agents, producers and directors to scout for new talent. First thing this morning I get a call from my agent who tells me that last week Lucille Ball sent someone to check me out at a small theatre-in-the-round, where I'm performing in *Blue Denim*. Apparently, she wants me to join her new repertory company being assembled at Desilu Studios. What a break. Just imagine. Lucille Ball wants to meet me.

On the day of my appointment, I'm more than a little nervous meeting her as I vividly recall the Lucy of my childhood. A week never passed that I didn't watch *I love Lucy* on our television set Uncle Zack won in a poker game. I spent the first week just trying to figure out how people could move and talk inside that little box. Meeting a memory in the flesh is no small thing. Waiting here, my thoughts retrogress to the many times Joan Crawford, Aunt Lowee's pet red hen, sat on Uncle Zack's shoulder and never missed an episode of *I Love Lucy.* That hen was Lucille Ball's greatest fan. I'd love to tell her about Joan Crawford, but she'll think I made up such a crazy story.

I'm so nervous sitting outside her dressing room, my face begins to break out in hives. I try and read *Daily Variety* to calm my nerves ... hard to believe I'm about to meet Lucille Ball, my Lucy. Suddenly, I hear a loud strident voice. I've no idea what my expectations are, but this can't be her screaming. I try to convince myself that no way does this shrill voice belong to the Lucy of my childhood.

Show Biz Here I Come!

I'm startled to hear a rough voice yell in my direction, "Well, don't stand there like a bump on a log. Get in here!"

Is she talking to me? She must be. There's no one here but me. With considerable caution, I walk into her dressing room and stare. I didn't ask to be here; she invited me. I go back and forth with myself, thinking surely this hard voice belongs to someone wearing a Lucy mask. No such luck. She cuts right to the chase and begins her pitch, that if I sign a contract with Desilu, I'll get more theatre experience. The carrot she dangles is the promise of placing her repertory actors in the many sitcoms Desilu grinds out. Even though she has already handpicked, even signed up quite a few established actors, this is no big turn on for me. I'm loyal to my heroines but this one is going down fast. My trusting nature, or whatever naivety is left in me, has its heels put to the fire with this encounter. I watch her ultra red lips move against a mop of freshly dyed, fire red hair, eyelashes I could trip on, and realize she isn't the same Lucy I remember and loved.

Once reality sets in, clearly her offer will knock out future opportunities that might come my way. Binding myself to a long-term contract for an iffy project that only pays scale doesn't make sense. She promises the moon, but does she think I just got off a banana boat? Truth is, I don't like her. She senses my hesitation and begins to rant about my agent who either was, or I suspect still is her agent. She looks directly into my eyes and screams, "You're so damn stupid, you don't understand he doesn't want you involved in our project because his commission would be shit! I know him like the back of my hand!"

I'm stunned she talks like this to someone she doesn't know. The Lucy I loved would never say "shit." After this tirade, she dismisses me and states with utmost confidence, "Think about it and get back to me!" To insure hers is the last word spoken, she screams, "Soon!"

I leave her office fast as my legs will take me while chewing four sticks of gum at once. I know for sure it will be a cold day in hell when I ever get back to her. Shattered dreams are harsh realities to face. The Lucy of my childhood was only a television character, quite different from the woman I met today. I call my agent from a payphone to let him know I'd rather have my hooters shot out of cannon, than sign a contract with someone I don't trust. If I go with Desilu I could be stuck there forever.

Lucille Ball is a great comedienne. I'll give her that. *I love Lucy* ran from 1951 – 1957, one of the most watched shows on television. This afternoon, Lucille Ball spoke to me at length about how hard she worked to be the star she is today, how she saved her money from every paycheck, and how she never stopped trying to better herself. I take my hat off to her for that. I also admire her grit because she's married to a man who can't keep his pants up. Maybe loving him made her like this.

Once I recover from the shock of losing my childhood heroine, I drive straight home, crawl into bed without taking off my clothes, pull the covers up over my head and cry.

Show Biz Here I Come!

Ronald Reagan and me

Even if I tried, I could never forget Ronald Reagan. He is the moderator and star of *General Electric Theatre*. I am the ingénue lead in one of the weekly shows he oftentimes stars in. I'm really nervous because this is my first lead role in a major television show that first aired in 1954, and still ahead in the ratings. The irony is that my first paycheck came from a thirty second bit part on *Jane Wyman Theatre*. I died. That's it. I was on screen only fifteen seconds when they pulled the sheet up over my head, but it paid the rent for a month. Jane Wyman was Ronald Reagan's first wife.

From the moment I arrive in makeup at 7:00 a.m., he's there waiting for me. He gives me a firm handshake as he introduces himself. I immediately notice his eyes twinkle when he smiles. They have deep creases in the corners from laughing, probably at a joke he's told a million times before, then cracked up again the next time around. My grandpa was like that. He loved to tell a good joke, and laughed as much as the listener, probably more. Mr. Reagan is the same way. His presence is formidable yet he seems more like a favorite uncle who leaves nickels and quarters in the corners of a chair he always sits in when he visits, knowing children will find them when he leaves. There's something about him that makes me feel that no matter what, everything will be OK.

After I, "Yes sir" and "No sir" him half to death, he finally puts his hand up as if to say, "Stop!" He pauses a moment then says, "How about this young lady: you call me Ronnie, and I'll call you Tharon. Fair?"

I'm somewhat taken back as I was taught to respect my elders, but Mr. Reagan insists I call him Ronnie. He has a natural way about him that immediately puts me at ease, unusual in this town.

Throughout one week of filming I'm never out of his sight. He's bent on teaching me the various techniques every actor must know. Television is shot on tight budgets. Reshooting a scene due to an actor's lack of technique is a surefire means of never working for that studio again. Ronald Reagan is the kindest person I've ever met in show business. For example, we have one scene coming up, a long shot of just the two of us riding in an old buckboard wagon with a team of horses. Long shots are usually done by extras or doubles, but Ronnie thinks it would be fun to do. The next thing I know, he tells the director he wants to drive the team of horses himself, over-riding his objection. "You are the star," the director reminds him, "Why waste your time since your face won't be seen in a long shot." Nevertheless, the handlers bring a team of horses, along with an old buckboard wagon for us to climb aboard the wooden seat. I honestly don't know how the early pioneers had a butt left after those long treks across the prairie. The high birthrate is baffling. Ronnie turns to me and says, "Well, Tharon – not easy on the old behind is it?"

The telephone rings. It's my agent. I have an interview at 1:00 this afternoon with Jerry Wald, an important producer at Twentieth Century Fox. This is a huge break, and hard to believe it's happening to me. I put on my best outfit and drive to Twentieth.

When I enter his suite two other men are present who right away get down to business, and check me out like I'm the lox and bagels they just ordered from Cantors. They dissect me from head to toe as though I'm not here. Slowly, the conversation segues onto the subject of my name, that it doesn't meet the standards of other great show business names. Jerry W. says in a thick accent, "Tharon Ann? It's got no b'zazz!" Who ever heard of a name like that? You listening? I named Jennifer Jones ... see the rhythm? You gotta have a three syllable first name and a one syllable last name."

I'm standing here, a cadaver in the midst of an autopsy, watching my birth name fly out the window. The only sound that comes out of my mouth is, "Yes sir, that's fine." The young girl once named Tharon Ann, someone I began life with, is dead. I'm suddenly frightened. I want to resurrect her ... why did I cave in? ... why did I allow him to change my name? Tharon was my father's name; it's all I have left of him. Then again, what's in a name? So what if my ambition caved to a loudmouth star maker. So what. I'll bury Tharon

Ann once and for all. I'm not her anymore. Don't I have my foot in the door of a major movie studio? This is what counts.

I sign a contract with Jerry Wald for his upcoming film, *Mardi Gras,* starring Pat Boone, Tommy Sands, Christine Carrere, Gary Crosby, Dick Sergeant, Sherrie North, Fred Clark, Barry Chase and me. From this point forward, everyday I drive to Twentieth for wardrobe, hair, makeup, schedules, meeting with various cast members, and rehearsing the musical sequences with a choreographer. Jerry Wald parades me around Twentieth and introduces me like I'm his new toy poodle. Who minds being a poodle? I don't. Woof! Woof! I'm in heaven.

I have an important interview today. Jerry W. makes a point of telling me to wear the yellow dress from *Mardi Gras.* He urges me to be very polite to one of the two most influential women in Hollywood, Hedda Hopper. Louella Parsons and Hedda have gossip columns. They make and break careers with a word, wielding their long, vengeful, sword-like tongues. In 1958, they own this town. People around here treat them like the second coming.

We walk over to the set where Hedda, as famous for the hats she wears as her scathing tongue, holds court. Jerry W. bows low and kisses up to her,

"Hedda, love of my life, I'd like you to meet another little lady who loves hats."

The only hat I like is my old baseball cap, but today I'm wearing a pale yellow cloche style to match my dress. He continues,

"She's going to be in *Mardi Gras.* This one has the makings of a star."

Unimpressed, Hedda gives me a quick glance, just enough for me to look into her unyielding steel-blue eyes. For a brief moment, if ever a pissant froze to death inside a popsicle, it's me standing here right now. She hates me. In an attempt to salvage the moment, I grab hold of my composure, and strain to harness enough sunshine to send a Kodak smile to this powerful woman wearing a hat reminiscent of a rooster chasing a barnyard hen. In a calculated move, Hedda slowly turns her head in my direction, and gives me an icy look that clearly represents her instant opinion of me, which is: "Drop dead you little bitch!"

In silence, I recite the alphabet ten times in wait for sound to come out of her draconian lips. She whispers in the vicinity of where

I'm standing, "How nice." Her head does a three quarter turn, as she summarily dismisses me with a flip of her hand.

Someone once told me I'm too direct with people, that it makes them uneasy. After my lackluster introduction to the Queen of Hollywood I pretend to be dead, and stand there like someone waiting at a red light, who dies two seconds before it turns green. Jerry and Hedda continue to plot about exclusive dirt he'll give her, only if she will *not* print something he doesn't want made public. This town specializes in the game of tit for tat. It's easy pretending to like a person when they pretend to like me, but hard even being cordial to someone who hates me right off the bat.

When he's finished his arm-twisting, brown-nosing chat with Hedda, on we go to our next stop which is the makeup department. As we walk along he tells me how many stars he's made, pausing long enough for me to acknowledge the double entendre. Once there, he introduces me to a well known man who is polite and eager to please – rare in this town. Everyone has an agenda. What you see ain't necessarily so. No one around here can point fingers if they're completely honest.

He takes one look at me and says, "Now little lady, wait here for a moment. I'll whip up a custom eye shadow that will be perfect for you."

After his last remark, my introspective, philosophical thoughts jump headfirst out the window. I need the wait for my ego to orbit back to earth. I'm just being honest when I say, "I'm so in awe when I think of me."

When anyone in Hollywood uses the expression, "I'm just being honest," it's usually right after they've insulted the crap out of someone, and I'm just being honest.

Performing in television and film is boring as all get out, not at all like theatre where performance is live and in sequence, as opposed to film where scenes are shot out of sequence, with the exception of live television. All I do is sit all day in wait for my scene to come up. My friend Barrie Chase is also in *Mardi Gras*. She was Fred Astaire's dance partner on a much anticipated television special they performed together. *An Evening with Fred Astaire* was awarded nine Emmys. Oh, these long waits on the *Mardi Gras* set.

Like clockwork, at least one or two of the Crosby brothers visit the set each day to hang out with Gary. He never tires discussing the same subject over and over: how much he hates his father, Bing Crosby. Day after day, he paints an image of a man quite opposite of the easygoing, warm person he projects on film. No matter his fame and money, Gary's yesterdays are his life. Without them he'd be lost. I try hard not to look back at a past I can't change.

Maybe 1958 is my lucky year. I'm a regular visitor to a psychiatrist. So far, the only thing I've discovered is that one hour doesn't equal sixty minutes. It equals fifty five. At this hourly rate, two years is enough. I'm determined not to live my life repeating the "poor me" mantra to everyone I meet.

Live television is a scary bitch. After a week's rehearsal and showtime arrives, it is performed live, and in sequence with no place to hide. If during a scene, the actor suddenly feels the urge to pee and can't hold it, the best he can do is pray the television screen covers it up. This happens to someone I'm working with. We're performing a drama on live television when I notice a waterfall on the front of his trousers. I'm so startled, I can't remember my next line – on top of that, I come close to blowing the scene by laughing when I look at the expression on his face. Everything happens so fast, like a play within a play. We perform this scene on live television as rehearsed. I'll never know how we got through it.

Once the scene is over my dresser grabs me in the wings, stands me at attention with my hands outstretched like a scarecrow, while she strips off the old costume. I'm in the process of being re-dressed for the next scene with people mulling around backstage. No one pays the least bit of attention to me or anyone else for that matter, as the other actors are being re-dressed in the same way. Someone else takes me by the hand, and leads me to the next set to make sure I don't trip over cables, or whatever else is on the backstage floor I could break my leg on. All this takes place in two minutes or less. There's no safety net for failure on live television. If a mistake is made chances are, the viewers will see it. I pay my dues the old fashion way by performing small parts in shows like *Playhouse 90* and *Studio One*.

Give my regards to Broadway

It's a done deal. Finally, I'm making the big move to New York and leaving Tinseltown with no regrets. My roomy and protector of sorts is Lovie, an iconic writer with friends around the globe so it's not like we're moving to some obscure place as strangers. New York is a dangerous town to live in, particularly for a young, inexperienced girl like me. Oh, and lest I forget Lovie is a dictator; he hovers over me like a mother hen – just what the doctor ordered.

Looking for an apartment in Manhattan is a nightmare, but hooray we've just hit the mother lode. Lovie and I are now the proud renters of a third floor walk-up in an old brownstone on a beautiful treelined street on West 11th in Greenwich Village. We live directly across the street from Ann Bancroft and her husband, Mel Brooks. One morning when Lovie and I are having coffee on his side of our apartment, I look through the front window and happen to catch a glimpse of her as she's leaving the house. My fertile imagination conjures up different scenarios where I introduce myself as a new neighbor – you know, natural-like, "Oh excuse me Ann, sorry to bump into you like this, but I want to apologize for Marlon Brando, my roomie's half poodle, half chihuahua dog who pees on your tree everyday," or "Well, I'll be a monkey's uncle, since we're neighbors, how bout' coming over for coffee and a piece of my homemade Bundt cake – hot out of the oven." I never made a cake in my life. Truth is, I can boil water for great instant coffee, so isn't that sort of like cooking? I remind myself of groupies who hang out at the backstage door of theatres to catch a glimpse and an autograph of their favorite actor.

New York in the sixties is quite the opposite of LA, the City of Angels not. I can vouch for this. It's also the cradle of that grand old lady – the Actor's Studio, at 432 W. 44th St. in Manhattan; no frills there, just electrifying creativity inside the closed doors. I'll audition once we're settled. This is a filthy city with nothing but highrise buildings that stretch out far as the eye can see, and masses of people walking shoulder to shoulder. Midtown trash pickup is something not to experience; refuse piled on sidewalks by the curb, the putrid odor mixed with perspiration of those walking in close proximity along narrow sidewalks, is definitely not a new perfume by Chanel. The foul smell is something you either don't notice because you're so used to it, you're wearing a gas mask or like me, you're blind to her faults.

What I like best are the sidewalks always teeming with people. I get lost walking side by side, block after block in this parade of sweating humanity from Central Park to Midtown Manhattan to Greenwich Village, until finally winding up in the East Village. This is Mecca to me. It is the beginning and end of my goals, and whatever semblance of happiness I dream of having in this life. People either enjoy an intimate relationship with this city and accept it as is, or they move on. When I watch the body language of New Yorkers, I'm at a loss how best to describe it. Sometimes it's poetry in motion, other times it's the most eclectic dance of untalented aardvarks I've ever watched in a B movie. What others consider a negative, I view as a positive undercurrent in a metropolis of addictive style and elegance. New York is my town.

One morning as I walk up Lexington Ave. and late for an audition, I happen to notice a small wildflower growing out of the concrete. I've little time to reflect on the life of a weed; still, the irony of it makes me stop for a moment. I look around just long enough to notice the sidewalk filled with people whose feet more than once, trample it down – yet it continues to pop back up again and again and again. How can anything be so contained within itself? How can it possibly survive against all odds, what life is so determined to throw its way? Is one insignificant wildflower's ability to survive in concrete greater than my own struggles, given a similar circumstance? If a common weed can survive all that is thrown at it, surely I can withstand every assault laid at my door. I quickly dismiss my uncharacteristic train of thought as I'm late for an audition. Why think this way? I've better things to do than stand here worrying about a weed.

It's easy to nail someone who isn't a New Yorker by the way they walk. One hundred blocks a day is the norm for natives. Tourists on the other hand, are an easy mark because they wear the wrong shoes, the worst imaginable for the sidewalks of New York. I can tell by the grimace on their faces, their feet hurt to the point of extinction.

Few New Yorkers have cars. Their daily commutes are by subway, crosstown buses or taxis. Few are masochistic enough to wear white in this city. By noon, white shirts have morphed into gray from the polluted air. Black is a New Yorker's best friend – nothing more elegant than a simple black dress with a strand of pearls, black leather shoes, and understated leather handbag. Shopgirls waiting for the crosstown bus have better taste than the rich and famous I meet at parties who wear whatever fashion dictates. Even if "what's in" makes them look like clowns, they'll spend fortunes to look absurd. On the other hand, a savvy shopgirl who is low on funds but high on smarts, studies her body and is selective enough to only buy clothes that accentuate her best features. She saves up for that one perfect dress to wear for any occasion – to work, to the Met, anywhere. Shopgirls know how to accessorize. They best define what I love most about New York.

My best pal Rene heads an upscale fashion house. We used to hangout together in Hollywood when neither of us had enough money for bus fare. His point of contention was, American women seem clueless when it comes to fashion. They follow trends whether "what's in" is good for their body shape or not. It's OK if their ass is the size of an elephant, or their knees like weathered driftwood; guaranteed, come hell or high water, they'll wear tight slacks, leotards and mini-shorts anyway.

Back in our Hollywood days, every Friday night Rene and I watched old *Tarzan* movies unless one of us had a date. We spent long nights smoking pot, eating, and laughing at how I created my own fashion statement, a retro Salvation Army look for under two dollars – mixed with my own designs. Once he flipped up the hem on a top I'd made, and threw a hissy for fifteen minutes based on my slovenly job of hemming. Oh golly gee, someone forgot to take out a straight pin! But his point was well taken. Details are everything. From God's mouth to Rene who says, "Without them, you're as useless as tits on a boar hog!" After that we'd share a joint, make spaghetti, and pork our way through another *Tarzan* movie.

There is the small issue of noise in Gotham, a cacophony of sounds twenty four hours a day like a Tibetan prayer wheel. Had Henry David Thoreau lived in Manhattan, no doubt he would have blown his brains out and I would never have read *Walden,* my childhood favorite. As for me, I love Manhattan street sounds, a lullaby rocking me to sleep each night, winding as they do through windows covered with wrought iron bars and doors with triple locks.

My big Broadway break

I'm in New York trying hard to find work in the theatre, and coming up against a brick wall wherever I go because my Hollywood credits mean zilch in this town. So what's the first job I get? I finally get a chance to perform comedy on a *DuPont Show of the Month* starring Art Carney, Walter Matthau, Frank Gorshin, Jonathan Winters, and yours truly playing the female lead. But the most difficult job is to survive working with some of the best funnymen in the business, each attempting to upstage the other – especially during breaks. We rehearse in old lofts, anywhere the studio can find that's cheap. Laughter is what keeps me going.

The most unpredictable comic to work with is Art Carney – scary too because he forgets his lines, yet he's so right for this part the producers cast him anyway. The director can easily cover for him by writing his dialog on cue cards, or anything with a surface including the ceiling, on the underside of an actor's hand including my own, on a chair cushion, on a butt, not mine, anywhere and everywhere. How great was he in *The Honeymooners* with Jackie Gleason.

I'm crazy about Walter Matthau. During our weeklong rehearsal period, each day I look forward to having lunch together, just taking a break from it all. We eat at a diner around the corner from where we rehearse on the Lower East Side. He describes in detail the struggles he's faced in his life; gambling in particular, almost destroyed him. As I listen to Walter, my thoughts go to all the people in my professional and personal life who've suffered through drinking, gambling and drugs. Addiction is no respecter of persons. People only see the glitter of show business; so far, I've never met a genuinely happy person. As for me, happy and sad aren't issues. I don't analyze my life. I'm in the flow of it trying my best to hang on. To be cast in quality shows, and tutored by some of the best comedy actors in the business is happiness enough for now – that, and paying the rent. Finally after so long a time, I'm beginning to luck out. But you never know, up one day, down the next, here today, gone tomorrow – that's show biz.

People are clueless when they say actors who perform dramatic parts have a more difficult task than those who perform comedy; the truth is quite the opposite. Great comics usually make great dramatic actors if they get a halfway decent director to reign them in. The personal lives of most comics are riddled with sadness.

OK. So I am just an understudy to the understudies but so what? Come on. This is my big break. It's 1963 and I'm actually sitting in a real dressing room in a real Broadway theatre, in a real Broadway show. *One Flew over the Cuckoo's Nest* stars Kirk Douglas as Randall Patrick Murphy and Gene Wilder as Billy Bibbitt at the Cord Theatre. Being called at the last minute to replace an actor who was just run over by a bus is my worst nightmare, but this job pays the rent with enough left over for acting and dance classes. May these understudies live forever. We share a dressing room many flights up. Am I in heaven or what. Whoo! Whoo!

If an actor is lucky enough to perform at the Cherry Lane Theatre, it's as close to Broadway as it gets. Many great playwrights and directors came out of this small theatre in Greenwich Village, along with industry people who cover new plays and scout for talent. I've just been cast in a new off Broadway play, *The Dutchman* to open soon at the Cherry Lane.

The producers are quite savvy in their bold decision to showcase new actors, directors and playwrights like Harold Pinter. I love to sit in the wings and watch other plays in rehearsal. Down the road I'd like to direct, but for now this is where I've always wanted to be. It's not the money because off Broadway only pays scale, at least for me. It's belonging to something grand, something bigger than life. I'm judged by what I produce, not where I was born or what I look like, and surely not for the size of my boobs. I lack self-confidence, except in performance when I'm no longer me. My one and only psychological epiphany, the result of visiting a psychiatrist for two years, is that I don't need one. I always feel more comfortable being someone else, someone outside myself. Truth is, I have enough ego to make up for my low self esteem, words coined by my psychiatrist to keep me shrink-poor for the rest of my life.

The Dutchman is a two character play written by Le Roi Jones a.k.a. Amiri Baraka, a central figure in the Black Arts movement, and stars Robert Hooks and me. The fact that we improvise some of the dialogue he wrote may account for his uptightness most of the time. It's not unusual for actors and directors to improvise in rehearsal as the text doesn't always translate into the performance of it. We improvise the script to make the dialogue flow in a more realistic way. Many professional writers and directors encourage this method as a means of character development. Bobby and I work well together. His easygoing nature, coupled with a good sense of humor makes him fun to work with. I'm probably the only actress in New York he hasn't hit on. Our relationship is strictly professional. We're good friends. "Bobby the Babe Magnet" describes him to a T. I'll miss him when the play completes its run.

Tonight's opening of *The Dutchman* is electric with anticipation from the producers on down. We get rave reviews. I've hit the gravy train for sure, as it is the first play of its genre to be presented on stage. A psychotic white girl uses black, racist street language and provocative body moves, to seduce a middle class black student on the subway. He, on the other hand, tries to contain himself and avoid being killed by her.

This is an incendiary two character play and the reviews reflect it. The *Village Voice* has awarded *The Dutchman* an Obie for being the best new play in 1964. I receive the World Theatre award for best actress in this same play. Well go damn figure me winning that. My career in New York has finally given birth. The role of Lulu is the most challenging part I've ever tackled.

Not long after opening night, the famous director Elia Kazan drops by the Cherry Lane to check out my performance. He is one of the most sought after directors in both theatre and film, having to his credit such films as *On the Waterfront, East of Eden, A Streetcar Named Desire, Viva Zapata and Splendor in the Grass* along with founding the Actor's Studio with Cheryl Crawford and Robert Lewis in 1947. Oddly enough, I learned the technique of method acting when I was five years old. Early in life, I discovered how to dive within and create imaginary characters to camouflaged myself – a ploy to keep from stuttering. At the same age I began to read body language. Had I known Kazan was in the house, my usual panic attacks would have accelerated to the point of informing the producers I had a brain tumor and couldn't go on. My new understudy would have dropped dead, because much of what Bobby and I do is improvise off each other.

Two weeks later after much back and forth between the Cherry Lane management, my agent and Elia Kazan, the two of us begin work. We rehearse eight hours a day in a loft on the Lower East Side, before the first dress and light rehearsal with the original cast members at the Lincoln Center. *After the Fall*, a play written by Arthur Miller, and directed by Kazan, is based upon the life of his deceased ex-wife, Marilyn Monroe. I'm being rehearsed to replace Barbara Loden in the lead role of Maggie, four performances a week, while still performing *The Dutchman* at the Cherry Lane.

Do I have what it takes? That is the question. I reassure myself Kazan would never have chosen me had he not seen a spark of something. Still, there are so many talented actresses in this town including Barbara's understudy, Faye Dunaway. Why me and not her? What does he see in me? I find this rehearsal period unsettling, and plagued with doubts I won't do justice to Kazan, or to the memory of Marilyn. I've done so much research on her life, on her temperament – still, I'm unable to find her center, that defining motivation in her life that colored her. On top of all this, I'm wiped out from rehearsing eight hours each day for *After the Fall*, then performing *The Dutchman* at night plus matinees on Saturday and Sunday. I'm insecure about everything. One day when I'm beating up on myself as usual, I realize these are the very feelings Marilyn Monroe lived with her entire life.

There was the movie star Marilyn, a persona she contrived in order to achieve the maximum desired results her fame demanded. In addition was the neurotic Marilyn whose insecurity never allowed her to triumph over her childhood, her marriages, her career, anything of importance. When Marilyn didn't get her way, she forced those around her to prove themselves by their acceptance of her unprofessional habits, specifically her chronic lateness on the set that so often held up costly productions for long periods of time. She fell in love with men she considered better and smarter than her. All this, and so much more was Marilyn Monroe.

Diving within the character is always the first step in preparation for a role. This type development equates to understanding what drives that individual. Every human being wants something. To this day, the abuse I experienced in early childhood colors everything I do. I've protected my personal demons for so long a time, that to peel off layers at this juncture is akin to being skinned alive. Still, this is the process I follow with Kazan in the development of Maggie. Each day at the end of rehearsal, I feel depressed. The greater my depression, the happier Kazan is with my performance because he's getting results.

In rehearsal today, Kazan gives me an uncharacteristic pat on the back. In the same breath he urges me to join the Actor's Studio without delay. He thinks I have a great future on the Broadway stage as well as film, and makes a point of saying he has plans for me in the future – whatever that means. I've learned to take what people say in show business with a grain of salt. Another thing I've discovered about Kazan, is that whatever he says is always measured for the affect it will have on my performance, otherwise known as "the means justifies the end" result. He urges me to utilize my own life experience to breathe life into Maggie. He surprised me the other day when he confided one of the reasons he cast me in this role, was that I have the same vulnerability and sense of loss Marilyn had. Doesn't sound like much of a compliment but at least now, finally, I've something to work with. I have my own sense of unworthiness, of going through life feeling unwanted. Now that my personal fears have come forward, I'm as miserable as Kazan is thrilled over my discovery. There is a coldness about him that only looks to the end result. It is to that end he can be ruthless.

Anyone who ever worked with him knows he is an actor's director. If he can't achieve the desired result out of me for a scene, he improvises a similar situation, based upon memories dredged up from my past to be transferred to the character. And even though I'm finally on the right track, I leave rehearsal each day feeling worse than the day before. He couldn't care less about my mental state as long as it remains a useful tool to broaden the character. His *only* concern is the end result. I'm awed by him, but I also hate him. I do. I really hate him. Some days I dread going to rehearsal. Those are the times when I feel like such a pawn in this life, I could walk away and never come back.

I have a rough time separating my past from the present. I can read twenty books on method acting but this is it in a nutshell. I fast-track the process by using what I intuitively know, the rest I learn firsthand from Kazan. I want to please him, but method acting isn't easy as I've blocked out so much of my life. Working with Kazan forces me to remember things, long forgotten. I'm not sure it's worth it. After rehearsal each day, I go to a neighborhood bar for a couple of martinis, then walk the rest of the way home wondering where the joy is. At the end of a day, the only words that come to mind are, "Maybe tomorrow will be better."

Marilyn Monroe and Arthur what's his name?

I look at Arthur Miller's gaunt, lifeless face checking me out in the darkness of the Lincoln Center during my first run-through with the original cast of *After the Fall*. He's waiting to see if I measure up. I'd sooner read *The Ladies Home Journal* backwards than *Death of a Salesman* – that's how morbid his writings are to me. Maybe I just don't like him. What did Marilyn see in him? Like me, she lived her life with aloneness, and went for men she considered better than her. Maybe that was her attraction to Arthur Miller. I'd just as soon wrap my legs around a buffalo than crawl in bed with him. Really. I admire and respect Elia Kazan more than any director I've ever worked with, but it seems to me some in this crowd are self-serving for want of a better term.

Kazan sold out many of his friends by naming names during the McCarthy hearings in 1952. Some of my friends were blacklisted from working in Hollywood, their professional lives destroyed. Kazan didn't believe in Communism, more importantly he didn't want to be blacklisted. This I understand. Still, I feel nauseous when I think of how they used and betrayed each other. Every time I make up my mind to audition for the Actor's Studio, something stops me. I don't know if it's my insecurity of performing in front of my peers, or the mixed feelings I have about Lee Strasberg.

It all began when Kazan introduced an insecure and confused Marilyn to his intellectual crowd of friends, including several well known psychiatrists. This type therapy is designed to make the patient dredge up repressed, painful memories buried in the subconscious; to face them and be free to move forward rather than remain a lifelong victim. In Marilyn's case, she was willing to undergo such treatment in order to understand, and rid herself of negative personal issues. As an added bonus, she was convinced it would give her performances greater depth.

Was it worth it? Was Marilyn the better for it? Was she happier submitting to a psychiatric tractor with a bucket in front, digging up her past? In my opinion, her psyche was too fragile to undergo this type sustained psychiatric treatment, compounded by another failed marriage. When Arthur Miller fell in love with someone more his intellectual ilk, Marilyn had nothing to anchor her.

Method acting utilizes life experience to give reality to the character. In Marilyn's case, I believe such intrusion into her psyche pushed her even closer to the edge. The qualities of pathos and humor she naturally injected into every character, were not enhanced as a result of this type therapy. It isn't for everyone. Her life slowly went downhill after the divorce from Miller. Although her career was still in full swing, she had little self-esteem. In the early years, she used men by allowing herself to be used by those in positions to advance her goals. She had lots of company on that score. Marilyn's body was her greatest asset, and she used it to full advantage to garner attention, anything to fill the emptiness she lived with. It's no mystery she knew too much. Toward the end, her life became tawdry at best. Sperm Donors appear in every walk of life. They can be of tall, short, skinny or plump stature. But the one thing they all have in common is a willful lack of personal responsibility. Just as Marilyn manipulated others to advance her career, so was she used and dismissed by the rich and famous of the day. On August 5, 1962, Norma Jean Baker, best known to her fans as "Marilyn," died at the age of thirty six, an empty bottle of sedatives by her side. The actual circumstances of her death remain a mystery.

To this day, her presence fills the screen with a face and body the world will never forget. Still, her neurotic mind-set and bad work ethics turned off many professionals who worked with her. From my perspective, I doubt she needed the Actor's Studio. She was made to believe, that to be respected as an actress she required an in-depth method of character development. But with it or without it, the people she created on-screen would have come out the same. Today, years since her death, her screen image is still magical. Marilyn Monroe was a natural. The world is filled with those who prey on the frailty of others; predators empowered by weakness. When all is said and done, it was about them all along.

It's insane to burn myself at both ends like this. Performing the lead role in two plays week after week is a killer. What is the matter with me that I always need a mountain to climb? My understudy picks up the slack at the Cherry Lane when I perform in *After the Fall* at Lincoln Center. Some days nothing seems right.

Show Biz Here I Come!

Performing in Germany

Flying to Germany with bad hangover ... smoked joint before boarding ... flight takes forever ... I'm famished ... spaghetti sounds good ... me and Bobby performing *The Dutchman* in West Berlin ... on German TV – whatever ... gotta stop drinking so much ... my head hurts ... need a drink ... tall blond men meet us at airport ... I climb in back seat of Mercedes ... need sleep ... gotta get my head together before I go to the studio ... staying at old castle outside West Berlin.

Now that I'm here, it's too dark to see anything ... countryside blanketed with snow ... comes down hard ... real hard ... too much snow ... try to get out of the car ... stumble ... my face caked with snow ... German man helps me ... pull myself together. Please ... let me do it ... stand by myself ... steady ... steady ... where am I?

This ungodly cold kept me up all night, that, and the worst hangover ever, no heat in our rooms, and wiped out from no sleep. I have the worst hangover ever. Didn't I just say that? I'm two clicks away from freezing to death on cold sheets. The wind blew through a crack in the window all-night. Even though I put on every sweater I brought with me, icicles have formed in my veins. Nothing more sobering than the prospect of freezing to death which reminds me, when's breakfast around here? There's a sharp tap on my door. A voice in broken English says, "Time to get up!" The voice continues, "Your driver will be here in forty-five minutes. Get up!" OK, I can do this.

There's a gorilla jumping on my head. I manage to sit up in bed, the snow still coming down outside my window; a lone cardinal perched on a branch caked with snow, his red plumage announcing his manhood. The dowdy ones are females. If he's as hungry as I am, he'll peck a hole through the window. My head hurts, I'm hungry and so cold, I might as well be dead.

As my hangover pounds away, I slowly make it down a long, spiral staircase to find a buffet of juice and rolls so rock-hard, they could break my teeth. Our driver looks nervous. He has the unfortunate responsibility of getting Americans to the studio on time. We're a motley crew. About now, I could go for a bag of potato chips, and a martini to swill them down with.

Hard to believe, it only took two hours for the Germans to build *The Dutchman* set. We're blown away because it takes at least two American stagehands to remove one chair in a Broadway play. The Germans pride themselves on punctuality. The U-Bhan subway train is precise, down to a hair-raising-split-second arrival and departure at each destination.

Finally. We've been granted permission to visit the East Zone via Checkpoint Charlie, a name given by the Western Allies to the Berlin Wall crossing point, that separated East Berlin and West Berlin during the Cold War in 1961. Our purpose is to attend the famous Berliner Ensemble founded by Berthold Brecht who was forced to leave Germany upon the rise of Hitler, along with composer Kurt Weill. He presented the famous *Threepenny Opera* in eighteen languages, and gave over ten thousand performances on the European stage before coming to America. West Berlin feels like New York with Coca Cola billboards staring me in the face, along with other American products being hawked to a German public. The anti-American sentiment in Europe is sobering. I've never thought much about what it means to be an American in a foreign country, much less one so disliked.

We're frisked by Russian soldiers who carry guns with bayonets pointed at us. They treat us as though the war is still ongoing. Apparently not much has changed in the East Zone since World War II. I see nothing but rubble scattered everywhere, a broken tank by the side of the street, ruins of buildings destroyed by bombs, and few places to eat. Our German guide strongly advises us not to ask the Russians any questions. He says we'll find a cafe nearby.

I've made one bizarre observation, and that is the fondness Germans have for any edible that smacks of sausage. Regardless of where we go, I discover limitless versions of it. Here we sit in a small cafe in East Berlin, and the menu features bratwurst – surprise, surprise. Whenever I try to pronounce German words, they come out sounding like a mouthful of hot potatoes. I'm utterly hopeless. Our guide assists with the bill. We can't be late. It's freezing cold; the snow begins to come down again as we walk towards the theatre along winding, neglected streets still cluttered with remnants of the war years, but we arrive just in time. The curtain goes up in three minutes.

I'm fascinated by the East Berlin Theatre, particularly the architecture and history behind it. We've cut through so much red tape to be here tonight, finally we'll see the Berliner Ensemble in performance. I don't recall the exact name of the play only that it concerns Russian struggles during the war, and the narration by a soldier. This play is so tedious, it's a struggle not to fall asleep – that is, until a Russian tank barrels onstage into a major snowstorm. Talk about a wake-up call. Afterward, we meet the cast in the Green Room where we're served Courvoisier, for which I've developed a sinful taste. It takes several drinks and conversation, before they warm up enough to explain in detail how dangerous the climate remains in East Berlin. I listen intently as they speak in hushed tones. Although I've heard all this before on U.S. News, how so many East Berliners have lost their lives trying to escape; still, what's being said tonight is firsthand. They seem anxious to relay stories of friends and fellow cast members who died in their unsuccessful attempts to escape East Berlin. They confide that only last week, one of the actors made it to the West Zone. They don't, however, bring up the subject of World War II – its end, not so long ago. I'm embarrassed at how blasé I am about the freedoms I enjoy. My aspirations seem rather petty when compared to the millions of lives destroyed by that war. No one is anxious to say goodbye, but we've been ordered to return at a specific time. This evening has exceeded all my expectations.

It's snowing as we walk back to Checkpoint Charlie, where we're met by Russians and the Red Cross. One soldier almost knocks me down as he jackboots his hands under my coat, while another points his bayonet in my face. No doubt small compensation for a small Russian phallus, and a free feel.

I leave with a different attitude than the one I arrived with.

Lovie'n me, hooting it up in Manhattan

There's no place like home – for me it's Manhattan. I love all the trappings of glamour, especially the fast pace of daily life; I can't imagine living anywhere else. There's always something to do, dancing, acting and singing classes, going to the New York City Ballet, the Met, the art galleries, the museums, the great jazz clubs in the East Village, and the fabulous parties.

My roomy, David Vandergras better known as Lovie, is through-the-roof witty and equally savvy. I'm of the opinion, every woman should have someone like him in her life; gay men make great friends. They know more about women, what makes us look good, and what makes us tick than most of us know about ourselves. Lovie is very attractive with tousled auburn hair and chestnut eyes. He's teaching me to rejoice in the fact that I'm not normal. "Jen," he so often says, "Just be your usual crazy self."

The other perks of our friendship include the fine art of networking, how to dress, how to make an entrance, what to say, what not to say, when to say it, and when not to say it. In short, I'm learning how to market myself in a business that only pays homage to the rich and famous. I've never mastered the art of being tactful – not good, because honesty isn't a virtue at parties where everyone networks to get ahead. No one listens in social situations unless it's about them. This proves itself out when Lovie and I are guests at a party hosted by a well-known movie star who recently survived a messy divorce with an Italian movie star. Her trademark is a loud, abrasive, shrill voice that makes it impossible to hear names when introductions are in order. Her face is never focused on the person she's introduced to, her squinty eyes forever dart towards the front door to size up the new guest who has arrived. Lovie prepared me for her. During introductions, I decide to test my theory of social unconsciousness on her. She greets me with, "How are you?" –

Show Biz Here I Come!

clearly the other side of, "How's the weather?" Her eyes dart everywhere except on the one she is introduced to.

I smile sweetly and gingerly respond, "I was diagnosed with brain cancer this morning when a bus ran over my ass outside the doctor's office."

Toward the middle of my one second response, her radar suddenly hones in on a famous couple who await recognition at the front door. Panicked, she turns in their direction, her chunky robo-arms outstretched like elasticized bowling pins, every corpuscle in her donut-loving body alive with anticipation; every vein and sinew leapfrogs to the new arrivals, leaving her Amish barn ass to finalize the conversation we never had,

"So happy to hear it," she says, as pudgy fingertips refresh her mauve rouge with a pinch on those famous fat cheeks. She quickly turns from me, and walks towards the front door, her voice trailing off ... "So utterly fab meeting you." In addition, I receive the bonus of a small hand-flutter as she waddles off to a greener, more lucrative pasture.

Lovie lives by the rule of boldness, to break rules meant to be broken – fashion in particular. For example, we're invited to an upscale party after an evening at the Met. I can expect a ballet of tuxedoes, women with long black gowns, furs, and a front-end loader of diamonds. The minute he tells me where we're going, I fall back on my bed, and proclaim, "Oh Lovie, I've absolutely nothing to wear!"

My remark, the impetus for his right eyebrow to take on a life all its own, and like the phoenix rising, his lips purse out, their finest sibilant S exclaims, "Oh Reeeally, we'll just see about that!"

The next thing I know he calls his friend, a fur buyer at The Plaza. They gossip for a minute, then it's down to business, the guest list and other details, including my immediate need of a floor-length sable for one evening at the Met, and how fast can he whiz it over. Within hours, I not only have the sable but a velvet gown to die for – a perfect fit. Lovie gives the gown a probing look, and exclaims, "Absolutely not acceptable, and don't look at me like that! You will wear a floor-length sable, jeans, white silk blouse, and cowboy boots. They'll look at you as a goddess with musical notes coming out your ass!"

Lovie's right. It's all about playing the game.

I'm looking for my favorite couple from Texas who always attend these parties, and sound like rejects from the *Grand Old Opry*. Connie is in her early fifties, hair tinted a soft honey, and cut in a bob reminiscent of young ice-skaters, a style accentuating the waddle beneath her chin. She's more ill at ease than her husband, Bubba Earl someone who dresses like he just came off a duck-shoot. They're wealthy enough to buy Manhattan. Old money is revered but new dollars are better if free flowing. All that counts is – they have it.

My favorite couple from Texas own oil wells. Even though they are big-time spenders of objet d'art, and don't know the difference between a Jackson Pollock and a horse's ass, they are the overnight darlings of upscale parties. In short, Mr. and Mrs. Bubba Earl have arrived. Connie only wears high-end clothes, never steps out without her Kelly bag, and would submit to a cyanide induced coma before she'd wear off-the-rack. She reads *Women's Wear Daily* like Christians read the Bible, and prefers hari-kari to missing a trek to Paris each spring. She's greeted by her first name at fashion shows; designers know her by the checks she writes. Even though she buys everything that isn't nailed down, she still looks like the chubby girl wearing an ill-fitting hand-me-down, hanging on cousin Jim Bob's arm at the Senior Prom.

Poor Connie. I feel sorry for her. Who knows better than me how it feels to be out of place. She buys into all the compliments afforded her from the same people whose hands run deep into her pocket, those praying to God, Connie and Bubba Earl continue to open their wallets. These two are nothing more than wealthy groupies, trendyites who buy into the assumption, that associating with successful people in the arts automatically morphs them into the same. I feel the urge to grab one of the fat rolls under her arm, and whisper into her diamond studded ear, "Feel like going out for black-eyed peas and grits? I know just the place." Whoops. Lovie gives me a warning glare from the other side of the room. To see him work the crowd at parties is a vision to behold. Success is all about networking; still is, unless you're Gandhi's love child or the baby Jesus.

While Lovie fetches me a plate of hors-d'oeuvres and another Martini, a wisp of a man who has been staring at me for the past ten minutes, is headed my way. He stands in front of me, quiet for a moment, then speaks in a breathy almost inaudible voice, "Jen ... caught you last week in *The Dutchman*."

Andy Warhol

Here I stand in one spot for what seems an eternity, looking at the strangest man I've ever met. I don't know who he is, what he does or what spaceship he arrived on. His presentation of himself is a contrived maneuver to keep the attention focused on him alone, while I struggle to figure out what is wrong, if there *is* anything wrong, or if it's just a figment of my imagination. His bow tie is cocked to one side, his hair more like a fright wig gone askew – a dash of corn starch sprinkled here and there, his left eyebrow a few centimeters off, and the length of his jacket favoring the left side. Each time he shakes his head, an avalanche of dandruff cascades downward onto his shoulders like those glass snowballs with Santas in them, that when you turn them upside down, white snowflakes generously fall. His pale face looks like it's been douched in formaldehyde. Before I can open my mouth, Lovie says, "Jen, have you met Andy Warhol?"

Before I have a chance to answer Andy jumps right in, "Have you seen my underground movies?"

His strange speech pattern makes me envision the Rock Island Line barreling through tunnels of his excruciating long pauses between words. I remember a socialite whose name escapes me at the moment, who made one of his underground movies. The title of his avant-garde film is *Sleep,* and that's what they did on screen for five hours and twenty five minutes: slept. It catapulted a New York socialite into a wannabe rock star whose career fizzled as fast as her voice.

Truth be told, to look at one of Andy's artsy movies for five plus hours is more than I could stand, so I reply, "Not yet, but lookin' forward to it."

In the same moment we begin to play a game. I find myself liking him despite his terminal demeanor, another ploy used to hypnotize the clueless. I steer away from more discussion of his films which seem tedious and uninspired next to Andy himself standing before me. In a breathy almost hypnotic voice, he begins the following conversation. He says, "Will you star in my next movie?"

"What's it called?"

"*Kiss*."

"Who will I kiss?"

"Anyone you want"

"For how long?"

"For two hours non-stop"

"What if I have to pee?"

"Sure, but you can't stop kissing."

"I appreciate your offer but it doesn't sound like a plan. Thanks anyway."

Andy offers, "Think on it. Next week then, we'll get together."

Before I can answer, Lovie jumps in, throws his hands in the air with a feigned note of exasperation, and in the same breath tells Andy he loves the idea, and we'll definitely get together in the weeks to come. Andy, a faint smile on his lips, is still focused on me. The game isn't quite over between us.

After we leave the party, Lovie starts in on me. He's furious I just dismissed the most famous artist on earth. There are no grays in his world. It's either black or white. True, I don't think much of Andy's five hour, long-take footage, anti-films, but I like him personally. Outside of being a marketing genius, he seems content in his own skin. I envy him that. I can't stand being around Lovie when he's like this. Even though we're best friends, there's a new distance between us. Andy and I will probably get together next week.

Afterward, Lovie and I head for an obscure place in the East Village where writers and painters hang out. As we weave in and out Lower Manhattan, it's easy to get caught up in the street life where musicians and out of work professionals play on corners and store fronts. Some prefer the underground subway station because of the acoustics. Passengers show their appreciation by dropping money in a hat before they get on and off the subway.

I don't even try to keep up with Lovie, who is still uptight and walks briskly ahead of me. He's mad I didn't take advantage of a career opportunity. I tune him out same as when I was a little girl, and got called on the carpet for something I'd done. I leisurely walk behind him to deaden myself to his vibes. My thoughts, now alive with memories of Grandpa Leo and me strolling hand in hand through Westlake Park, of poets reading T.S. Elliot, of sitting for hours watching my grandpa play chess, of listening to an old jazz musician play the clarinet, and remembering the music of Bessie Smith.

I feel better now.

Larry Rivers

We're still not speaking as we head for a club in the East Village where I meet Larry Rivers, another well-known artist, poet, jazz musician and film maker of sorts, with an emphasis on the last two words. Lovie still nursing a mood, spots a writer he knows and leaves me to spend the entire evening listening to Larry describe his transcendental life as an embryo, up to and through this evening. As he drones on, I begin to visualize myself dead, approaching rigor mortis as I attempt to close the lid on my casket. Larry stands beside my coffin still talking about himself. People hover over my body, and say things like, "Pity ... she was too young to die," "I don't like her foundation," "Her last play was a bomb," "Who did her hair?" Another replies, "Monte." Finally, Larry comes up for air and asks if I'd like to go to the theatre tomorrow evening. I quickly forget his redundancy and accept.

No, I haven't forgotten the fur Lovie borrowed for me. How could I forget that? The doorbell rings. A disheveled and slightly hungover Cinderella wearing one of Lovie's old chenille robes, opens the door to our third floor walk-up. Ever-so-promptly at 7:00 a.m., I place the sable back in the hands of the evil courier from The Plaza. Very slowly, I turn around and crawl back into bed ... oh, let night come quickly ... at the very least, give me a new head without an ape jumping on it.

Later that same evening when the doorbell rings, I open it to find my date standing in the doorway. Larry Rivers is a vision to behold. His tie, abruptly cut off under the knot, grins from ear to ear and stares at me. Heaven and earth could have been created in the time I wait for him to speak. One of us should break the ice. *Roget's Thesaurus* trolls through my mind in an effort to recall a synonym for "like." Nope, can't find a thing. My turn: "Larry, I like your new look."

"Yeah," Larry responds then quickly adds, "It's where fashion's going."

After this remark, I feel like jumping out the window into traffic. He suggests we grab a bite so we head for a bistro nearby. Once there, we sit down and order. While waiting, he looks deep into my eyes and says, "Beautiful lady, do you know what the very best thing is about meeting someone new for the first time?" He continues to gaze into my eyes, then reaches over and takes my hand.

I look into his eyes, shrug, and reply in my softest voice, "No Larry," thinking he's on the precipice of voicing a sublime remark about me, my heart begins to throb with anticipation.

Finally, after an eternity passes, he replies, "It's getting to tell my whole life story all over again."

To say that I am stunned, and yes, mad as hell by his remark about himself rather than about me, is beyond expression. However, I manage a faint smile at his obtuse turn of phrase, and respond by saying he has a Pulitzer wit, but silently pray his sandwich has poison in it. What I'd really like to do is to jump on him until he's half dead for building me up to such heights, only to talk about himself. How egotistical can one person be? Really.

After a boring evening at the theatre, we push on to another party frequented by painters. Throughout the evening, Larry continues to hold himself in eulogy, in between attempts to run his hand inside my blouse. By now I'm not just bored, I'm nervous because he's drunk and aggressive. What he wants is obvious, but it will never happen. I want to go home but Lovie is out for the evening, and I don't trust Larry. Finally we leave. As soon as he hails a taxi, I slip the cabbie Sandra's address – my girlfriend who lives at Kips Bay. I'd called earlier to ask if I could spend the night.

In the elevator going up to her apartment, he begins to press his body against mine. I try to get away, but he blocks my attempt by taking both hands, shoves me against the door which, to my horror, opens and we fall headlong on top of Sandra and her next door neighbor who holds a blueberry pie as they chat in wait for the down elevator. The four of us, now sprawled over the hallway, Larry with the neighbor's pie running down his shirt, me trying to explain my dilemma to Sandra as we run to her apartment, and quickly open the door. Before he has a chance to put his foot inside, we slam it shut. Nightcap my ass!

When anyone is nervy enough to say, "When life gives you lemons make lemonade," I want to hurl. Yet, I've always been able to make something out of nothing with little more than grit and imagination, never more evident than when I accepted an invitation to a trendy party with no clothes fancy enough to wear. I bought a used sewing machine at the Salvation Army for ten dollars and immediately put it to good use after I borrowed, and I say that loosely, a blue velvet curtain from a hotel ballroom. In no time, I whipped up a floor length velvet gown trimmed in Cluny lace under the long sleeves, with a slit up one side. I didn't feel guilty about the curtain as it was old, torn and needed to be replaced ... or so I rationalized. Come to think of it, last week I discovered a warehouse on the Lower East Village that sells vintage raccoon coats. I bought one for thirty dollars. One of my friends, an over-the-hill supermodel, confides that models don't buy designer clothes for themselves. They shop at places like Filene's Basement and thrift shops. Glad to hear it. Ha!

Lovie is a great talent but jaded to the bone. I'm beginning to think we're no good for each other. All the hues of his personality have become part and parcel of my own nature. This happens to people like me who are fed up with everything. Every now and then I take inventory of myself and gasp at how ambitious I've become, but seconds later I forget all about it. I pretty much live in the fast lane. I wish I could get off, but I can't. Not now. There's got to be more to life than this. I can't see God but I can see my career. He'll have to find me if he wants me, and why do I say, "he?" Why not, "she?" If I was God the first thing I'd do is clean up 42nd Street.

Lovie keeps his personal life to himself. Hard as he tries, he can never override my will even if what I'm doing runs contrary to my career.

Theatre people rarely take their evening meal until after the show. Sometimes Lovie comes backstage, and we go out for dinner, swill a couple of martinis, and maybe smoke a joint before going to a party – like the one tonight. Someone who resembles a butler opens the door, and invites us in. As soon as George something – I can't remember his last name, spies Lovie and me standing in the doorway, he motions for us to come over. He's very gracious, and introduces us to Jackie Kennedy who stands beside him. I imagine half the people here are Secret Service.

Show Biz Here I Come!

Honestly, I'm so stoned I can't stop myself from staring at her famous face. Up close, it's quite different than the elegant one I've seen in magazines. In person, her eyes are so far apart her face resembles a fish. Standing here like this, stoned and staring for what seems like hours, a slideshow goes through my head of all the fish I've ever known personally, seen pictures of, or even heard about. I'm trying hard to figure out what fish suits her best – to no avail. She manages a faint smile at Lovie, who insists we've already eaten, but in the same breath, admits it was only hors-d'oeuvres. I ignore his response and politely answer, "Sounds yummy … and a martini would be nice." Completely out of it, I turn to them and say, "So nice meeting you but I feel sort of queasy. Must be the corn dog I ate. Please excuse … I need to sit down."

You'd think I just dropped the A-bomb from Lovie's horrified expression over my corn dog remark. He glares at me, quickly grabs hold of my arm as I'm about to sit on the floor, and eases me onto a French provincial love seat. Quite content, I flip my shades down from the top of my head, and take a nap. An hour or so later, almost hyperventilating from anger, he pinches me hard on my arm and peevishly growls, "Let's go!" He's livid that I slept instead of hobnobing with the elites in attendance. In silence, we ride the subway back to the Village.

The tension between us escalates as we stroll along the crowded streets of Greenwich Village, when suddenly I hear strains of "Tiptoe through the Tulips." I glance over to see a strange man sporting a large hooked nose with a mane of long, stringy black hair, standing near the curb. He plays a small ukulele, and sings the same song over and over in a high falsetto voice. Lovie is still so uptight, he won't even look at me. He's forgotten we were invited to a surprise party for Tennessee Williams, rumored to be in town. It's my fault. Of course. I guess the surprise will be if he shows up. I pull Lovie over, cover his eyes with my hands, and coo into his irritated ear, "Lovie, I'm sorry. Come on, I have a makeup treat for you."

Lovie's mood has become boring even to him. He lightens up, and walks with me over to the curb where the man is still singing. I go through the introductions, and ask for his name as he continues to sing "Tiptoe Through the Tulips." He giggles, and puts his hand over his mouth like someone trying to cover up bad teeth. We hardly know what to say before he giggles again, and confides his name is Tiny

Tim. Lovie asks if he would like to come to a party with us. Giggling, he nods in the affirmative. We hail a cab and head back Uptown. Throughout the ten minute ride, he never stops singing "Tiptoe Through the Tulips."

We arrive to a packed house and signal Tiny to take his ukulele and move swiftly to the ornate living room. We usher him to the upstage right corner where a pink marble water fountain in the shape of a lotus, whose centerpiece, a knockoff of Michelangelo's David, stands aloof in the center. David is peeing a gentle stream beside the "who's who" of New York, all busy with gossip and drink, along with clusters of gay men laughing and toasting each other. "Go Tiny." I whisper encouragingly, "Go over there and sing "Tiptoe Through the Tulips." I count to ten for the time it takes every head to turn and be mesmerized by him.

A star is born this auspicious evening as Tiny stands alone, shaking his long mane of black hair, and singing his lungs out deep into a Manhattan night as the jaded guests listen in bewilderment and awe. If Tennessee is here, then he's in a closet somewhere. Lovie and I haven't seen him, and neither has anyone else. Doesn't matter. Tonight's spotlight is focused on a stringy-haired, hooked nose Village street singer who warbles in a high falsetto voice, and plays his mini-ukulele beside Michelangelo's David. Everyone squeals with delight over their new find. After tonight, Tiny performs on many television shows, including *The Johnny Carson Show*. For sure, he's a bit strange but Herbert Buckingham Khaury, a.k.a. Tiny Tim, is for real.

We've decided to get separate apartments at Kips Bay Plaza near the United Nations, complete with a doorman to walk his dog, Marlon Brando, when Lovie goes out. Lex Luther requires no such attention. My mongrel kitty is overly fond of his new digs, and crawls daily through louvered glass panes. He sits blasé, if you will, on a small ledge for hours on end with no fear of heights, even though my apartment is on the eighteenth floor.

I can't find Al Hirschfield's sketch; it's missing from my apartment. Before the *Diamond Orchid* Broadway debacle of Lawrence and Lee's short-lived play detailing the rise of Evita Peron, the First Lady of Argentina, Al drew one of his famous caricatures of me performing the title role of Evita Peron. His wonderful sketches of showfolk line the walls of Sardi's. He gave it to me as a personal gift on closing night. He explained how he embeds the name of his daughter Nina in such a way, that it's virtually hidden in every sketch. Naturally, Jerome Lawrence and Robert E. Lee, the same producers who adapted the novel *Auntie Mame* for the original stage production starring Rosalind Russell, think it belongs to them. Sorry, it doesn't. It belongs to me to keep as a reminder of just how hideous a review can be, how miserable one human being can feel who gets the worst review any actor could ever receive, and still maintain their composure. After the much publicized opening of *Diamond Orchid*, the cast heads for Sardi's to punish ourselves during the long wait for reviews. They are so hideous, I'm surprised they aren't featured in *Ripley's Believe it or Not.* Living hell would be a welcome relief to being in Sardi's tonight. I need a drink. I'm the type no one suspects. My close friends call me, "Mama Gin Sling."

I like Edward Albee. Some find him cold and indifferent. People can say what they want, but it doesn't make it so. I see him as a brilliant, quiet man. His most famous work, *Who's Afraid of Virginia Woolf* won a Pulitzer for drama in 1963. I feel at home working in plays his team produces. They always treat the cast with appreciation after the run of a play. For my performance as Melba Pussy, a rock n' roll singer in *Malcolm,* another ill-fated Broadway play adapted from a novel by James Purdy, I'm given a sterling silver mirror with the title of the play, and my name engraved on the front.

Performing at the Spoleto Arts Festival in Italy

Gian Carlo Menotti has invited *The Dutchman* cast to represent the United States at the Spoleto Arts Festival in Italy. Performers the world over will represent each country's finest in their respective field of art. He founded this festival in 1958 with the idea of bringing established, as well as young promising artists together. Spoleto is a small, picturesque, Italian hilltop village where townspeople go about their daily lives walking back and forth on steep narrow streets. Nothing out of the ordinary happens here, outside of the landscape which changes in the summer months when the art festival barrels into town. For a short while this small dot on the map is alive with the performing arts, its countryside splashed with colors of vermillion and gold far as the eye can see. On my way to the theatre each morning, I walk past the winery where locals line up in wait for their glass jugs to be replenished.

This would be the perfect summer if my cousin Francis hadn't tagged along. No one ever called him Fran or, God help us, Franny. Grandmother said people named Francis should always be called Francis. I told him up-front, he could join me in Spoleto *only* if he reigned in his hormones, if he didn't wear high heels in public, and if he didn't get stoned every night. This is not happening. Francis parties all-night, and slips into his red high heels every chance he gets. He also travels with a large suitcase of money earmarked for a shopping spree in London and Paris. He claims it's for his business.

What a royal pain he is, particularly his incessant nags about my smoking in public. He promises to buy me a new gown in Paris if I stop. It's the "women smoking in public" attitude that bothers his old-world Southern charm, otherwise he couldn't care less if I die from lung cancer. I say, "Francis honey, this is nothin but a goat path. Who's gonna see me smokin?"

Show Biz Here I Come!

He is utterly maddening. Francis never gives a direct answer to any question. That would be too easy for his obtuse brain. No, he must first visualize an old movie before making his point. Once the scenario is clear in his mind, he gives me a silent stare while he slowly pulls out a strawberry lip gloss from his linen vest-pocket, and methodically applies a heavy coat to his lips, before throwing his head back like Bette Davis in *All about Eve.* All the while, his touched up black roots and heavily sprayed mane of blonde curls, never moves an inch.

Several pregnant pauses later, Francis finally replies to my question in a pronounced Southern drawl, "I can see you Tharon Ann and so can your grandmother. She's rollin over in her grave lookin at her only granddaughter walkin around with a cigarette hangin out her mouth – in public. It is so common, it is downright vulgar!"

Just to get him off my back, I agree not to light up again in exchange for a new, size six gown from Paris. OK Francis. Done.

Each night, a few of us, along with some dancers from John Cranko's Ballet Company, get lost drinking wine and dancing all night at the local disco – usually to "Baby Love." Francis tags along until he lucks out and meets someone; after that, I don't see him until the next day. When I came home last night, I found a note slipped under the doormat which read, "Sending you a gown from Paris. Tda, Francis." I won't hold my breath. He left in the middle of the night, his suitcase and red high heels with him. I'll miss ol' Francis.

I'm introduced to Ezra Pound, one of twentieth century's most influential voices in English and American literature. He's come backstage to congratulate us after watching our performance in *The Dutchman.* I look at this famous figure standing in the doorway, and think of my Grandpa Leo who would have loved the idea of his granddaughter chatting with literature's bad boy; of Westlake Park, where as a young girl I listened to fiery poets recite Ezra Pound. Grandpa admired his genius, but never understood his support for Mussolini. In 1958, his Fascist broadcasts during World War II led to his arrest and long confinement in a mental institution. To see him now, he hardly seems the iconoclast of yesteryear, rather a tired old man years have worn down. I notice a woman standing slightly behind him to his right, perhaps his wife – maybe not. There's talk his famous *Cantos* will be recorded in Spoleto. I'd love to ask about his complex relationship with Yeats, but I won't. He invites Bobby and I to have a drink at a local café.

I'm meeting well-known poets, opera singers, actors and ballet dancers from several countries, including the New York City Ballet. Some days, I sit on the back row and lose myself for hours listening to the Italian Opera Company in rehearsal. The baritone will limp through his performance tonight. Poor dear, apparently he fell into the orchestra pit during a light and sound rehearsal.

Today, I have an interview with an Italian tabloid which should be interesting. The interviewer speaks no English, I don't speak Italian, and there isn't a translator. I understand there will be lots of photos.

Nice meeting you Mr. Sperm Donor

I met the Sperm Donor during the short run of *Malcolm.* It's hard to find the right words to describe him. It isn't his looks, more his talent and personal magnetism that draws me to him. I see his potential as a director, his acting ability and creative projects at the Actor's Studio. I'm convinced he's more talented than me, yet he finds acting jobs hard to come by – outside of small parts in television and Broadway plays. It's hard to say why one person gets a break and another doesn't. Even more difficult is knowing what attracts one person to the other. Outside of our careers we have little in common, yet I am attracted to him in ways I find impossible to understand. Lovie incessantly warns me to stay away from him, but his words fall on deaf ears. What right does he have to tell me who to love, and who not to love. I don't understand his rabid dislike for someone he just met. He never comes over anymore unless I'm alone; our relationship isn't the same. My attraction to the Sperm Donor is such that I can't see his faults much less my own. When the lease is up, I'll move from Kips Bay to a larger apartment near Riverside Drive. Lovie can stay where he is. What am I thinking – how does anyone get along without a best friend? All I do is say goodbye.

I have one of the lead parts in an artsy television show with Jason Robards and Hal Holbrook. The script is an embarrassment; the characters recite morbid, stilted poetry, with each actor performing multiple roles. Yesterday, Hal confided it takes at least five hours to apply his own makeup for his performance in *Mark Twain Tonight*. But my all-time favorite is Jason Robards, exceptionally witty, a heavy drinker, and a golden piece of work. On the set, his favorite topic of conversation are the photographs of Humphrey Bogart hanging on the walls of his home. If I was married, and not already a drinker, looking at the many pictures of Bogie throughout the house would drive me to drink, same as wearing the first husband's wedding ring, and calling out his name when making love to the second one.

After a tiresome rehearsal today, Jason invites me to have a bite and a few drinks before we share a ride home. To say we get royally soused is an understatement of mammoth proportions. I'm not sure how either of us can stand up long enough to hail a cab. When we arrive at my apartment and I attempt to get out of the cab, he leans over and shouts, "Honey, will you marry me?" while in the same breath warns my neighbor, out walking his dog, that he is on the precipice of belching in middle C, then almost falls on the curb before I catch him by the arm. He proclaims in a loud voice, "Jen, I really love you. Can we get married before you kill yourself?"

I look at his famous face lined with deep wrinkles more from hard living than age, revealing more than I need, or even want to know and I answer, laughing more than usual, "Sure honey why not, but first let's check with my husband."

"That's what I like about you girlie – straightforward all the way. See you tomorrow at rehearsal if my head's still on." Off he goes into the midnight hour to Lauren and Bogie.

The Sperm Donor never asks about my career. He has no interest in anything I do, which includes staying out late. There's room for only one in this family. My drinking doesn't bother him, but cigarettes are another matter. He's convinced secondhand smoke will kill him. Not me. Just him.

In the world I move in, people are defined by the success or failure of their last job. For a short flicker of time I move on up, but always with a dark cloud of bad reviews looming over my head. Not remaining on top of the heap means one slip, and my telephone stops ringing, and the invitations stop coming in. It's over. I've spent my entire life chasing dreams, but this one isn't what I bargained for. When it all comes to an end, what will I have to show for my life that mattered? I know I'm more than this, but then I look at my life and wonder where "more" is.

I feel better about myself touring the summer circuit in theatre-in-the-round, performing Molly in *The Unsinkable Molly Brown*. The conductor rehearsed with me privately for one month. He made me promise not to smoke or drink, and insisted I run one hundred blocks daily to handle the rigors of performing with dancers, singers and an orchestra. I don't even want a drink. This musical is the biggest challenge I've ever tackled, and certainly the most fun. I need to be in top shape physically as Molly sings and dances in every scene. We play to packed houses every night. My vocal chords are forbidden to make friends with old habits. I'm happy.

My short-lived happiness has come to an abrupt halt. After little sleep and full body aches, I long to hear a kind voice. I call the Sperm Donor to explain just how difficult it is to perform a musical in theatre-in-the-round without a smoke and a drink, and how much I wish he would come stay with me for a few days. He cuts me off before I have a chance to explain how much I miss him, how much I need him right now. He doesn't listen, instead he begins to tell me about an actress who starred in a Brazilian film that won the Palme d'Or at the 1959 Cannes Film Festival as well as the 1960 Academy Award for Best Foreign Language Film, and the Golden Globe award for Best Foreign Film, and blah, blah, blah, blah, blah, blah, blah ... *you're cheating on me.* I've suspected it for a long time but I could never work up the courage to confront him, instead I sugarcoated his cheating by making excuses. I reassured myself that he would never lie to me, and why accuse him when I didn't have rock-solid proof, but this time it's different. My wild side was more appealing than whatever he sees in me now. He only wants to talk about how beautiful she is. *Dammit don't say you're just friends!* I'm so upset, I hang up. Oh God, what's wrong with me, why did I hang up, I need to speak to him. I dial the number again but he doesn't pick up. Why isn't he answering? Finally, he does; I hear a woman's voice in the background. I hang up again ... *they're having sex in our bed.*

The rare flicker of happiness I experienced in *Molly Brown* has vanished by the same door it entered, replaced by severe laryngitis – the result of stress. The producers hired an expert to bring my vocal cords back up to snuff through breathing exercises. No doubt she can fix my voice but she can't repair my trust. Nothing ever will. I look like a dog's dinner, my eyes red and swollen from crying. I don't possess the gene for loving just a little. It's always the same for me, a freefall with no safety net. It's never considering the facts, or even the smarts to protect myself. I loved my stepfather this way. I waited for him to come back for me, but he never did. I may just be the stupidest person alive. I don't know how to change.

The Sperm Donor is the type that if I say, "It's a sunny day, come on, let's take a walk through Central Park ... you know, hold hands like sweethearts do. Look at that couple over there. Come to the window honey, can you see the old couple across the street? No? You're looking in the wrong place. Look at the bus stop. They're holding hands."

He responds to this type remark with a question that has nothing to do with the point I'm trying to make. Those two old people probably live in a rent controlled building; they can't afford a cab, probably scrimp to make ends meet, probably eat peanut butter and jelly sandwiches until the end of the month when their social security checks come in, probably in their nineties – but they still hold hands.

The Sperm Donor never looks me straight in the eye. He's always in a hurry to answer the telephone, or dash out the door to work on endless make-believe projects at the Actor's Studio. He never commits to time as though it's something, once mentioned, he can no longer harness. Time, that illusive fairy godmother aiming her middle finger in my direction, points out that at twenty eight, I'm no longer young with crow's feet in the corner of my eyes and a husband who can't keep his pants up. There was a time when I couldn't walk down Sixth Avenue without cabbies whistling at my long legs. Is my value to be weighed like a slab of meat, one thigh versus the other, one set of legs versus another? There must be more to life than meeting the same man again and again in the name of love, of being thrown off a cliff praying for death, to arrive at the bottom only half dead. I worry about losing what I never had. I worry about all the things I don't have today, and will never have tomorrow.

I'm off to Spain – a movie for him and a niño for me

Finally, something tangible and wonderful. I'm pregnant. Just imagine, I'm going to be a mother ... something I've always wanted. I need to put his affairs behind me. Far as I know, there are no parts being cast for a crazy lady who looks like a beached whale. I'll go to Spain with him and have the baby there, in the hope starting a family will change things; maybe he'll grow up. Paramount just cast him in a film starring Robert Mitchum, to be shot on location outside Madrid. He's landed a decent part. I'm crossing my fingers that acting jobs, spotty at best, will start rolling in for him. I'm good with taking a backseat. Maybe I'm to blame for our problems; maybe my career is in the way. Doesn't matter. I'm strangely content these days, pregnant with our first child. Maybe now we can be a real family, although he doesn't look as good as he used to. Living with a cheater can do that. Time douches the bloom off a cheating rose.

My gynecologist told, or should I say, ordered me to stop smoking if I want a healthy baby. Not easy. I've smoked since I was seventeen, and now up to four packs a day. The Sperm Donor is fiercely anal about what he eats, keeping fit, and not inhaling secondhand smoke. Him! Him! Him! It's always about him. OK! I've got it: smoking causes cancer. Got it! If I don't stop smoking my lungs will collapse. Got it! If I don't stop, my ass will turn into a cornball! I've got it! I've got it! I've got it! I need a cigarette dammit!

I'm more than a little nervous about having our first baby in Madrid. Part of me wants to buy into his reassurance that it isn't a big deal, but the other part wants to put saltpeter in his coffee for the rest of our married life for making such a lame remark.

It's a balmy evening in Madrid. The siesta long over, merchants have reopened their shops, and the Italian couple in the apartment directly above us have stopped throwing furniture at each other. Life is going on as usual when the first labor pains come roaring in five minutes apart. I look at the Sperm Donor, my cheeks flush, my hair standing on end, and tell him with as much sweetness as possible, "This isn't at all like the book said it would be. They're five minutes apart, hardly time to drive to the clinic." My gynecologist in New York explained that the distance between the first labor pains, and when the final ones arrive depends on the woman. She also advised that when the five minute labor pains do arrive, I should already be in the hospital because the baby would be due any minute.

Her words "should already be in the hospital" have an inexplicable hormonal effect on me I can't explain except to say, while it's true I appear calm, inside me dwells a woman with hot lava flowing through her veins. I give the Sperm Donor a determined, probing look as he continues to read, oblivious of what is about to happen. I repress a sudden desire to scream, and calmly remind him that our baby is on the way, and no time to waste.

Men haven't the faintest understanding of this hormonal, psycho, transcendental morphing that some women go through during labor pains. Times like this, if I hear a man so much as whisper the words "*We're* having a baby," I can actually envision myself clubbing him to death before my rational self kicks in.

The only place worse on the nerves than driving in Madrid, is driving in Manhattan where cabbies consider their middle finger a right-hand turn signal. As we race through the streets of Madrid, we come close to having an accident, me shouting in the Spanish cabbie's ear, "Step on it redneck or I'll have this kid in your lap!"

As the pains grow more severe, the Sperm Donor continues his mantra, "Calm down Jen, calm down, calm down," like some primal chant he learned from his two previous marriages.

If a poll was conducted as to how women really feel when they hear the words "calm down" during extreme back labor, and if they're honest they'll tell you there is a moment when we actually get a rush at the thought of killing the man who says it. Yep! Track him down woman! Shoot him dead, and throw his ass in the desert for buzzards to eat!

The closer we get to the clinic, the more nervous I become. Apparently, I make our cabbie the same way because the second we arrive, he stops short of driving his taxi through the front door of the clinic, and certainly would have except for one thing: the doors are locked! The cabbie hears me yelp a bloodcurdling scream that signals him to slam his foot on the brakes. That jolt pushes the baby even closer to delivery. Sweet Jesus, it could roll down the steps. I hold my stomach with one hand, and bang on the door with the other yelling, "Is anyone home? I'm having a baby! Open the door!" The new hormonal me spins around and observes the Sperm Donor in a state of shock and bewilderment. I shout, "Wake up hombre! You said you knew all about this!" I tell him to either put his foot through the door or be ready to catch the baby when it slides out.

Mercifully, a sour-faced nun resembling Pope Pius VI in drag, opens the clinic door, mumbles something in Spanish and pushes me into the labor room. Nun Sourpuss has a blasé, what's-the-weather-like attitude and if my Spanish was better, I'd tell her where to put it. My back pain is so severe, it feels like razor blades going up and down my spine. These nuns speak no English except for one word: Push. I'll never go through this again. I'll adopt an orphanage before I get pregnant again. Is it fair only women suffer labor pains? Why doesn't nature kick in and give him some of it? Better still, I'd like to see him have a "peckergram" on PBS! Hold on girl, here comes another.

Inside the labor room, my body signals the rest of me to put the hammer down and push. But the more painful my back labor, the greater the Sperm Donor's attempt to calm me down by chanting, "Now just calm down, calm down, now just calm down, calm down." I beg them to give me something, anything, for this excruciating pain. Instead, I'm given some type tranquilizer.

Every time the words "calm down" come out of his mouth, I vaguely recall sitting up and throwing a book at him, me looking and sounding like Gamera, the flying crime-fighting turtle with fire shooting out it's ass, and screaming throughout the intergalactic world, "Come near me again, and I'll shoot that ding-dong right off your body!"

Suddenly, without warning, the Supremes enter my room, their black habits morph one into the other … Oh, Diana … she smiles at me … I'm here, over here Diana … she signals Cindy Birdsong and Mary Wilson to sing, "Stop! In the Name of Love" … just for me.

I look up to see the Sperm Donor being escorted out of the labor room by three beefy nuns looking less like the Supremes, more like world wrestling champs, and the Sperm Donor like a man in need of Preparation H. The nuns try to calm him down by reassuring in Spanish that he need not worry, that it's perfectly normal for "La Mujher" to behave like this, that having a baby is as normal as squatting to relive oneself. I'm sure their endearing words are a source of great comfort since his Spanish is limited to barking our hotel address to a cabbie, "Quintana Veintidos!"

The next thing I know, Rome is born. My sweet little man is here ... it's over. Nothing more to worry about. I must have passed out from the ordeal, because I have no memory of being wheeled back to my room – only looking at him. When the nurse puts him in my arms, I glance down at my first child, and feel a surge of love I've never before experienced. But the more I look at him, the greater my heart palpitations. I thoroughly expected my first born to look like all the pictures I'd seen of the baby Jesus, instead he looks like a pintsize squirrel. In Spanish, I ask the nurse if he's abnormal as I fear the worst. Outside of resembling a squirrel, he makes strange hand motions, rolls his eyes and smiles all the time. Maybe all this smiling is a good thing. I ask, "Is it a good thing he smiles all the time? Is it?" She explains, smiles are merely gas. I jump right in, "I would never have guessed it. Really? Seriously, I never would have guessed that." She continues to reassure me, there's no cause for alarm. "Really?" I inject, "And why is that?" Once more, she answers as though I didn't hear her the first time; again she patiently explains, that my niño is a perfectly normal baby. I have my doubts.

No sooner do my thoughts advance to his enrollment in Harvard, than the nuns whisk him away. They return minutes later with an older Spanish doctor who speaks English about as well as I speak Spanish. He says, "Hokay, how I gonna say dissa ting? Hokay, you hub'n u gotta de blood dat no likka de odder'n dat why el niño lello. We gotta changa de lello blood widda muy bueno blood ... hokay?"

I express my gratitude, "Muchas gracias – lo entiendo." Why am I shocked the Sperm Donor and I have incompatible blood types, or even surprised that our whacked out blood caused our first born to be jaundiced. Why did I say, "lo entiendo," when I *don't* understand. Say it again please, "They're what? They're going to change his what?

How do they do that? Does it hurt?" Smiling, the doctor shrugs and leaves the room.

I could build a bridge in the time it takes the nurse to bring back my niño. Earlier in the day, I further endeared myself to the staff by tiptoeing into the nursery. I pushed his wicker crib back into my room to keep vigil over him. Now I'm starting to worry. If I could so easily walk into the nursery and remove him without them knowing it, then maybe someone switched babies and this one belongs to, well, OK, maybe a gypsy, or someone … abnormal. But the longer I look at him, the more I know he's mine. I can't sleep for wanting to gaze at him – such tiny hands and feet. It's hard to believe I gave birth to something this precious. He still looks like a squirrel but after the initial shock, I wouldn't care if he had four ears and a tail. In my eyes he is perfection.

The doctor walks back into the room to let me know the blood change went well, and not to worry about anything. Rome is a healthy baby boy except for the little matter of circumcision. The last part he explains in his own language, while miming the procedure. Apparently he is concerned that his mother language won't properly convey the experience this particular organ is about to have. I cry when my niño is taken from me once again. I always thought women had it rough during childbirth, but the mere thought of my munchkin having the foreskin whipped off his little pecker is more than I can bear. I need a cigarette.

The Sperm Donor works on the outskirts of Madrid today. No problem. I bundle Romie up, hail a cab and bring him home alone. I enjoy this part of motherhood although I am a bit stir-crazy. A quick shopping spree at the Galleria Prethiodos should cure that. Cooped up for so long, I've forgotten what it's like to be out and about. He hired a young English au pair with blue eyes and peachy cream skin to help for the first two weeks.

As I wander about looking at this and that, trying on hats, sampling every perfume in the store, I buy something for each of us – and forget the time. When I get on the down escalator, I notice the woman in front of me holds an infant. She reaches into the diaper bag for a bottle to stop the baby from crying. No sooner does my body hear it's cry, than it responds by releasing the milk stored in my breast for Romie's noon-feed. Suddenly, with no warning whatsoever, liquid begins to run down my stomach and legs. Romie's lunch is gone. I use my umbrella to cover the front of my dress, and quickly leave to hail a cab, "Por favor, Quintana Veintidos!"

Tonight at dinner, I notice the Sperm Donor's eyes stray up the au pair's legs. She has visible chin hair, no waistline, short neck, not even cute but cute enough for him to have a quick roll in the hay. I forgot to mention she doesn't shave her armpits, her boobs bulge from her sweater like overgrown eggplants, and I want her out of here! I'll take care of my own baby.

After two weeks of no sleep due to Romie crying each and every night, I conclude he must be terminal. When I call the doctor, he laughs and explains my little squirrel enjoys his new habit of being rocked in my arms all-night. The crying begins the instant I put him in his cradle. This bothers the Sperm Donor who is due on the set at 6:00 a.m. I have no choice but to fly back to Manhattan with three week, Spanish-American Romie, and leave the Sperm Donor alone in Madrid to complete his film, no doubt thinking, "Free at last!"

Saying goodbye isn't easy

I wish I could say my life has changed since I returned from Spain, that Romie somehow fills my unrelenting emptiness compounded by my husband's lechery, that – and my jealousy of faceless women whose appeal I can only surmise. Mainly, I consider my own shortcomings, and wonder what is wrong with me.

I enjoy the rewards of motherhood, the sweet, baby fragrance of my little son, dressing him up, popping him in a stroller these autumn days, and walking to Central Park where I sit for hours every afternoon with other young mothers, my thoughts faraway from show business. I take refuge in their prattle – having a second child, life after the third, Cindy had her tubes tied, what really works for diaper rash, their husbands, his job, what to have for dinner, how to turn last night's leftovers into supper tonight, and when to stop breast feeding – at three months or when the baby is thirteen.

Peggy, oldest of the park women, becomes animated each time the subject of breast feeding arises. She reaches over, slides her hand into the stroller, the back pocket overloaded with peanut butter crackers, spare diapers, baby formula, sun tan lotion, and pulls out an obscure periodical on the advantages for breastfed babies. Earlier in the day as she waited to see the doctor, she felt a sudden urge to tear out the article but leave the magazine; she stopped short when it occurred to her this might be construed as stealing, after all the periodical did belong to the doctor, "Oh, what's the big deal," she mutters, "He always keeps me waiting. Dammit, wouldn't you know this is the one day he's on time. I'll finish the article in the park today, and return it next month when the baby gets shots."

I enjoy these afternoons, basking in sunshine and watching our children. What a strange group of women we are. What I like most about the park women is when they say hello – they really mean it. I think less about my career these days. I don't know why. Will my last spoken word on this earth be "why?" My thoughts seem to rest on the same old question, "Is this all there is?"

There is a certain freedom in being superfluous, no luggage, no questions – just me and my niño in Central Park watching the crisp autumn leaves waiting to drop, like old people who refuse to embrace what time they have left ... just how I feel.

I'm stuck in the never-ending sixties and I can't get out – 1968 seems to go on forever. It's doubtful I'll last to the seventies. But here I am ... still here, and rehearsals about to begin. I'm playing Helen of Troy in *Tiger at the Gates,* directed by Anthony Quayle, to open at the new uptown, permanent home for the Lincoln Center. A few days into rehearsal, he takes me aside and says, "In chemo are we? My dear, we're dreadfully thin. Helen hardly looked skeletal."

There was a time when this type remark would have sent me through the roof; today I think nothing of it. What do I care if I'm skin and bones. The costume designer created a gold lame, floor-length gown with transparent fabric down the sides, offering the effect of nudity. I know by Quayle's tone, I have to regain the lost weight before we open. Gotta look good y'know ... I feel like hell. If I can gain weight I will; if I can't I won't. I can't stop crying.

Each morning I wake up depressed, my eyes swollen and bloodshot from the night before, and I wait for my wonderful streetwise housekeeper. Each day she takes the subway from Harlem to rescue me from myself. She reminds me of Mama. From the moment Ida Mae walks through the door, she takes over. It's all I can do to pull myself out of bed, and get to rehearsal on time. She's twenty two, and married to Lenny who works at a Harlem dry cleaning plant. They have three kids, two in school, and a four year old she calls "Tootie," who comes to work with her each day. Everyone, including the hospital staff, knows her premature birth was a miracle. I never saw Ida Mae cry, until she tried to explain her feelings when Tootie was born, so tiny she fit in the palm of her hand. Each day she rubs oil over Romie's little body from head to toe, same as Mama did with me so many memories ago. He loves Tootie and toddles beside her wherever she goes. She's my friend in ways I can't describe. I'm falling apart, but she's always there to catch me.

I work regularly in New York, and earn a living without having to take part-time jobs to pay the bills, as most show people do in between work. However, I can't run away from the fact that I drink more and smoke four packs of cigarettes a day. There are times when I could walk out of the house and never come home again. The only thing that stops me is my little guy. I thought life would be different once my career took shape, that I'd be happy with just a tiny bit of achievement. Nothing is ever what it's cracked up to be. Outside of Romie, my life can be summed up in two words – wasted years.

This morning, Ida Mae takes my hand, sits me down and speaks to me like I'm five years old, "Miss Jennifer, you not right in the head. I think you having a breakdown. You needs help."

Ironically, last week one of the actors I'm working with mentioned a chiropractor who helps people in show business. I'm more than skeptical, but I'll try anything.

When I stroll into his office, he stands up from behind the desk, shakes my hand, and asks me to sit down. He says my chart has been reviewed, and he can pinpoint the problem by looking at my skin, while adding to this on-the-spot analysis, his conclusion, "Your eating habits are the source of contention; tell me, does your diet include meat, fish and eggs?"

I've no idea where this is going, and snap back, "Sure does!"

Undaunted by my snotty retort he begins to lay out instructions for my recovery. Is he crazy? I just walked in the door and already he's telling me what to eat, and what not to. I doubt seriously he's a real doctor when I hear him say, "I strongly suggest you stop eating animal flesh, including meat, fish, eggs or anything that contains them. I also advise you to eat green leafy vegetables, such as broccoli, collard greens and spinach, along with one baked yam every day. Do this, and you'll feel better in two weeks."

That's it? You quack, I'm here twenty minutes, and you'll bill me an hourly rate. Great. I mumble something incoherent about the cost of a twenty minute office consultation when he casually answers,

He smiles, "It's on the house – just give it a try." As an afterthought, he continues, "Why so anxious to make your body a graveyard for animals?" What did he just say?

Visibly shaken, I'm not prepared for this remark as I've eaten fried chicken, and anything else that wiggled, my whole life. Anyway, what I eat is none of his damn business; I didn't come here to be lectured, but still he continues, "When living creatures are slaughtered, they have the same fear of death humans have. That fear goes directly into your body when you eat them, not to speak of serious health issues, the least of which is a heart impervious to their suffering." He adds, making me feel even worse if that's possible, "If it begs for mercy, don't eat it."

I find the first part of his sentence about their "fear of dying going directly into my body," very disturbing. I remember when Grammy wrung a chicken's neck, its headless body hopped around the barnyard until it collapsed, and Uncle Zack cutting the heads off fish he'd caught. Once I was in a seafood restaurant, and watched a customer choose her dinner. After she picked out the biggest lobster, the owner yanked it live from the bucket. I remember its agonizing cry as it was dropped into boiling water. It's all coming back. During the cab ride home I begin to reason that if I'm afraid to die, wouldn't all living creatures fear death as well; that if I would suffer being thrown into boiling water, wouldn't a cow or a chicken or fish experience the same?

From this day forward, Ida Mae brings me collard greens from Harlem, then slow cooks them to perfection. True to his instructions, despite my sarcastic doubting nature, I eat one yam each day for two weeks. I have a hard time explaining this vegetarian business to Ida Mae, whose idea of fine cuisine is to put fatback in all things green. However, the good news is, two weeks to the day I feel better, which makes Ida Mae case up on the issue of fatback. Romie and I are now vegetarians, something I can't say for her. Each night I say a silent prayer of gratitude that cigarettes and martinis aren't made from living creatures. Seriously.

No sooner does the Sperm Donor return from Spain, than he's hired for another movie in Italy with Gina Lollobrigida. I'm desperate to leave New York. Even though the chiropractor helped me physically, from a mental perspective I'm two clicks away from a nervous breakdown. I cry endlessly for no reason, even in my dreams. Our marriage doesn't exist except on paper, and my life – just one catastrophe after another. There's no escaping it, no where to go, and no place to hide. I'm contracted to perform in *Tiger at the Gates* until the end of its run, which can't come soon enough. Each night my dresser shoots questioning looks at me, like I should be locked up in a loony bin instead of here. Maybe she's right but who cares? I don't. There was a time when people's opinions mattered. No more.

Show Biz Here I Come!

All my dreams do come true in the short time I've made New York my home. I get it all for one fleeting moment. The opiate of my ambition fuels every inch of the way; small triumphs ushering in the aftereffects of my expanding void, an abyss that requires recognition as fulfillment. I am the recipient of those things which accompany success. However, the few moments of elation never supersede my gripping loneliness. Some mornings I wake up feeling as though I just came off a bad acid trip without ever taking the drug. The highs and more lows in my personal and professional life have left deep scars. I need help. Maybe it's too late. I have no one. No one.

Shut your eyes ... Shut your eyes and don't wake up ... Hail Mary full of grace ... I want to die ... can't leave Romie like this.

I need to hear her voice. It's been a long time since I spoke with Aunt Lowee. I'll call between the first and second acts.

I nervously dial her number; she picks up on the first ring. My hands are shaking ... this dresser is too damn nosy ... watches everything. The moment Aunt Lowee answers the telephone, time begins to slip away, to cheat me of reconciling a past not far behind, happy days short-lived, and my future little more than a burdened past. The sound of her voice makes me sob. She struggles to understand why all she can hear on the other end of the line is crying. I just listen as she tries to make out who the caller is, "Tharon Ann, that you? T. Annie, is this you?"

Almost whispering, I answer in hushed tones so my nosy dresser can't hear, "Aunt Lowee, I'm in trouble. Can I come home? Please, let me stay with you until he finishes in Italy?"

"You never have to ask to come home. When the play's over just bring the baby and come home. Please, don't cry ... I can't stand hearin you cry like this ... everything will be all right ... come home ... pack up and come home."

We talk a few minutes more. She reminds me of my desire to have a family, that I have a beautiful son and a husband to consider, that I work as an actress in New York, and live the life I always dreamed of.

"Isn't this what you always wanted? For goodness sake Nanny, why aren't you happy?"

My answer isn't calculated. It is a reply that flies out of me as naturally as breathing, "I can't find him."

"Who Nanny? Who can't you find?"

"I don't know what his name is – God, whatever … I can't find him."

Aunt Lowee is childlike and a bit eccentric but tonight, speaking with her like this, all the hell years she suffered through alcoholism is the sum total of that experience reaching out to my rescue. As she continues to speak, an overwhelming sense of relief comes over me. For the first time in a very long while, I have something to look forward to. I can't wait for this play to close, to be out of Manhattan and back in LA with Aunt Lowee, for however long it takes to pull myself together while he's in Italy. We'll pick up some television shows when he joins me in LA. It's not like I'm never coming back, although people in show business have short memories.

Today, I was almost late getting to Lincoln Center. I sat for hours on a park bench in Central Park wondering if this human experience is about what I've loved the most. I tried to find something to hold onto, when I remembered the smell of Grandpa's pipe tobacco. For a few moments I felt better. Most of the time, I teeter on the precipice of a cliff, whereby the slightest breeze could push me over the edge. I have to get out of New York.

The heart is the loneliest place in town like a child's ball gone askew, rolling here and there, trying hard to avoid the open drain in city streets

Part III

A New Beginning

I'm back in East LA

I just spent the last five hours reliving my entire life, a roller coaster ride in neon memories through the past thirty years. I'm so tired I could sleep for two weeks, and still wake up exhausted. Yet despite all the changes going on in my life, something subtle happened when *Tiger at the Gates* closed, and I flew back to East LA to be with Aunt Lowee, in that my perspectives began to change. I felt lighter. Suffice it to say I don't feel today, the same as when I first arrived. I'm afraid to question this new state of mind for fear it might vanish.

Yeah, I still get panic attacks if I think too far into the future about what role, if any, the Sperm Donor will play in our lives, and I still think living in New Jersey is the closest thing to being in hell. For sure I'm still a crazy lady, but my eagerness to once and for all bury the past is evident in a newly discovered exuberance, that when I least expect it bubbles up inside me like fresh well water drawn to the surface in a bucket. In the midst of so much uncertainty, something inexplicable has happened, as though someone is listening and protecting me from all the dark aftereffects of my past. As a potter beats the clay from the outside, and moulds it from the interior wall of the pot, he paves the way for a new beginning; a play going on within a play.

It's clear to me now, that when I left Manhattan I was edging towards the end. The emptiness I have experienced since birth had come full circle, and no matter how hard I tried, my personal efforts could never fill the void, a longing for something beyond myself. Burnt out, clueless where to search for answers, my incentive for living was gone. I've no idea what triggered this emotional breakdown. Everything I had worked for, the fast-paced lifestyle I couldn't get enough of, the loveless marriage I held onto, suddenly became meaningless – if not worthless. In the end, I had nothing to anchor me ... not even myself. My life changed the day I met Mary Blakemore. In this final hour before waving my last goodbye to the Sperm Donor, my thoughts go to the events that occurred two weeks before I met her.

Since childhood, I've been very attached to Aunt Lowee. When the plane lands on California soil, all I can think of is how good it will feel to see her again after so long, that, and my resolve to leave my problems behind. The minute she wraps her arms around me, I'm relieved. She's eager to know if I ever bumped into John Wayne, flabbergasted at how much Rome talks for his age, and anxious to hear the inside dope about show business once, that is, we're home and have coffee in her new teacups. Our relationship is the same. Her once curly dark hair is now touched up with henna in the attempt to disguise an avalanche of gray, but Aunt Lowee's temperament hasn't changed. Her loving nature was always the constant in my life. Nothing has changed on that score. I've found my way back home.

My grandparent's old home in East LA is still eclectic, and overflows with antiques. She still rescues stray dogs, still shops at thrift stores for "treasures" and still rearranges the living room furniture twice a week. This makes my cousin Sue crazy everytime she wants her to wrestle freeway traffic for an hour, just to help move the living room couch back to the same place she helped move it from the week before. Some things never change.

I love this Mexican neighborhood. They're good neighbors. The aroma of hot tamales invites me to come in and have one anytime of day. My Okie family should have felt out of place in this neighborhood, yet generations later we're still a perfect fit. I envy their ability to be happy in the small things. In the evening after work, the men gather to play their guitars and sing, their wives sitting beside them on the stoop.

Each day when Romie and I take our morning walk, I'm filled with wonderful memories of my grandparents who once lived in the home left to Aunt Lowee – colorful flowers and orange trees everywhere I look. I was running so fast, I couldn't stop long enough to notice anything. This narrow street might be the result of an earthquake long ago that split this mountain in half, and created a passageway in between. "I'm-pregnant-again-Maria," our next door neighbor with a dozen kids, says Mexicans come over these mountains each year to find work. No doubt they're illegal. No one around here cares. In the hot summer months, the city burns the grass to prevent brush fires from spreading and destroying homes. Sue and I used to drag cardboard boxes to the top of the mountain across the street, climb in, then slide downhill on burnt grass in our make believe go-carts. So many memories.

At breakfast this morning, Aunt Lowee decides, somewhere between the first and fourth sip of coffee, to throw her antique "Doll and Bear Tea Party" on Saturday afternoon. Each year, she dresses her "children" in their Sunday best for this auspicious annual event. Some have flowers and satin bow ribbons in their hair, small books of poetry in their laps, one with haiku, others holding toys, a beaded purse, and laundered lace hankies. She alternates the seating arrangement by rotating every other doll in a chair, the young bears in makeshift high chairs. Together, they sit around an oak table covered with an antique lace tablecloth, and embroidered rosebuds on each corner. Each child has its own teacup, complete with nametag, and two heart-shaped, home-baked cookies made by Aunt Lowee.

She bought, stripped, stained and reupholstered a small love seat for her favorite dog Jempsy, so named for the Cherokee woman who helped deliver her twin brothers back in Oklahoma. According to Aunt Lowee, she can do no wrong. She is 100% certain, Jempsy is the only child in the world who likes haiku. Matter of fact, she always refers to her as "my little girl" – never as a dog. She can pee on her foot, but Aunt Lowee makes little of it. Without fanfare, she wipes up the piddle with one hand, and takes small sips of coffee with the other. Jempsy always gets the favored seat next to her at the "Doll and Bear Tea Party." No doubt this makes the other kids jealous from time to time. No doubt.

The placement issue is a real brain-twister, as only Aunt Lowee knows who wants to sit where. I avoid any discussion of seating arrangements as the word *why* might come out of my mouth; her answer a sure-fire means of getting a migraine that would last into the night. Everyone in the neighborhood gets an invitation. Whoever is home that day comes with a gift. Last year, I'm-pregnant-again-

Maria, brought all the kids a plate of hot tamales. My heart laughs to see Aunt Lowee happy in her own skin. Quite a difference from the years she scrimped to put food on the table. When the first day of school rolled around, Sue and I always had new outfits to wear, and colorful lunch boxes, although Aunt Lowee never owned a winter coat. I can never forget how she took me in when I was nine years old, and shared what little they had.

Is it wrong to feel happiness when someone dies, to feel content Uncle Zack no longer lives on this earth? He died of cirrhosis of the liver. Aunt Lowee and Sue are free now. In his last days, I went to the hospital, and sat beside his bed for the longest time. No tears would come. I sat quietly holding his hand, and prayed to a God I didn't know, to the God of my childhood. I prayed for his love to comfort Uncle Zack, to bless him wherever he is. May God have mercy on his poor soul.

For as long as I can remember, Aunt Lowee has rented the small apartment upstairs to the same Mexican family. Every night, just when my eyelids begin to close, I hear multiple warning shots of volcanic explosions, the precursor to a mighty eruption soon to be released from the husband's nether region. These walls are so thin, I can hear him flush the toilet three times to dismiss the remains of fiery chili his wife made from the hottest jalapeno sold in East LA. He turns up the radio.

Son of a bitch, there he goes again. Now I'm wide awake. I give the ceiling a few thumps so hard with a broom handle, a piece of plaster falls on my head. I shout, "Callate la Boca!" Yep, I'm back in East LA.

One new thing around here is Aunt Lowee's participation in a group that teaches meditation through Kriya Yoga, or spiritual awakening through the practice of breathing exercise and meditation, whatever that means. Bless her nutsy heart. When I first arrived, she was so alarmed at my condition, so eager to help me straighten up, she paid three hundred dollars in advance for me to attend a yoga retreat near San Diego; four days of meditation, solitude, contemplation, and great vegetarian cooking. The food sounds good, and meditation will be a new experience, something different. Anyway, what's the big deal about this meditation business I hear so

A New Beginning

much about? I mean, come on, all I have to do is close my eyes, and there you have it. What's to lose? I've been sermonized, baptized, lectured, dipped, dunked, and others with too many consonants to mention. One third of my nicotine-loving self will go to please Aunt Lowee, and the other cynical two thirds is strictly for the food. I'm losing weight again. I hover around one hundred pounds, so I'm thinking more about my stomach than my soul.

I board the bus with a backpack and a prayer, searching once again for answers to questions I've stashed in my psyche since childhood. I love to ride buses, trains too, getting lost in the journey, without pangs of guilt over what I should be doing, not doing what I didn't want to do in the first place, and wouldn't have done anyway.

As the bus pulls into the depot, I look out the window to see if anyone from the retreat has come to meet me. Surely someone will be here holding up a sign. I quickly surmise the young boy picking his nose, the pregnant teenager, and four Marines aren't for me. It has to be the youngish man with a shaved head, leather sandals, white pajama pants, and a style shirt that exposes his pale bare chest. The willowy girl beside him wears a longish orange dress, and colorful bangles up to her elbows. I like her ankle bracelet with small silver bells. No doubt they jingle when she walks.

As I step off the bus, they give me a three quarter smile, and introduce themselves as Om and Yemini. They seem friendly enough, although I find their quiet unspoken holiness disarming, and the red dot between her eyes baffling. Still, these two are my guides for this retreat and if I have questions, their insistence that I shouldn't hesitate to approach them, meets with an OK on my end. Outside of Yemini humming the Beatle's song, "Nowhere Man," for ten minutes, the drive to the retreat is uneventful – like waiting in the dentist's office without a magazine to flip through.

Once we arrive, I'm pleasantly surprised to find myself in a tranquil setting lodged in a wooded area, where people can meditate and chase their dreams without the clamor of city noise crashing in on them. What was I thinking? I love it here! The more I breathe in the ambience of this environment, the happier I am to find myself ensconced in nature's bosom. How will I ever thank Aunt Lowee enough for such a treat? I can't wait to meditate. It's possible I won't do anything else while I'm here. As we walk along the wooded path leading to my cabin, their pointed questions clearly suggest they think

I'm a seasoned practitioner of Kriya Yoga, questions like, "What stage are you?"

I reply, "Your point is?" My nondescript answer intrigues them, as well as clouds my state of "duh-ness" as to what they're even talking about. To my relief they seem impressed, as though my response comes from the mouth of an enlightened monk with no interest in divulging her spiritual height. If they only knew. As we continue to walk, I set aside my usual acerbic retorts as I'm totally committed to giving the next four days my very best effort. I owe it to Aunt Lowee.

By day's end, without a doubt I am convinced this retreat is not for me. No way is it. Not. Ever. Outside of my clandestine flights into the wooded area to sneak a cigarette, one of the cardinal rules is to spend as much time as humanly possible in meditation which is, contrary to my preconceived notions, misery incarnate. If I slept on a bed of hot nails, it would be easier than sitting quietly in meditation. I'll take it to another level: sitting quietly is impossible for me. Now add "in meditation" to "sitting quietly" and there you have it – my stay here is a veritable nightmare!

I'm giving it my best shot, really I am, but when I try to meditate, all I think about is cigarettes, cigarettes, cigarettes. I visualize a cigarette tasting contest to vote for the best blue ribbon cigarette pie at a county fair. They march in front of me as best friends forever present to comfort me, to give me solace in my time of need. I dream of flying back to LA on an intergalactic cigarette shaped spaceship, decked out like Mr. Spock in a white robe and Trekkie ears, with cigarettes sticking out each one. After this dream, I begin to obsess over diverse ways to escape without disgracing myself. After two days, enough is enough.

We're required to meditate crossed-legged on a hard floor several times daily for at least thirty minutes without moving. Come on. Anyone who squirms and meditates less than that needs work. I try my best to be respectful – not to speak of unnoticed, by sitting in back near the door. But the minute my watch hits the thirty minute mark, I bolt out of the hall, polevault over the bushes, and head straight to the woods for a cigarette. My tailbone aches, and I mean emergency room pain. I'm sick of being forced to sit in this unnatural lotus position, and what does a flower have to do with anything? And please tell me why they don't call it like it is: the torture posture! Why

A New Beginning

can't I lie down and meditate? Every time I try and meditate in the lotus position, my nose runs, my throat feels like gravel, my legs ache, my face itchy, my legs cramp so bad I'm not sure I'll ever walk again. My condition is such that it's highly probable I'll roll forward, and squash the tall, skinny woman with a skinny pigtail hanging down her back. She wears a long white gown hiked up above her bony kneecaps, and sits directly in front of me in the torture posture. When the clock hits thirty minutes, and I attempt to unlock my legs to stand up, it's a crapshoot at best whether I'll roll over, and seriously injure the woman by throwing her back out of alignment as she chants, "Om ... Om ... Om."

Hey lady, here's my chant, "Om, I need a cigarette! Om, I need a cigarette!"

What sane person sits like this? Outside of the mentally disturbed, I can't think of anyone. Another bothersome tidbit is that my mind goes ballistic each time I try to be quiet and focus. Instead of experiencing the tranquility and bliss the brochure promised, all I can think about is the delicious meals they serve. At night, I dream I've become a glutton from overeating, and grow an enormous beer belly. Due to my new spare tire, I'm laughed out of casting offices, and forced to join an exercise class to unload two hundred pounds of stomach blubber. In the end I'm unable to walk. Dragging my gigantic stomach on the floor has resulted in jumbo bunions the size of watermelons, on both feet.

By the second day, I've made up my mind to board the next bus headed for LA ... but after dinner. As strict vegetarians, they use soy to create dishes that taste like chicken, beef, even fish. They get an A+ for cooking, but I'm still leaving two days early, same as when I tried other religions or paths: let down, and disappointed. Kriya Yoga may be the answer for some, but it's not for me. I feel guilty because Aunt Lowee pre-paid for this four-day retreat. They won't refund her money for the last two days of cosmic, tailbone, back-breaking yoga seminars, avatar lectures, and grueling meditation time I didn't complete. I'm here only two days, and already I've overdosed on chanting, and the many ways to twist my legs around this nicotine filled body to last me a lifetime.

I'll bet if yogis and avatars are so blissed out, it's because they've stashed a Marlboro in their loin cloth. It's impossible for me to concentrate on anything outside of smoking. No matter how sincere, these people exacerbate my desire for a cigarette. I'd be willing to give meditation another shot if I could smoke at the same time. All I can think of during this tortuously long bus ride from San Diego back to LA, is buying a carton of cigarettes. As the bus rolls along, I laugh out loud at the thought of Aunt Lowee trying to meditate in the lotus position. I'd like to see her do that for five seconds.

Sitting on the edge of Aunt Lowee's bed, I glance down at my hands. My fingers are yellow, and I can't take my eyes off them. Surely they belong to someone else. My hands aren't model-gorgeous but they aren't freakish either. I'm horrified to realize these ten putrid, nicotine-stained, yellow fingers are mine. I begin to see myself as the addict I've become, rather than the free spirit I've always thought myself to be. In this moment, all I can see is a weak, jaundiced woman who can't travel on a subway longer than ten minutes without getting off to smoke a cigarette before she gets back on again. Strung out on four packs a day, nicotine is such an intregal part of my daily routine, I've become blind to its addictive nature. Truthfully, there is never a moment when tobacco isn't center stage – one way or another. I'm either smoking, thinking of smoking, or devising ways to escape long-winded conversations before having a smoke. Worst of all, I love secondhand smoke, and make a point of standing next to other cigarette fiends in a crowd.

I remember one embarrassing nicotine filled moment in New York, when I went into a Catholic Church to sit quietly and de-stress myself. I'd just lost a part I wanted, and felt like throwing myself off the Brooklyn Bridge. I sat in a hardwood pew listening to the Latin mass when before I knew it, I was lulled into such a peaceful repose that I dozed off, and began to visualize the Marlboro man as Jesus sporting a Stetson, his long hair flying in the wind behind him, with a cigarette dangling out one side of his mouth. As he rode his white stallion across the sands of the Mojave, he blew smoke rings with the precision of a metronome. Suddenly, I had the desire for a cigarette, which jolted me out of my self-induced reverie. In the attempt to go outside for a smoke, I nearly knocked unconscious two elderly people on their knees in prayer. As I continued to push in front of them, I whispered in hushed, sing-song tones, "Hail Mary full of grace, please excuse me; sorry, hail Mary, nice purse – here let me pick it up for you; whoops, sorry again, please excuse." As I plowed my way down the long narrow aisle, I bumped into every arthritic kneecap in that row. I couldn't sit for ten minutes without a cigarette.

Maybe big cities are the same the world over but after living there awhile, New York began to affect me this way. There was never a time when the streets didn't pulsate with faces who carried the same mental luggage as me, and probably wanted to be anywhere but here. Sometimes the noise was so intense, it felt like the sidewalks were caving in on me, and I wanted to run. Times like that, I needed a quiet spot to clear my head. But no matter where I went, I was always there to greet myself, and have a cigarette. On one such occasion I got caught in a downpour, and stepped inside a Christian Science Reading Room to wait until the rain stopped.

The moment I walked in, a cordial man at the front desk put his forefinger up to his mouth and whispered. "Shhhhhhh." He looked at me dripping wet and smiled as he handed me a long plastic bag for my umbrella, before giving me a copy of Mary Baker Eddy's book, *Science and Health with a Key to the Scriptures*. He ushered me to a small room for contemplative thought and study. After reading a few pages I fell asleep, and began to dream of Joan of Arc and Mary Baker Eddy having a swim together at the YWCA. They were laughing and smoking cigarettes while doing the butterfly stroke. I was startled by a tap on my shoulder. When I looked up, it was the man at the front desk who politely remarked, "Miss, if you've completed your study of Mrs. Eddy's writing, you might consider giving someone else the opportunity."

I was embarrassed. The other people sitting there were sincere, whereas all I wanted was to detox my nerves and escape the rain. He handed me my umbrella, and ushered me to the door. The rain had stopped; now I could smoke outside.

Enough dammit. This is my last cigarette. No amount of logic, of scare tactics, of photos of a smoker's lung, none of it mattered as my addiction to nicotine was greater than any fear of cancer. Over the years smoking has become a strange type of security, a crutch I can always depend on. The gradual weaning off cigarettes no longer exists. It's all or nothing. I know withdrawals won't be easy, but the time for options is over.

Aunt Lowee stands in the doorway holding her little mongrel dog Jemsy, and tries to figure out why I just cut all the cigarettes in half – from the carton I bought yesterday. "For goodness sake, T. Annie, what are you doing?" she exclaims, as I flush the last one down the toilet.

"This is my last cigarette." Her sigh of relief says it all.

"Don't worry about Romie, I'll help." Now that issue is out of the way, what excuse do I have? Big resolutions are never easier to carry out than when I'm angry, and I am – at myself for being so pathetically weak. If I can make it through the first week, I'll be OK – not one hundred percent but on my way to it. I'll kick this habit the old-fashioned way – cold turkey.

I hope there's a God out there somewhere, otherwise I'll never make it through this first week of withdrawals. If there's such a thing as hell, I'm in it. I don't know what to do with myself ... don't know what to do with my hands ... want a cigarette so bad ... please God, give me a damn cigarette! Am I in my right mind to give up smoking and drinking at the same time? Why do I set these impossible goals for myself? In the past when I held a cigarette in the right hand, my left hand lusted for a martini. So what do I do? I give up drinking to make my right hand stop wanting a cigarette. Why do I always need mountains to climb? Why do I endlessly punish myself?

My new resolve makes me feel better. The telltale sign will be when I no longer have the urge to uproot every tree in sight to smoke it's trunk. It's too soon to pat myself on the back. This is the first time I've ever faced up to a fault without sugarcoating it. How can I overcome what I can't see, or purge myself of a flaw I don't admit to? I've smoked my last cigarette and toasted my last martini. Aunt Lowee says it's OK to have a glass of wine now and then, but no thanks – not even wine. There's no in-between with me. Slaying the dragon feels good.

Aunt Lowee prods me to get out of my doldrums and enjoy a night out in Hollywood at the yoga restaurant, her favorite vegetarian hangout. After my retreat debacle, I have no recourse but to say yes. After Uncle Zack passed away, she morphed into a flower child. Now she's come full circle, and two serious clicks away from being an old hippie on her way to a Dylan concert. She thinks my moods are unhealthy, that I need to get out more. I'm content being my usual quiet, cynical, bored self who wears the same sweats two days in a row, no makeup, and matted hair. I do floss, do brush my teeth, and do make excuses for my dismal physical state as being no more than an old smoker's rehab center. But … I no longer smoke and drink. This afternoon, just to please Aunt Lowee, I'll say adios to the sweats I've worn going on three days. I'll take a bubble bath, wash and blow-dry my long, slightly tangled hair, and that's about as good as it gets. In the past I always guaged my weight by how tight my jeans fit but I've lost so many pounds, the back of my Levi's look like an empty butterfly net. Ready for a night out, we drop Romie off next door to be spoiled by I'm-pregnant-again-Maria and the kids.

She's adamant about driving … seeing as it's her car. It's an hour's drive into Hollywood and she's confident I've forgotten how to get there, but I hold my ground. Driving on the freeway with Aunt Lowee behind the wheel is more than my nerves can stand. She weaves in and out lanes like a bat out of hell, as though the freeway is exclusively hers. I quickly draw the line and state in my firmest voice, "I drive or the deals off." Simultaneously, we put our hands on the door handle of the driver's side. I add in a low, quasi threatening voice, "Aunt Lowee, I drive."

"No, Tharon Ann," she growls, "It's *my* car. I drive!" Aunt Lowee always calls me, "Nanny," or "T. Annie," but never Tharon Ann unless she's angry – very angry. Her insistence upon driving has more to do with it being trash pickup night, than me behind the wheel. Once a week, the City of Angels picks up old furniture left by the curb. Trash night is her primo source for "treasures" as she fondly calls them. Tonight is the night.

"I won't go if you drive."
"You don't know how to get there."
"I can drive to Hollywood blindfolded."
"I might want to stop."
"Like where?"
"Like somewhere"
"Fine!"
"Fine!"
"OK by me."

Here we stand, neither of us gives an inch until finally she says, "All right Tharon Ann, you drive!" Looking like Greta Garbo in

Camille's death scene, she reluctantly skulks to the passenger side, opens the door, and slides onto the front seat. She's given in just enough to release her hand from the handle, but not enough to admit defeat. Aunt Lowee pouts for ten minutes or so until she glances out the window, and spots an old cane chair propped up against a trash can. She grabs my arm and pleads, "T. Annie Stop! Please Nanny, it'll fit in the back seat. Pleeeeeze with sugar on it." The good thing about the two of us, is that we never fight with each other. We quibble but it's forgotten in minutes.

I answer as though there was never a dispute over who sits in the driver's seat. "You forgetting the time they close?" That does it. We're back to normal for the rest of the drive.

Finally we arrive.

The fragrance of sandalwood wafts through the air as we enter a foyer filled with handcrafts, love beads, scented oils, packaged incense, along with photographs of dark skinned yogis, their legs twisted like pretzels around each body part – all for sale on a display table against the wall. I begin to laugh, not knowing whether to stop or pretend I'm dead. These people make Tiny Tim look normal. We don't have to wait – a table is available. We're lead to a center spot by a vanilla looking waitress. The only one out of place here is me. I quickly scan the menu. "Aunt Lowee, everything looks great. You order."

"No Nanny, you order."

"You order ... for both of us. OK?"

After our usual back and forth banter, she selects enough food for ten people. No sooner does she order, than I notice a young girl up front, standing by the cash register. She has the type look that readily sizes up any friends who might be here. Her long hair with bold strokes of blonde highlights, conjures up visions of California sunshine right before a tsunami hits. She smiles; obviously there's someone here she knows, and heads in our direction. As the girl approaches our table, I glance over at a smiling Aunt Lowee. She is the stereotype rich brat girl from the San Fernando Valley with accent to match, and here I go again judging people before they get a word out of their mouth. Maybe I'm a little jealous of her youthful exuberance, and yes, her friendship with Aunt Lowee who never seems thrilled to see me these days.

A New Beginning

She starts to get up but "Brat Girl" won't allow it, instead she bends down and gives Aunt Lowee the type hug that would have sent me to a chiropractor. It's all I can do to keep my cynical thoughts in check ... although I must admit, they do seem a nice fit. It's obvious they know each other, probably from Kriya Yoga class. It's plain to see, Aunt Lowee comes here often as several people wave to her. Her lovable, eccentric nature attracts all ages.

While the two of them laugh in between endless chitchat, I grow increasingly bored until Brat Girl begins to describe a place she visited the week before. My napkin graffiti comes to an abrupt halt the moment she mentions an older woman called Mary who discourses on a far eastern philosophy every evening in the back of a small shop. Brat Girl refers to these informal gatherings as "satsangs." She goes on to say, this woman is a mystic who sold everything she owned to pay for a plane ticket to India, as well as helped twenty two young people meet their teacher in the Punjab, India. The stories she tells about how they bought tickets and secured visas, is nothing short of a miracle as none of them had money. She speaks at length about Mary's recent return from India.

The moment I hear her name, my every stress related problem fast-tracks into a single desire to find the woman called Mary. I nonchalantly ask for an address where the meetings, or satsangs, as they're referred to, are held, "Sounds interesting, can you give me the address?"

"Wow, bummer, it's like somewhere on Fountain Ave."

"Thanks, I'll start tomorrow." Brat Girl is confident I'll know it's the right place if I see handmade items such as love beads, keyrings, clothing and books in the storefront window, and she's really sorry, but she can't remember the name of the store. She continues, "You guys feel like hanging out at Barney's Beanery? We can like hang for awhile after we split from here."

"Nanny, let's hang ..."

"Aunt Lowee, I can't. Write down her telephone number and we'll do it another time, I promise."

I'll make it up to her. We wouldn't get home until midnight, way too late to pick up Romie. I'd be terrible company, as all I can think about is Mary. I have to find her.

Looking for Mary

For the first time in a very long while my mind is at ease, and the long drive home a happy one. I don't understand the "why" of my feelings, outside of the fact that I'm experiencing something new – hope. Aunt Lowee is back to her old self. She's already forgotten her irritation over the lost night out, and wants to meet Mary too. It's illogical, I'm so anxious to find someone I've never met and know nothing about ... yet, that's how it is.

Once again, Aunt Lowee comes to my rescue. She offers to watch Romie when I drive into Hollywood to search for a storefront on Fountain Avenue; a place where someone who works there might help me find Mary. She volunteers to do this – no matter how long it takes. Will tomorrow ever come?

The neighborhood kids love to chase Maria's pet rooster who runs loose in their front yard, and more times than not hops over the fence into Aunt Lowee's yard, until Jemsy chases him back into his own. Like Pavlov's dog, he predictably greets each day with the rising sun. The moment he crows I bolt out of bed, splash water on my face, comb my hair, slide into jeans and t-shirt, and leave in enough time to avoid bumper-to-bumper traffic.

Every morning, I drive from East LA into Hollywood to look for Mary. After I park the car, I walk up and down Fountain Avenue looking for a storefront that fits Brat Girl's description. When I return home, Aunt Lowee looks at me a few moments and says, "Nanny, let's me and you sit out on the veranda and have coffee in one of my new teacups." She knows from my expression, I've spent another fruitless day looking for her. By the end of the second week, I begin to feel a huge let down, as though Mary is just a figment of the girl's imagination.

I've looked for this storefront since early morning, and same as other days – nothing. My feet hurt. I sit down on the curb and begin to think how nice it would be to have a cigarette about now, and where is that pot of gold at the end of my rainbow? Worse still, do I even have one? For no apparent reason, I glance over to my left and see a piece of paper taped to the door of a small storefront called the Sweetheart Tree. I get up, and walk over to read a hastily scribbled note that says, "Out to lunch, back at one." I peer through the front window and notice hand painted leather keyrings, jewelry, and a few books on display. This is it! Of course, my cynical nature inevitably rears its doubting head every time I approach something new. My mind warns me that what I seek doesn't exist, and this time is no different, that it's all about money and self-interest. It's long past one o'clock but I'm so relieved to at least have my foot at the door, there is no way I won't see this through and return. I can hardly contain my joy. Tomorrow I'll surely find her.

Predictably, Maria's pet rooster is up at daybreak crowing his head off – my signal to jump out of bed, and begin preparing myself to meet Mary. Instead of my usual Levis and t-shirt, I decide on a modest skirt and blouse; rather than let my long hair fly loose, I pull it back in a ponytail.

Same as other days, I battle the early morning freeway traffic to Hollywood. Once there, I luck out and find a parking spot close to the Sweetheart Tree. As soon as I walk up to the front door, I begin to feel apprehensive for no reason. When I turn the doorknob, small bells on the handle jingle when it opens, but I don't see anyone – only a small room with unusual handmade items, Indian style kurtas, pants, bracelets, a few paintings, and books. I'm not sure what to do, and my feet refuse to go any farther, so I continue to stand near the front door. As my eyes scan the room, I immediately notice a photograph of a man hanging on the wall. He has a compelling face, a long beard, and wears a white turban. A young fellow walks up and stands beside me ... but volunteers nothing. His solemn face provides a canvas for an outstanding nose. I can't help but wonder if English is his first language, as eons pass before sound comes out of his mouth.

"Hello," is all he says. When I ask about the photograph, he mutters in an unfamiliar language that sounds like someone pulling marshmallows out their nose. He's putting me on. I'm beginning to feel like a person on speed asking a sleepwalker for directions. Maybe I'm in the wrong place.

A moment or so later, a cheerful face comes out from back of the store, "Hi! I'm Robert. Need some help?" This one appears normal.

"I'm looking for Mary. I don't know her last name. I don't know where she lives. I don't know how to reach her," and I almost say, "I don't know why I'm here."

He smiles, then laughs and replies, "No problem, just turn the corner and stop at the first castle." When he sees the expression on my face, he explains, "Look, just go around the corner. It's the first small apartment building on the left. You can't miss it. It's the only Irish castle on the block," and laughs again.

I'm glad he clarifies this remark otherwise I'm out of here. I've had enough phonies to last me a lifetime, the ones who take money and give nothing. Thanks, but no thanks. "What does she do?"

"She manages thirty two rental apartments in an old Irish castle." He grins at the look on my face and continues, "See for yourself. Mary does everything from plumbing to painting, to cleaning toilet bowls, to pruning the bushes, and mowing grass. Go see her now if you want."

I'm somewhat taken back when he describes her daily routine because, based on Brat Girl's description, I picture her wearing a flowing velvet gown, a red dot between the eyes, and a halo that travels above her head wherever she goes. She'd be anything but an apartment house manager, who cleans toilet bowls and paints vacated apartments. Now I'm really intrigued. "I can't just drop in. Would you tell her someone wants to meet her?"

It's as if every breath of my life has led up to this moment. What if she's busy? What if it's all a scam? After my last negative thought, I hear bells jingling on the front door of the Sweetheart Tree. Robert walks in with a big smile on his face when he says, "Mary would like you to come see her now." He hardly finishes the sentence before I turn, run around the corner, and stop only at 1343 Catalina.

A New Beginning

Meeting an American mystic

"Man, Thou art God. Awake and realize thy glorious destiny."

Charan Singh Ji Maharaj

Robert's remark that I would recognize Mary's apartment building is validated the moment I walk up the front steps, and notice the manicured surroundings. Everywhere I look there are Birds of Paradise, and the fragrance of roses lingering about the walkway. I open the entrance door to a freshly painted hallway with inexpensive reproductions of Renoir and Matisse on the wall.

I stop at the first apartment where a small sign to the left of the doorway reads, "Apartment Manager." I stand for a moment to collect myself. I've traveled this road so many times before, and I'm more than nervous as I begin a mental countdown of what to say, and the questions I will ask. Lost in my thoughts, I finally ring the doorbell. After a moment, it opens. Dressed in a confetti print housedress, the type older women might buy from JC Penny, she looks every bit like a petite grandmother with white curly hair cascading down to, and barely touching her shoulders. I am at once struck by her eyes. Words cannot do justice to those indescribable blue eyes that immediately penetrate the core of my being, without giving them permission to do so. They let me know right quickly, my thoughts are little more than transparent glass to her – all this in the time it takes to breathe in and out again. She looks at me, puts her hands on her hips, then smiles and says in the softest, most inviting of Southern accents, "I've been waiting for you."

The robotic look on my face doesn't deter our one-sided conversation in the least. She keeps the ball rolling, and says she's been at it all day cleaning up after a renter, who only this morning left the apartment in this filthy condition, that she just cleaned all the appliances, and scrubbed the kitchen and bathroom floors on her hands and knees, and without pausing to take a breath, that it will take her at least a week and then some, to shampoo the carpets, and paint the entire apartment, but for now she just has to stop and ..."Honey, don't you want to come inside?"

I manage to squeak an inaudible, "Thank you," as I walk into her apartment, one so small I could easily bump into myself if I turn around. No sooner do I step inside than she mentions something still cooking on the stove, and continues to speak in a familiar way as though we are old friends.

"I need to check the stove ... come on Jenny ... I'll give you the tour ... Lordy, am I tired ... my day begins early, and I work straight through," her voice trails off one subject, then on to another, "I'll tell you this, my only salary is this rent-free apartment, and that's about it." Once again she segues mid-sentence to another matter, "When I found out what Mr. Nurenberg – he's the owner of the building, paid contractors to paint one apartment, I told him I'd do it for half the price. So now I paint and vacate the entire apartment for twenty five dollars, and I'm here to tell you it's damned hard work. Now, he laughs all the way to the bank thinking about the money he's saved since he gave me the job." With this remark comes robust laughter that embraces the listener, and has waited until just this moment to express itself. How does she know my name? She just called me Jenny. I didn't mention my name to anyone at the Sweetheart Tree. How does she know it?

Her living room leads to a smaller area with a comfortable upholstered chair, a television on one end, an oak table with a drop leaf, and four matching chairs on the other. There is a small bouquet of flowers in the center – maybe from the rosebush out front. She explains in great detail how she managed to convert a small bedroom into this combination den and dining room. At the same time all this is going on, she leads me to a small kitchen where she's frying something in a skillet, all the while explaining how people today cook on too high a flame. "Jenny, see how I'm cooking this? I've turned the heat down low because food tastes better slow cooked, don't you think?" Not waiting for my answer, she interrupts this train of thought and says, "Nothing tastes good if you forget to add the main ingredient. Know what it is?" Her smile tells me she's enjoying herself. Mary speaks to me as though she's known me forever.

On my end, I am mesmerized by this lady, yet clueless as to what it's all about. "No mam."

A New Beginning

"You will." I want to know more about the secret ingredient, but now isn't the time since the only words to escape my lips are, "Yes, mam" and "No, mam." She glances up from the skillet and says, more an affirmation than a question, "You a Southern girl."

"Yes mam."

"You know Jenny, I love the sound of those words, "Yes, mam" and "No, mam," then out of the blue she segues into, "Say, I feel like a Coke – you want one?" Not waiting for my answer, she takes two from a squeaky clean refrigerator, pops them open, reaches in a drawer for two coasters, and motions for me to follow her back into the living room. I'm struck by the cleanliness of her home as opposed to my own helter-skelter way of life.

By now all my anxieties are gone. I'm standing in her kitchen discussing everyday matters. She wants me to relax, and ushers me back to the living room sofa. I sit down beside her and wait ... not sure why I'm here – only that I am compelled to be at this very place, at this very time, yet I can't speak. I wait for her to make the next move.

"Jenny, how bout' a cookie? I baked them this morning."

"No, mam. I'm fine M ..."

"Blakemore ... Mary Blakemore," and hands me several perfectly baked chocolate chip cookies anyway.

"Thank you Mrs. ..."

"Oh, don't be so formal ... just call me Mary." She's so natural. With little effort, she puts me completely at ease. I note a familiar photograph on the end table. It's the same Indian gentleman wearing a white turban that I saw earlier at the Sweetheart Tree. I can't stop looking at his eyes.

"Well Jenny, tell me all about yourself." I had jotted down every question I've had since childhood, but at the moment I can't remember anything. Instead, I cover my face with my hands and cry; unable to even look at her. I can't say a word. All my pent-up emotion for so long pours out to her. She listens without questioning, without saying a word. Most people listen *at* what is said, whereas Mary listens deeply. She listens *to*.

Very gently, she lifts my hands away from my face, eyes red and swollen from tears, mascara running down the front of my cheeks, and while holding both hands in her own, she looks into my eyes and says, "Jenny, everything will be alright."

I lay my head on her lap and we sit like this for the longest time – two old friends meeting once again in this life, picking up where we left off, and a feeling of déjà vu comes over me. It is the same contentment I experienced after I stopped drinking and smoking, a sense of being lifted upwards ... only weeks before meeting Mary today. It is the same experience I had as a young girl sitting on Aunt Lowee's ivy covered front porch; an understanding that someone was with me, a memory that haunts me still.

"How did you find me?" she asks. I describe in detail everything the girl in the restaurant told me about her, how I bolted out of bed each morning when the rooster crowed and made the long drive into Hollywood to find her, how this continued for two weeks. She finds this amusing and responds, "I've been waiting for you. What's taken you so long?"

Silence again on my end. How do I answer this question? Didn't we just meet? This is the second time she's made this type remark. Mary notices me looking at the photograph on her end table. She smiles, then casually offers, "That's Charan Singh Ji Maharaj, my spiritual teacher," and volunteers to answer any questions I might have. I'm eager to know more about her, her life, absolutely everything because all my preconceived notions are wrong. She is so down to earth, natural, and easy to talk with as she begins to tell me about her life as a young girl growing up in the South.

At sixteen, she married Art Blakemore who was twenty three years her senior, a widower with three children, the eldest only six months younger than Mary. Despite those differences, their marriage was a good one. They raised more children and grandchildren than some people can count to. More importantly, he respected her desire to find a spiritual teacher, one who could show her the method of accessing her own spirituality within. He encouraged her to seek out various religious orders and philosophies, in the hope that one day she would find an answer. But everytime she returned home he knew from the look on her face, it was another dead-end. "No soap?" was his standard question. "Not even a bubble," was her reply.

Her husband was an engineer and helped build the Gatun locks in the Panama Canal. Mary loved to travel with him. She never wanted for anything during their thirty three years of marriage. He died only one day before they were scheduled to leave for a holiday in

Switzerland. The last thing he ever said was, "Mary, you'll find what you are looking for soon."

"Art, what do you mean soon?" He couldn't answer ... he had passed away.

She buried her husband; afterwards, she neatly folded and packed away fragments of their married life, and gave all their belongings to the children. With two suitcases and limited funds, she boarded a train, and traveled west to California to begin a new life. Mary led a normal householder's life for thirty three years yet in all that time, she never stopped searching for a living spiritual teacher.

This sunny California afternoon, Mary answers every question I've carried with me since childhood – all to my satisfaction. Old issues are finally put to rest, and the *why* of this upside down world finally makes sense. She speaks to me about meditation, of reincarnation, of death, of karma, of destiny, of the positive and negative powers and critically, the necessity of being accepted into the fold of a true, living mystic ... a spiritual teacher, something I've always wanted. She goes on to explain, that since time began all true mystic teachers have come from the same ocean of love. She points out these teachings do not conflict with any religion I may have embraced. Mary further explains this philosophy is not a religion, but rather a soul science. It is a state of awareness to be achieved by human beings, and proved through individual meditation as taught by a true mystic who is one with the divine consciousness. The mystic way embraces rather than judges. As she continues to explain this balanced way of life, her words don't seem at all strange. She has placed a stamp of approval on what I've always known.

I've waited a long time to hear someone speak with authority on what I've always felt, that great souls walk this earth who have firsthand knowledge of the divine. I press further, although hesitant to even say the word God, as I've been angry with him for so much of my life, "May I speak to him one on one?"

Without blinking an eye she answers, "Of course you can." She speaks as though having a two-way conversation with God is as easy as falling off a log, and continues, "You may speak to him and he'll speak to you – same as we are now."

Honestly, I can't believe my ears because the issue of being unable to have a two-way conversation with God without a go-between, has been a point of contention since childhood. I always felt that if it's really true God is my father, then why would any real father not speak directly to his daughter?

I muster the courage to ask the last question that has plagued me the most, and no doubt will be the deal breaker, "How much will all this cost?"

She looks at me and smiles in a way generally followed by peels of laughter, as though anticipating my reaction to her answer before she says the words, "God is free."

I've never been able to reconcile the checks and balances of religious institutions, payment for helping another human being find their way to the divine. The words "God is free" rolls off her tongue as easily as "please pass the mustard," making it sound rather matter of fact, more like the fourth ingredient down in a recipe than the headline news it is to me. I ask, "Do you belong to this?"

"Sure do." she answers.

Without hesitation I ask, "How do I go about it?" I've never read a book on this philosophy, yet here I am asking for initiation into a path of mystic truths based upon all Mary has explained to me. Am I naive to make such a request without giving it thorough study? After all, embracing this path isn't the same as joining the YWCA. This is forever. But, I know what I want and cynic though I am, I haven't an iota of doubt about Mary Blakemore *or* the mystic way. We are old friends. This path is what I have searched for my entire life. I always knew that when I found it, I would recognize it immediately, and without hesitation.

She proceeds to explain the four vows that are simple enough, to my great relief. I am expected to lead a good, moral, ethical and principled life, to refrain from alcohol and mind expanding drugs, and to be a strict vegetarian. Really? I mean if that's all there is to it, this path is a no-brainer – don't have to hold my nose, don't have to jump off a cliff repeating om, om, om. I mean come on, is this all I have to do? Hold on ... what did she just say? There's another one? ... a fourth vow? No sooner does she explain the vow of sitting in meditation each day for two and one half hours, preferably at 3:00 a.m., than my heart almost flatlines. I recall the yoga retreat, and my struggle to sit still in the lotus posture for even a minute without falling over and knocking myself senseless, along with the woman sitting in front of me. All this flashes in the forefront my mind. I can't meditate for five seconds, let alone two and one half hours. To put it another way: I am to vow, that I will sit still for one hundred and fifty minutes daily. Every day? Oh my God, come on she can't be serious. Then it comes to me, that she must mean those two and one half hours will be spread out over one month, as in thirty one days of the month divided into one hundred and fifty minutes. OK, I might be able to work up to five minutes a day ... in time. But Mary, reading my thoughts, offers reassurance that I will have no problem meditating for 2 1/2 hours each day. Oh really? She goes on to explain that meditation is nothing more than sitting quietly in prayer with my best friend. Meditation is still a hot topic, as the memory of my two day stint at the yoga retreat remains fresh in my mind, but my trust in Mary Blakemore supersedes any qualms I might still entertain.

Even though I'm eager to be initiated today, right this minute, she explains that a seeker must thoroughly study the teachings, and read at least three books on the philosophy as well as practice the vegetarian diet. If I can do this, and after a period of three months being satisfied, only then may I ask for initiation. After this explanation I look into her eyes and ask, "At the end of those three months, will you sponsor me to this Path?"

She smiles and replies, "Of course I will."

This late summer afternoon sitting beside Mary, I am content in the acceptance that I have waited twenty nine years of my life to find my friend of long ago. She is the only person who has given real answers to lifelong questions that I can prove to myself by practicing the art of meditation. I have always known there would be no haggling or intellectual wrangling if I ever found what I was looking for, that my acceptance of the truth would be immediate. I'm already a vegetarian, but is it a coincidence that I've stopped smoking and drinking in this short period of time before meeting her?

It is sundown when I leave her small apartment, a time when daylight acquiesces to night, and despair finally surrenders to hope. She's given me so much of her time this afternoon. Her parting words as she hugs me, "Jenny, never miss going to satsang, and never miss one day calling me."

I have no idea what satsang is much less what to expect from attending, but from this moment forward Mary is my spiritual teacher, spiritual disciplinarian, mystic mother and conduit for all good things to follow in years to come.

Words pale at any feeble attempt to describe my state of mind as I drive back to East LA, gliding as I am through California twilight. Whatever remnants of the midday sun remain are pouring into the front seat of Aunt Lowee's car, bathing me, and the unseen passenger who sits beside me – the one keeping me company on the long drive home.

I explain all that has happened to Aunt Lowee. She listens intently, then asks if I will arrange for her to meet Mary. I'm eager to read the book she gave me. Once started, I can't put it down; the tenets of this ancient philosophy are so familiar, the words almost jump off the pages. When I finish reading the last page, the whole of the universe feels near. No truer words were ever spoken than those of Mary Blakemore as I left her apartment, "The simplicity of God confounds the wisdom of man."

Having spent the entire night reading, I have my first cup of morning coffee in bed. As I reflect back on all that occurred yesterday, I am suddenly aware of the same divine presence who was with me as a child, is now having coffee with me. Throughout the day, it is with me no matter where I am, or what I'm doing, whether taking a bath, walking to the car, or sitting beside me in the passenger seat when I drive. This isn't my imagination. It is a personal experience of living moments in the presence of the divine, a gift of unearned grace to a desperate soul. Anyone who knows me will agree, that up until now, I have lived my life on the cutting edge of ambition, too much time on the wild side, always cynical, and more times than not, angry with God Himself.

It's hard to put into words, how this summer has impacted on me. Although my personal life has gone from bad to worse, the Sperm Donor still unable to keep his pants up, but the difference between now and other times, is I am happy in the discovery of a path I've taken to like a duck to water. After so long a journey, I have discovered rays of hope in the midst of hell.

A New Beginning

There is an old saying, "When the student is ready, the teacher appears." Indeed she is here and her name is Mary, a mystic who possesses that great magnitude of love who will guide me through the years ahead. In satsang today, she referred to the present time in which we live as the Iron Age when so many seek the mystic way. It is rare to have this type of close, teacher-pupil relationship. Given my track record, I'll never understand why I had the good fortune to meet her, and be accepted for initiation by Charan Singh Ji Maharaj of Dera Beas, her Guru, now mine as well.

Growing up in the South, I never heard of the four divisions of time. I'm eager to know more. She further explains, the Hindus divided time into four yugas, or cycles named Sat or Krita Yuga – the True or Golden Age, Treta Yuga – the Silver Age, Dwapar Yuga – the Copper or Bronze Age, and Kali Yuga – the Dark or the Iron Age. The world now passes through Kali Yuga, the age of darkness when moral virtue and mental capabilities reach their lowest point in the cycle. Mary further explains, the famous Indian epic *The Mahabharat* describes Kali Yuga as a period when the "World Soul" is black in hue, when only one quarter of virtue remains which slowly dwindles to zero at the end of Kali Yuga. One thousand yugas make a Maha Yuga, a great age or incomprehensible length of time. One Maha Yuga is regarded as one day of Brahm. When I asked if the end of the world was near, she just laughed and said, "I wouldn't worry about it Jenny, there's no shortcut for you."

Some mornings I wake up feeling like the first in line to the throne. Robert from the Sweetheart Tree, laughs when I describe my state of mind. He explains, this period is commonly referred to as the "honeymoon days," a time when I can do no wrong just before the gargantuan task of ego crushing begins. According to Mary, ego is the greatest obstacle on the inward journey. It exists in all human beings, and manifests through vanity, lust, anger, greed, and attachment. While I understand all this in theory, I really need to be honest when I say, "Come on, my ego isn't all that gigantic. I know me and it just isn't, and don't say I have a big ego because I know better. It's hardly anything – if that!"

These balmy California evenings spent in rapt attention listening to Mary discourse on the teachings of the mystics, are the most memorable days of my life. I never miss the long drive from East LA to Hollywood, seven evenings a week in the back of the Sweetheart Tree, along with many others in Mary's group, mainly young people from every walk of life, with the exception of one older man who drives ninety eight miles each way, and never misses a one.

This is satsang. Mary sits in a folding chair at the front of a long, narrow hallway while we sit on the floor, our feet outstretched to make room for others who sit with their backs against the wall opposite us. She discourses for hours; how many depends upon how focused we are. If she catches one of us looking at our watch, we're kept an additional hour. If someone else thinks about food rather than the discourse at hand, we're kept an another thirty minutes. We are a group of seekers bound in such a way, that no one believes these ties will ever be broken, not with Mary – not with each other. Not in our wildest dreams do we consider this could happen. People from every walk of life attend her satsang, like Jules of the group, *The Association,* who recorded "Along Comes Mary."

The knowledge of her deep, mystic insight is well known in certain circles. One afternoon, Dr. Werner Von Braun, father of the United States space program, pays her a visit. They sit together and enjoy her fresh baked apple pie and a cup of coffee, while discussing physics, philosophy, and his conviction that one day man will travel at the speed of light. Mary listens intently, and quietly offers the following in rebuttal,

"Dr. Von Braun, light is stationary. It does *not* travel at all, but man can travel *in* the light by entering therein. Just thinking of a destination, they are transported in the light."

A few moments pass. Dr. Von Braun nods in agreement but adds, the scientific world isn't ready to accept such advanced thinking.

They enjoy each other's company, as do many others with less impressive credentials; ordinary people, who many a night rap on her door during the wee hours of the morning, to discuss spiritual concerns. She is a buffet of mysticism, a homegrown American mystic who likes popcorn, Cokes, and Elvis Presley. Above all, she lives the life she teaches by serving God in all who come in contact with her. No one ever knocks on Mary's door and leaves empty handed. By summer's end, most fan out to go their separate ways, while others build their lives around wherever she lives. Mary moves to New Jersey, while another young man goes to Viet Nam. Some are musicians, some are students, one is a mathematician, one a college professor, another a preschool teacher, one an economist, two are writers, one sells flags from the back of a van on roadsides across America, one a beauty queen, another a Wall Street financier; the rest of us scrambling to find ourselves. No matter the road any of us take in the whole of our lives, we were in Mary's group. There will never be a time when her memory isn't so deeply embedded in our consciousness, that we aren't compelled to reach across the miles and turn to her for comfort, or whatever is needed to sustain the human spirit.

Mary knows everyone, but who can say they ever really knew her.

I've fallen in love with your myriad forms, always changing but forever the same, corn stalks swaying on a hot summer day, peaches so full of grace they burden the mother limb, and a lone red cardinal who sits outside my bedroom window in the holly tree. You are all that, and so much more. At the break of day as morning dew hardly settles upon this land, and sleep sits upon my brow, you appear as the face of dawn whispering to all who would hear, "Embrace me. I am here."

It's the Sperm Donor check out time

I'm worried about this clunker I'm driving. I wonder why, duh! The Sperm Donor says he'll keep our classic model Jaguar, leaving me to drive the old Chevy with an odometer that doesn't work, no luggage rack, an iffy radiator, and God only knows what else is wrong with it and, lest I forget, the air conditioner doesn't work. He claims he had it checked out, but any man who makes me sew a maternity dress out of our bedspread, had the carwash guy give it a once-over for ten bucks and a joint. Chenille to army blankets – the story of my life. He secured our largest suitcase to the top of the car by rigging up a makeshift luggage rack with chicken wire and rope, that has to hold up for a cross-country drive in the heat of summer. I'm tired, I'm cranky and I can't remember to do my simran, the part of this philosophy where I'm supposed to silently repeat the five holy names, that over time transmutes the negative mind into the positive mind. If that's not enough, I haven't slept all night reliving my entire life as though I'm not the main player. The kids are up, jumping their brains out on my bed. They want breakfast. Would someone do me a favor: just take me out to the woods and shoot me.

"What time is it?"

"Time to get up Mommy. Time to go."

"Guys, stop hollering in my ear. I haven't slept all night."

"Mommy, Willie talks on the phone but he won't let me talk."

"Who was it?"

"Mary. We're going on a trip."

"I'm four years old Mommy. I get to talk on the phone too."

"Not for a couple of months. I can still tell you what to do."

"You promised we'd go to the zoo."

"We'll go to the zoo in New Jersey."

"You said they don't got nothing there but gangsters."

A New Beginning

"Anything. They don't have anything."

"Mommy, you said bears come from Hollywood."

"Don't jump on me. Honey, please, no jumping! Romie, you're pulling me off the bed, stop pulling my nose, I can't breath. Willie, take him in the other room."

"Mommy, how are babies born?"

"They come through the mail."

"Mommy, Daddy's outside tying our luggage on top of the car."

"I'm up."

Bye Bye Sperm Donor

"Every day in every way, I'm getting better and better."
Inspector Dreyfus
The Revenge of the Pink Panther

There's still time left before we leave to meet Mary and the others in Hollywood. She'll drive in a second car with Patrick, a tall, charming, witty Irishman with no interest in the fair sex, and heir to a pharmaceutical fortune. Knowing him, he's waiting with baited breath for the day this inheritance falls in his lap. But for now, he's no different than the rest of us who've just enough money to get to New Jersey, and live for a month or so until we find work. I'll follow his car in my Chevy, Romie kicking the back of my seat to irritation, and whining, "Mommy, are we there yet?"

Cherie will sit with me in the front seat under the pretext of helping with the kids. At twenty one, she looks worn out and barely pretty with honey colored hair down to her waist, and blue eyes that never stop looking for a man – any man will do. She's the girl who stays too long at the party, the one in the backroom with all the guys. Her thoughts are habitually focused on men, meeting new ones, crying over old ones, and now misses some actor she left behind in Hollywood.

What a motley crew Mary is taking to New Jersey. I can't exclude myself. What could be worse than trying to elevate the attitude of a pregnant crazy lady whose husband just gave her the single digit salute as a fond farewell. Not one of us has an iota of common sense. We're all so in our own little world, Mary would have an easier time if she pushed boulders uphill. She is the glue that holds our traveling party together.

For the umpteenth time, I review my check-off list to make sure I haven't forgotten something. Rome and Willie are excited over the roll of quarters I gave them to spend along the way. When Mary asked if I was interested in moving to New Jersey to begin a new life, it took little effort to convince the Sperm Donor that Willie, our son by his second marriage, should come with us to be with his siblings; Romie – and the one on the way. Aunt Lowee is sorry to see me go, but that's about it. I need some private time to say goodbye to my mountaintop retreat, an old friend who never judges but accepts my tears as it's own. If I weren't a teetotaler, I'd pour myself a glass of wine and toast to the end of this dark chapter in my life.

Aunt Lowee and the kids stand by the car while the Sperm Donor fiddles with the luggage rack. After all that's happened, Aunt Lowee is still fond of him in a baffling sort of way. Last night I organized our luggage in the trunk, with the exception of one large suitcase which the Sperm Donor is, just now, at the very last minute, and right before we're about to leave, tying to the top of the Chevy. The kids are bathed, dressed and fed … can't get out of here fast enough.

My short walk down to the car feels like miles. The Sperm Donor, his arm around Aunt Lowee, is holding court and laughing with the boys. Mary said the worst thing parents can do in separations or divorce is badmouth each other to the kids. She urges me never to do it, although God only knows how much I want to. I'll make sure they send him postcards along the way.

I look at Aunt Lowee standing here waiting to see us off, and so many memories run through my mind. It takes everything in me to keep from breaking down … can't have that; I put my arms around her, and promise to write – don't know when, or if, we'll ever see each other again. I thank her for everything she's done for me. What else can I say … don't want the boys to see me cry.

The Sperm Donor leans against my car, his posture reminiscent of someone who watches too many Brando movies, and would rather give an interview to the *Hollywood Reporter* than see his family off. He isn't the least bit uncomfortable as he saunters over to the driver's side, and sticks his head in the window with a final travel tip, "Here's a notebook for the glove compartment in case you have an accident. Make sure to write down their license plate. You can keep the pencil."

I look at him in disbelief.

Truth be known, I suspect he hopes we'll all die, not all – just me. All smiles, I thank him then slowly turn the key in the ignition, throw my Chevy in reverse, and graze his big toe as I shift to first, and pull away. Not spiritual but so good. My Chicano neighbors can hear the dulcet tones of the kids trailing off in the background, their heads hanging out the back window waving "Bye Daddy" and "I love you Daddy," as I drive down this block for the last time.

From the rearview window, I can see Aunt Lowee and the Sperm Donor walking back to the house for a cup of coffee.

Driving across country with two kids and one in the oven

I'm one or two negligible minutes late, and the kids already want to know if we're in New Jersey yet. As I pull up to the curb in front of her apartment building on Catalina, I notice everyone is standing outside waiting for us. From the look on her face it's clear Mary isn't thrilled with Cherie. She's sitting on the curb displaying a full set of pink nipples through a sheer halter top she wears, as she checks out her split ends. Mary tells her to go inside and change clothes.

Before I have a chance to step out of the car, Mary walks over, opens the door, and sits down on the front seat beside me. I'm a little surprised because for some reason, she's been aloof towards me lately. I break the silence, and say something really stupid just to make conversation, "Go figure, I never thought I'd be driving across America with Mary Blakemore."

She gives me a look that makes me want to drop through the car floor and says, "Really? What do you want Jennifer?"

Strange she asks me this question since I tell her often enough, "I want God in my life."

"Really?" Just the way she says the word "really" makes me uneasy.

"Really. Now what do I do?"

Immediately she replies, "Just say, 'Let's go.'"

"That's it?"

"That's it. Just say, 'Let's go.'"

I don't understand the magnitude of what I'm about to say, or the commitment I'm about to make, let alone the impact these two words will have on the rest of my life. I look into her eyes, flash my best Hollywood smile and repeat what she instructed me to say, "Let's go."

Smiling, she nonchalantly steps out of the car, and walks back where Patrick is standing to review a few last minute details.

After our brief encounter, I have an ominous feeling that my glory days have come to a screeching halt; the honeymoon period when I could do no wrong, when Mary spoke of my spiritual potential, leaving me with the impression I had just been crowned princess of something. I've listened to enough of her satsangs to understand that ego is my enemy, and according to her it's got to go. But I would be less than honest if I don't admit to having a whole lot of trouble making this mystic path a way of life. I believe it. I have embraced it, I hold to my vows, but it's a bitch when I try to put it into practice. At this juncture, whatever I hear in satsang is little more than words; the same as reading a book on medicine won't make me a doctor; in like manner, attending satsang without living the life won't make me a disciple. I don't care what anybody says. To lead a balanced, spiritual life is easier said than done. It's one thing to talk about spirituality, but to live it is quite another matter. Something else I'm sick and tired of hearing so much about, is the word ego. Everyone has ego so why mention it in every satsang? Once in awhile, I'd like to hear something nice said about me. On second thought. What ego? I doubt seriously if there's much left in me to get rid of, although I do have a hard time remembering to repeat the five names – silently of course, like I'm so dumb I'd say them out loud.

Repetition, or simran as it's referred to, isn't new ... although God only knows it's plenty new to me. It's an ancient practice that dates as far back as 3rd century BC. Hindus made use of simran by the repetition of prayer beads to focus their attention in meditation, along with Buddhists, the Baha'i faith and many others, including the Catholic Church, who later adopted this method of concentration by renaming their beads the "rosary" for use in prayer. Well, hats off to the Hindus! Congratulations to the Catholics, good for them all, because I am sincere when I say, "What the hell am I doing here? What's this all about?"

If simran is so all time great, if meditation is such a big deal, then why is it so hard to do? On the other hand Mary explains, the five holy names when repeated slowly with love and devotion, have great power to protect, with the added bonus of keeping my mind from splintering in a million directions. Maybe my problem is that I've been doing the repetition too fast just to get it over with. It's so boring. In fact, I think I actually hate it. Why not own up, come right out and say it: I hate it, OK. I admit my attitude isn't all that great, and maybe that's why she's been so aloof towards me. I know it can't be my ego since I don't have much. She does say a focused mind throughout the day will help me focus when I sit for meditation in the early morning. OK. I'll give it another go. This isn't brain surgery.

Come on, this is ridiculous! I'm standing in the sun by my car for well over fifteen minutes, and I can't get through one round of simran as we wait for Cherie to change clothes. I can't focus long enough to repeat even a single round of the five names. Why is it so hard? For God's sake, I'm an actress who can memorize three acts in a play, who can easily learn five new pages of dialogue overnight for a television show.

Mary glances over at me and comments to Patrick in a voice that can be heard two blocks away, "Well just look at Jennifer. She wants to be treated like a queen. What she really needs is to have her butt kicked from sun up to sundown."

To say that I am stunned by her words is the understatement of the century, but I remain silent. Once again she aims her blue laser beams directly on me and says, "You are the *only* one who arrived late – ten minutes to be exact." I begin to feel the heat from her reprimand traveling upwards from my toes to my head, like being broiled in a five hundred degree oven.

Suddenly, I remember her question to me, "What do you want?" "Let's go," was my answer. I'm still clueless as to what those two words mean to her because at the moment, my only concern is what they're supposed to mean to me. For sure, this isn't what I expected. I hope she's not like this for the whole trip.

I've been on this path only a short time, and already I've met followers who bask in being treated as royal servants of the most high. The reality of the matter is that anyone genuinely interested in spiritual enlightenment, needs praise like a hole in the head – this much I know without any shadow of doubt. Clearly, someone like me was placed in the company of mystics because, despite my shortcomings, I am sincere. Perhaps this is the reason Mary came into my life. Maybe sincerity is the yardstick that measures those of us who can survive the up-close scrutiny, line-of-fire relationship with a true mystic, and others who find it easier to talk the path than walk it … and leave. I could be wrong but I don't think so.

Since time began, the spiritual teacher-pupil relationship, as mine with Mary, has been one of loving combat. If I can't see my weaknesses, how will I overcome them? To teach followers of this path the method of facing themselves, is Mary's only purpose in being here. The longest and most arduous part of the spiritual journey is to rid ourselves of ego, a huge hurdle for any seeker. She reaffirms in every satsang that ego is an insidious entity, or power, to be crushed; in so doing gives death to the negative mind, and birth to a positive mind – worth putting to the test. To be in the company of a true mystic is a rare opportunity to fast-track spiritual growth, but such relationships aren't for sissies. Owning up to my faults without sugarcoating or making excuses, isn't easy. There are times when I wish I was anywhere but here. Yet in my heart, I know this is where I'm supposed to be – but I don't have to like it. If I was a true spiritual person, wouldn't I like it? Well I don't and why say I do.

How to describe Mary Blakemore? Outwardly she appears to be a combination of Mother Theresa and General Patton, a unique blend of the kindest, most lovable grandmother imaginable. She is a folksy philosopher, an unrelenting taskmaster, a prison warden, and a tough-as-nails straw boss. But beneath that exterior is an enigma, a mystic of great spiritual height kept hidden behind the façade. She is forever a friend, and forever a mystery. Never one to mince words, Mary repeatedly warns me to stop being so gullible. I always thought people with spiritual inclinations were first-class in every way, lacking only angel wings. My rose-colored glasses have ceased to be useful. I am beginning to see people as they really are, rather than how I perceive them to be.

The great mystic Hafiz wrote poems about the turbulent years he spent in the company of his teacher, and referred to this discipline as having his nose broken many times – not to be taken literally. Although, I can honestly say a broken nose might be easier than this. To keep close company with Mary Blakemore isn't easy. People claim they want the truth but when the truth hits home, few remain.

A New Beginning

As we stand in wait for Miss Big Tits to change clothes, for no apparent reason Mary looks at the top of my car ... a coming attraction for the next six days. She's getting a bird's-eye view of my rigged up luggage rack the Sperm Donor hastily tied together with jute rope and chicken wire, reminiscent of the *Grapes of Wrath*. She takes a deep breath, then turns and announces, "I'll be standing on New Jersey soil in six days. That's with you or without you."

Is she serious?

Day One

I'm so wiped out from no sleep the night before, that it's all I can do to keep up with Patrick's car. Cherie does nothing but file her nails, snip off broken ends of her long hair, and check out the action each time we stop at a Texaco station for gas. I'm already sick of her. She asked to come on this trip under the pretex of helping me with the kids, but she's useless. Totally. The only thing she knows about children is they were born. Every minute on the hour the boys ask, "Mommy, are we there yet? I gotta go."

It's getting late. I feel like I could pass out, my lips parched from this God awful heat, and no air conditioning in the car; being pregnant doesn't help. As we head towards Death Valley, the heat passes one hundred and ten degrees. Mary puts ice cubes down Patrick's shirt to keep him awake. He's used to the highlife, and this trip isn't it. Despite his inability to help with the smallest task, outside of opening a car door, Mary loves him. She laughs each time he squeals from the ice cubes trickling down his back to keep him awake. I'm glad someone around here has a sense of humor. I used to have one, but I'm not laughing a whole lot these days.

This heat is stifling. Finally, we stop for gas. Cherie takes Willie into a convenience store to buy ice cream cones, but by the time he returns to the car, they've melted. The boys wail so loud, the entire desert population knows we're here. The mere thought of food makes me so nauseous I want to throw up; this heat only makes it worse. I hope we stop soon ... anywhere ... I don't think I can drive much longer. How will I make it to the end of this trip? Finally, Mary spots a Ramada Inn. I don't care if it doesn't have walls or even a roof, if I can lie down. For the next few days we'll sleep during the day, and drive at night to avoid the extreme desert heat. She's like a straw boss who keeps me one pointed on the job at hand, or maybe I'm dead and this is hell. I notice more and more blood in my panties. This pregnancy has been shaky from the start, spotting from time to time. At seven months, my greatest fear is that I might lose this child. My body is worn out. How will the two of us survive this trip? I'm so thin, people don't even know I'm pregnant.

Finally, we stop for the night. The first thing we do is find somewhere to eat ... everyone is famished. I'm so wiped out I can hardly chew. After that, we head for our rooms. Straightaway, I put the boys in the bathtub to play while I wash their underwear. Poor little guys are tired. I help them out of the tub, dry them off, and tuck them into bed. Tomorrow's another day. What good little troopers they are, to be cooped up in a hot car for such long hours. Afterward, I lie down in my hot bath and just soak for thirty minutes, thinking surely this must be as close to heaven on earth as I'll ever get. My body aches from head to toe. Suddenly I hear a knock. The words, "Come to the door." reverberates in my ears.

I throw a towel around me, water dripping all over the Ramada carpet, run to the door, and peek through the keyhole to see Patrick slumped over like the last rose of summer. Once again, he impatiently raps on the door, "Come to Mary's room. It's important!"

I think to myself, "Shut up you insufferable prig." My voice rises three octaves and insincerely responds, "Thanks hun, I'm on the way," as I quickly dry off, slip back into my jeans and t-shirt. The kids are fast asleep when I lock the door, and drag myself to her room next to mine. She looks refreshed in a soft blue robe. Smiling, she motions for everyone to sit down and listen carefully. Mary wastes no time explaining that we should never forget ego has holes in each letter, and that being the case, she is curious to know why we have such overblown opinions of ourselves. She pauses, then continues to explain that next to God power, sex power is the most formidable in this world ... something else we should never forget.

I'm like, that's it? Ego has holes in it? Is she serious? What does ego have to do with anything? I haven't the vaguest idea why she brought me here for something like this. If I don't get some sleep I'll never make it. I'm half dead, and the first to head for the door. On the way out I thank her, grumbling under my breath, "Got it ... mustn't forget that."

A New Beginning

Mary Immediately shoots me a look that tells me she knows what I'm thinking. Her parting shot preempts my shutting the door, "Jennifer, be ready to leave at 5:00 p.m. sharp. No excuses!"

Once again I thank her and hightail it to my room, still wondering why all this couldn't of waited until morning. Surely her statement was directed more at Cherie and Patrick than to me. Men are the last thing I want. If they had diamonds popping out every aperture on their miserable bodies, I'd sooner go to jail than get involved with another man. I don't even like how they're assembled. Let's see, did I forget anything?

Everything Mary says goes down like gravel these days. Still, I can't take her words lightly. Her ability to read my thoughts is disarming, something else I don't like. Matter of fact I hate it, who wouldn't? I used to be a free spirit, maybe a miserable one, but free nevertheless. Each day of this trip I feel more and more like a jailbird driving across country with the prison warden. And another thing, I'm sick unto death of her incessant talk about my ego! For crying out loud, isn't there something else we can talk about outside of that, and anyway ... what ego?

Day Two

Our daily routine is to telephone eight hours ahead, and reserve motel rooms in whatever town we'll stop in for the night. Once there, we buy cheese, milk, bread, chips, fruit, salad fixings, etc., to make a light dinner in the room. We have little money, so it's important to stretch out what we have. Mary thinks of everything, a fact she repeats with the regularity of a metronome. I'm so wiped out by the end of these long drives in an old car with no air-conditioning, that I sincerely don't know the difference between a head of lettuce and a turnip. Today she said I'm not operating on even half a brain cell.

Mommy! Our suitcase just flew off the car again!

Day Three

We set our alarm clocks to rise and shine for another nocturnal drive across America, sleeping during the day to avoid this damn killer heat. Mary raised nine children, and well understands how rammy they get when cooped up for long hours in the car. No matter how tired everyone is, rest assured we always stop to allow Rome and Willie some ice cream and playtime. Every half hour Rome kicks the back of my seat whining, "Mommy, I gotta go ... real bad!" I finally ask the waitress in a diner for two empty coffee cans, otherwise we'll never reach New Jersey.

On the third day through the Mohave, I hear the kids screaming the familiar, "Mommy look! Our stuff's flying off the car! It's all over the desert!"

"Great."

"Mommy, can I have a lizard? Can I catch one for a pet?"

"Mommy, I want a wizard too." Sweet Jesus.

I bring the car to an abrupt halt, and get out to see my underwear, clothes, the kid's clothes, and a few other unmentionables scattered over the highway, and in the sand. I begin to remember Mary's specific instructions in LA, that I leave everything behind except the needful. My art collection, blues and jazz collection, paintings, books, and all my personal belongings were left behind with Aunt Lowee. Mary had counseled, "You don't need old memories to begin a new life."

I'm pretty sure she won't consider my black leather mini skirt with matching coat custom made in Madrid, my gold leather pants and jacket from *Malcolm,* and two evening gowns from *Diamond Orchid,* "needful." I rationalized "take only the needful" to mean, I should only keep those items needed for psychological support, to take my mind off this move to hell's half acre in New Jersey. There is also the little matter of my scrapbooks filled with press clippings, playbills, photos, magazine spreads, and resumes now scattered over the highway and desert for disinterested road hogs and iguanas.

Honestly, we look like mad people scrambling on the hot desert floor for our clothes to throw into the suitcase before Mary drives back to see for herself what the latest holdup is now. What a sight we are, rooting about in the sand for panties, miniskirts, gowns from Broadway shows, and praying to God that Mary, by divine intervention, will keep right on going to New Jersey rather than drive back for us. Like that will happen.

Cherie quickly hustles to the top of the car with our large empty suitcase, now filled with sand and desert bugs. I begin tossing up our retrievables to shove back in, when I see Mary and Patrick headed our way. "Oh crap," I yell, "Hurry it up, she's here!"

They pull over to the roadside. Patrick opens the car door and stands for a moment like a man who has forgotten what country he's in. Mary doesn't move an inch. She looks directly at me, and I begin to experience the familiar heat rise from my feet to the top of my head, fast becoming her signature of annoyance.

Once again I recall her instructions to the Sperm Donor. She told him to buy a new luggage rack and have my Chevy checked out from top to bottom. On top of this disaster, Willie wants to pee again, a signal for Romie to do the same. I'm at the end of my patience and yell, "Come on you guys. Make it snappy!"

Willie chimes in, "Mommy, we want our coffee cans."

I shoot back, "Listen up. Pee, or get back in the car!"

Day Four

Mary is disgusted with all of us – me in particular. Everyone is exhausted to the point of extinction, and these kids make me wish I'd stayed a virgin. My luggage has flown off the car four times, the starter and water pump replaced, and now the radiator is smoking. Finally, we pull into a gas station and Jeeter something says, "Lady ya'll need a new radiator. I'll fix it but this here's gonna take two or three h'rs."

Mary is in no mood to hang around a gas station. Instead, she invites everyone out to dinner, and leaves me sitting on top of an oil tank in wait for Jeeter to install the new radiator. As the hours pass, I feel sorrier and sorrier for myself. After three hours, and most of my money, I drive to the motel where we're staying. I telephone Mary to ask if Cherie would bring the kids home, and apologize once again, for all the delays. I don't really mean it because ... is it my fault I'm driving this damn car from hell? Once again she lights into me about doing things right the first time, but I'm too tired to argue. I tell her I'm sorry, then hang up and wait for the kids to come back so I can put them to bed before I take rat poisoning. The point is, what do I ever do that works out? I'm damned if I do and I'm damned if I don't where she's concerned. Is it my fault the radiator overheated and blew up? Is it my fault the starter conked out? Is it my fault the odometer doesn't work? Is it my fault the Sperm Donor can't keep his pants up? Is it my fault I have a damn ego? Is it my fault I was born?

There's a knock on the door. I think it's the kids, and open it to see Mary standing alone in the doorway. When she smiles, and looks at me with more compassion than I can handle just now, I melt. She puts her arms around my bony shoulders, and speaks in a soft, reassuring voice, "Jenny, come on darlin now buck up. Look, I've brought you a pizza. Come on, eat it while it's hot; afterwards I want you to take a nice hot bath, and you'll feel better." This is the Mary I first met. As she continues to try and cheer me up, I begin to cry and thank her over and over. When she turns to go, as an afterthought she stops, does a three quarter turn, and makes the point, "I'll be in New Jersey on the date I said. If your luggage falls off again, or even if the car blows up, you'll be walking to New Jersey."

Day Five

Driving for such long hours makes my mind wander to better times and places. If I wasn't sick from this pregnancy, maybe I could look at things in a different light, but given a miracle I'm worried sick this baby won't come to full term. A miscarriage is my worst nightmare. As we near our destination, and just when I think the worst is behind me, I hear the sweet strains of, "Mommy, the suitcase fell off again! "Mommy, they're stealing your underwear!"

A New Beginning

I grit my teeth and pull the car over to find two truckers laughing as they try on my bra and black mini skirt. I scream at Cherie to stay in the car. Today she's wearing a cut off t-shirt that showcases her boobs when she holds up her arms or bends over. I jump out of the car, and working up a good set of tears, dash over to the truckers. I tell them such a sob story of being destitute with two kids and a dying sister, their mood quickly changes to embarrassment as they peel off my undies. I accept their offer to help us pick up our clothes – now scattered in all ten directions: that would be north, south, east, west, left, right, front, back, up and down. That adds up to ten! Afterward, they anchor my suitcase, and tie it to the top of the car. I thank my road angels as they climb back into their sixteen-wheeler, and take off grinning from ear to ear, tooting their horn, and waving as they pass us by.

By this time, I'm in no mood for Cherie who is intensely frustrated over the lost opportunity to display her hooters. She screams, "You're a bitch! Do you ever think of me?" She's got a lot of nerve talking like this in front of my kids.

I feel the heat begin to rise from the sole of my feet up to my head. Here she comes. Mary is on her way back to ascertain why the delay for the umpteenth time. The boys shouldn't be listening to this so I snap back at her quietly, "Shut the hell up you little slut. Get it out of your head the world gives a shit about your sorry tits!" I'd like to drop her off at the next truck stop. We don't speak for the rest of the trip.

Mary and Patrick drive up just as we pull out. No matter. She's fed up with our dimwittedness. Patrick has lost what little composure he possessed; he didn't count on this. He thought driving across country would be a hoot, that we'd browse in quaint antique shops, and snack in out-of-the-way places with local ambience.

Day Six

In Delaware, we pull into a gas station; we're only an hour out from New Jersey. I ask the attendant to check my oil, instead he claims I need a new engine. By this time I'm so wiped out, I lose whatever residual tact I possess, and go off on him, "Fill it with gas and oil! If my car breaks down, I'll come back and freaking kill you myself!" The LA doormat has flown the coop.

Welcome to the Garden State

The sign reads "Welcome to the Garden State" then another, a larger one about New Jersey being somewhere holly grows. Truth is, I'm so relieved to arrive in one piece, I'm almost happy to be here, if that makes sense. Mary wants us to stay overnight in a motel in Runnemead. Tomorrow we'll drive to her apartment in Lindenwold for lunch.

This is my first day in the great state of New Jersey, synonym for Mafia burial ground, and women with big hair. I've complained so much on this trip, I feel compelled to ingratiate Mary with humor. I tell her it's a known fact, that New Jersey women with big hair are closer to the Almighty. She ignores my feeble attempt to make her laugh; instead, she speaks in a gentle tone I haven't heard for awhile, "Jenny, I want you to stop worrying; it's bad for the baby. Tomorrow, I'll find you and the children a nice place to live."

My physical condition has gone from bad to worse. Who in their right mind will rent an apartment to a pregnant woman with no husband in sight, two small kids, no job, no bank account, no furniture, not even a bed, and no money for a security deposit? Who would? Undaunted, Mary tells me to wear something nice, and spiff up the kids so we'll look like respectable renters. I couldn't look more horrible if I tried.

After days of being cooped up in the backseat of a car, the kids have fun playing in the motel pool, but I'm so tired all I can do is sit, watch, and wonder what it would feel like to be a child again. My lips are so dry, they're cracked from the desert heat.

The next day, we turn left off White Horse Pike onto Gibbsborough Road, and begin to look for Coachman Manor Apartments.

A New Beginning

I park the car, tidy up the boys and anxiously walk to Apartment B3, the number I jotted down on the inside of my hand.

For a moment, we stand quietly at the front door before knocking. I'm very nervous and need to collect myself. A sense of cleanliness surrounds her apartment, the front door, the bay window that faces a walkway so clean it sparkles, and the fragrance of roses – yet not a rosebush in sight. I put on my sunglasses, in the hope she won't notice my swollen eyes from last night's crying jag. Finally, I knock. When the door opens, I experience the same uplift as when we first met in California. She looks at the three of us standing in her doorway, *worry* written across my forehead, then smiles and says in a soft voice, "Jenny, what's to be done is already done."

It's uncanny how she knows my every thought; there is no difference between what I think and the words I say. I never dreamed I would have to answer for my thoughts. To remain in close company with Mary is anything but easy, yet I'm drawn to her in ways I can't explain. Sitting here in this small, cozy living room, I notice mementoes and photographs of people from all over the world, of mystics I've only read about, along with pictures of her great-granddaughter's wedding, and other family members. There are cuttings of Ivy in a miniature jade vase standing alongside books that neatly hug a shelf next to a small kitchen. She brings each of us a Coke, and places a large bowl of potato chips in front of the boys much to their delight. Mary begins to emphasize the value of having a positive attitude where our future is concerned … and the new baby, "God works best when we're positive, otherwise it's uphill all the way."

What does she mean by that? What's to be positive about? My bones are tired, my eyes hurt, my lips cracked, and my ears don't want to hear anything smacking of God. At this point I don't know who he is or where he comes from. I'm so drained from this trip, I can hardly stand up, much less think about being positive. I know my attitude stinks, but I can't help it. I'm broke, I'm old, I'm ugly and dammit, what am I doing in New Jersey? Oh Mary, I've forgotten everything you try so hard to teach me. What's the use? I'm hopeless. I look up to see her smiling at me.

I came close to having a miscarriage during our grueling six day drive across America. No matter how uptight I get when she scolds me, I'm overwhelmed by her goodness of heart, and how she sticks by my depressed self like glue. We've been in New Jersey only two days, and already she's taken me to a Obstetrician who will deliver the baby. My weight loss is a concern, along with how emaciated I am in the seventh month of pregnancy. He confirms my fear that a September delivery could have serious complications; he urges me to rest and eat regularly if I want a healthy child. I feel as though a huge burden has been lifted from me.

Her response to his warning is predictable, "Well then, start eating." She continues, "That's the trouble with you people. You can't have it both ways. Either Lord is in everything or he is in nothing." When Mary first came to this path, she wrote a letter to her teacher in India, Maharaji Charan Singh Ji, and said, "I tied a knot in your coat-tail, and I'm hanging on for dear life."

I seriously doubt there will ever be an event in my life, death included, that she won't turn into a spiritual lesson to drive home a point, like the dream I had last night which began with a simple remark, "Mary, I'm dying."

"Didn't I tell you to spend more time in meditation – it's all that matters in the end."

"I'm always in trouble for not carrying an umbrella and not listening to the weatherman, but this morning I did as you advised. Have you noticed that even though I'm on my deathbed, I carry an umbrella today? "

"That's your problem Jennifer: you listen to the weatherman instead of your teacher."

I'm damned if I do. I'm damned if I don't.

True to form, Mary finds a new home for us, a first floor, two bedroom apartment in a country setting, only forty five minutes from her apartment. It has an environmental playground, a duck pond, tennis courts and plush green grass everywhere I look. The manager seems oblivious of the fact that I'm pregnant, with no mention of my husband, the Sperm Donor. The kids and I sit quietly beside Mary, as she charms away any objections the manager might have about renting to a pregnant woman with two kids, no husband and no job.

Already, I can see the boys happy just being children, playing and doing all the things kids do. I can't move in fast enough. For a short while this afternoon, I feel as though life can't get any better than now. How can it be that two days ago, I was exhausted, depressed, and didn't know how I could go on. Today, my world is filled with sunshine.

Although Mary has little money, her personal demeanor is such that everyone who comes in contact with her assumes she is a millionaire. Her reply to the question, "You're a millionaire aren't you?" is always the same,

"A millionaire? Why yes I am – mostly air." People laugh when she says this, but they never believe one word of it.

Mary insists I pay my hospital bill in advance, along with the purchase of two king-size beds for our new apartment. I've little money left. No matter. We're happy to have a home of our own, and the good news is: we move in today. It's hard to keep up with all that is happening to me. All my life I've chased happiness, now it's chasing me. It's Christmas in July.

Not only have we moved into a new apartment, but Mary decides to furnish it as well – with a little help from Patrick who is busy decorating his own. She has her eye on his latest purchase, a gold sofa and television set, and immediately calls him to say, "Patrick, who ever heard of anyone buying a gold sofa to match a carpet the same color? If it was me, I'd give it to Jennifer and the kids. They've nothing to sit on when they watch television. Matter of fact, I'd probably give them the TV as well – you know, along with the sofa. Of course, then I'd have to go shopping and buy myself new ones."

We are now the grateful recipients of a gold sofa and new television set. William is happy because he can watch *Mothra vs. Godzilla* again. Patrick went out the same day, and bought himself an expensive blue sofa with chair to match, along with a television set twice the size of the one he gave us. Everyone is happy.

I'm cleaning in the back when I hear the kids shout, "Mommy, Mary's here, Mary's here!"

I run to the living room and see the boys jumping up and down as they look out the pane glass door. There she sits in a white sixty seven Pontiac, complete with a small American flag attached to the antenna, and loaded to the gills with packages, folding table, chairs, dishes, cooking utensils, tablecloth, bedding, curtains, and so much more – everything needed to transform our apartment into a real home. What can I say about someone like this? I am a witness to the mystic path in action through a true devotee. The life she lives before me, is a living example of every lofty principle I've heard spoken in any church or satsang.

Just when I have exactly two dollars left, Mary finds me a job where I can work from home doing piecework for Robert, and still watch the kids. I'll earn five cents a necklace making love beads to be sold in Philadelphia. Some weeks I earn as much as eighty dollars, which helps on groceries and other necessities. I don't worry about anything these days except staying healthy enough to deliver my baby. But sometimes when I think of New York and my career, I begin to miss it. It never occurs to me that I should give it up. Quite the contrary. Last week Mary suggested once the baby is born, it might be a good idea to contact my old agent in Manhattan. I would love to see him again. Matter of fact, I could work in New York, get a housekeeper in New Jersey, and still be near Mary and satsang. I'll never leave her company. I'll just have both.

When I wake up each morning, I feel new pounds on my body. I eat regularly, but not so much as to give food credit for my sudden weight gain. My doctor can't believe the metamorphosis from war victim to whale, that's me. I am humongous! I need Willie and Rome to help me in and out of bed. It takes two of them to pull up a whale.

Each week Mary has someone drive me to satsang. True to form, she teaches from life experience. She's using my pregnancy to drive home the point of placing the needs of others before our own. She relates story after story about women who gave birth to plus-size babies without a whimper. Well, good for them. Honestly, I'm sick unto death listening to stories about how brave women were in "the good ol' days." When Rome was born I had so much pain, I vowed never to have another child. So much for that vow. My new one is, "Memo to Hospital: whatever's handy to knock me out, looks good to me. Morphine, I'll take it. Spinal, bring it on. Freeze me til it's over. Count me in. Knock me over the head with a broomstick. That too!"

I'm ashamed to admit how much I dread answering the telephone because I know it's Mary. She wants to discuss natural child-birth ... again. She won't give up. Maybe if I take classes that will solve the problem.

A New Beginning

She likes the idea. Tonight, she'll have Patrick drive me to the first natural child-birth class while he and the kids wait in the car, or go for ice cream. Although it's for couples only, the nurse-instructor reassures me I'll do just fine without my husband present ... like I didn't already know that. All I need do is give her a call when the first labor pains arrive. She'll stop whatever she's doing, no matter what, and drive to the hospital. Sure lookin' forward to that.

There are ten couples, plus me – who looks every bit like a beached whale. At the end of class, the husbands help their wives stand up to put on their coats. The happy pairs chat away with the nurse-instructor, while I remain stuck on the floor. I'm in my ninth month, and so big I need a blimpmobile to drive home in, and a forklift to stand me up once I arrive. But this instructor is too busy lollygagging to notice I'm still on the floor, unable to stand without assistance. If nurse smarty pants can't walk twenty feet to help me stand up after a class, what to say when I'm in labor? Who needs her. I'll scoot myself over to a chair, use it as leverage, then stand up on my own. Enough. This baby will come the old fashion way. I can just hear Mary saying, "Atta girl."

When I get home, the first thing I do is call her to say I'll deliver the baby naturally. She says, "Don't worry Jenny, when the labor pains come, I'll drive you to the hospital."

Pull off the road, I'm having a baby!

These last weeks of pregnancy have left me with a contentment I've never before experienced. I'd love to say it's the result of my deep meditation, but I'd laugh so much the baby might come prematurely. No. I'm the recipient of another's prayers, of someone sharing their happiness with me. It isn't that I have no worries; rather, they don't have me for a change. The kids are happy. They write the Sperm Donor every week but outside of that, they rarely mention him. They've grown accustomed to their father not being around.

I feel good about returning to my career after the baby is born. I'll contact my old agent, and ask him to send me on interviews again. Maybe I'll take some dance classes to get back in shape. Everything will be different now that my old destructive habits are behind me. I might go crazy if I thought I'd live here permanently. There is nothing to do. I mean, come on, it's New Jersey. Who lives in New Jersey?

As I sit at the kitchen table making love beads, I notice for the first time how subtle twilight rains its shadow on the cornfield surrounding this apartment complex. Nature just is – no stress, no pain, only contentment in itself.

I'm on the verge of a catnap when the first labor pain jolts me out of my reverie. They're here! True to form they skip the preliminaries and jump to the chase. They're five minutes apart when my thoughts flashback to Madrid, when I came close to having Romie on the clinic steps. Right now I'm so shook up I can't remember if I have a telephone, much less what room it's in. I run to the kitchen and call Mary to let her know they're five minutes apart. She's not the least

A New Beginning

unnerved; rather, she consoles me in a calm, loving voice, "Jenny, there's no time for me to drive forty five minutes to pick you up in Glassboro, then turn around and drive back another forty five minutes to the hospital, but not to worry – everything will be OK."

"Everything will be OK?"

"Yes, everything will be OK."

"Maybe I should call an ambulance. Oh my God, here comes another one."

"Honey, by the time the ambulance arrives it will be too late. No, you drive yourself."

"Drive myself?"

"Yes. Drive yourself."

"Drive myself where?"

"Drive yourself to the hospital. I'll meet you there and take care of the boys. Now get movin darlin, time's a' wastin." Before hanging up Mary adds, "Stay in your simran, and no harm will come to you."

At this point, I can hardly remember my last name, much less the five holy names. I overcome a moment of cardiac arrest, grab the packed suitcase I've left by the front door for the past two months, and round up the boys. The kids help me into the car while I silently pray the two dollars worth of gas I put in yesterday, is enough to get us to the hospital forty five minutes away. As we pull out, something inside me begins to speak … like God in silence.

The sun is going down fast as we drive along this desolate country road, my labor pains growing more intense, now at three minute intervals. I feel as though any moment this baby will fall down between my legs on top of the brakes – maybe I should pull over and have it in one of the cornfields over there. If hay was good enough for Jesus, a bed of corn is good enough for Zola, a name that's just come to me. I'm trying to stay calm but as the labor pains grow in intensity, it's hard to maintain composure with Romie rocking back and forth. He repeats in a monotonous sing-song voice, and rhythmically kicks the back of my seat in time with, "I want M & M's! I want M & M's!"

"You want me to have this baby here? Stop kicking my seat or I'll have it in a cornfield. Stop it!"

"I want M & M's! I want M & M's Mommy!"

Instead of repeating the five holy names, I begin to repeat, "M & M's, M & M's, M & M's."

Finally. I've just enough gas left to pull into guest parking at JFK Hospital. The pains are now one minute apart as I drive my Chevy up to, and almost through the glass entrance door. I waddle out of the car, grab the kids by their shirttails, the one still screaming at the top of his lungs, "I want M & M's," and announce to everyone within ear shot in the reception room, "I'm having a baby!" I throw the keys on the desk, and manage to say, "Park the car if there's enough gas!"

The nurses and doctors in the emergency room are shocked that I drove such a distance fully dilated. At this juncture, a baby doesn't care what the mother does or where she is. It only knows it's good to go. The nurse telephones Mary, who offers reassurance that she is only minutes away, for me not to worry, and to let Romie know she has a bag of M & M's for him. Everyone knows what he wants because the candy machine is out of order. As they wheel me upstairs, I hear echoes of his whiny little voice, "I want M & M's ... Mommy, I want M & M's!" If I could repeat the five holy names with the same focus this little boy repeats his craving for M & M's, I'd have it made.

I'm rushed to the delivery table, where my water bag immediately breaks. As the nurse wipes the sweat off my forehead, she whispers in my ear, "Your mother is here – just outside the door." The moment Mary hears his first cry, she ignores the doctor and nurses, and goes directly into the delivery room. She walks over to Zola and gives him darshan, an Indian word meaning divine glance or blessing. He receives her gift of love at the moment of birth. Like a warrior with his fists high in the air, my healthy eight pound boy enters the world. Despite all odds, a frank breech notwithstanding, my little son is here. Unlike a normal delivery, he came out with his feet pointed downward, his hands reaching up, and his head tilted back. His birth would have had serious complications had I not believed Mary when she said, "Jenny, stay in your simran and no harm will come to you."

How is it possible the emergency room nurse spoke with Mary in her apartment, at the same time I was being rushed to the delivery room? At my request, the nurse called her just as she was leaving Coachman Manor for JFK Hospital ... a distance of, at the very least,

A New Beginning

twenty minutes. The nurse clearly heard her say, "Tell Jennifer I'm minutes away, and make sure you tell little Romie I have his M & M's."

Within minutes, Mary was sitting outside the delivery room.

The maternity ward is packed tonight. Even though I paid the hospital bill in advance, I'm surprised to find myself on a bed in the hallway. After all we've been through together, I'm too happy to care where I am.

It's almost surreal, that only months ago we drove across America in the sweltering heat of summer. Zola weighed less than three pounds, and I was dangerously thin – yet here we are today, two and one half months later. I've just given birth to a healthy eight pound baby boy, we're out of that hellish life in LA, Willie has adjusted to his new family, Romie has his M & M's, and Mary stands beside my bed with two sandwiches made from her special mix, along with a fresh baked stuffed apple. My best friend is here. She looks at me tenderly and says, "Jenny, I was very tough on you when we drove across country. It was the hardest thing I ever had to do, but had I not, you would never have made it."

Miracles do happen

"There are as many paths leading to God as there are stars in the sky."

Doug Brookins

Until now my only concern was giving birth to a healthy baby, but now that he's here and life has settled in, I'm worried about how to make ends meet. I have no money left. Mary wants me to contact my agent in New York, in the hope he'll breathe life back into my career. Why not? Miracles happen, keeping in mind the old adage, "You're only as good as your last success." When I left Manhattan to go back to LA, I thought my career was over, but it isn't. It doesn't make sense to throw it all out the window. Why would I do that? Today, armed with a healthy body, a new attitude and renewed vigor, I've made an appointment to meet with Ben, my old agent, in two weeks. Manhattan, I can hardly wait to see you.

Mary sounds happy. She just called to say Robert opened a new boutique. He has a sharp two-piece wool pant suit she thinks would be perfect to wear on my audition in New York. "Honey," she says, "Why don't you and the boys come for lunch next week, and take a look."

I barely have enough money for gasoline, and what did she just say? What audition? There's no audition that I know of.

When the big day arrives the four of us get into the car, and just as I'm backing out I notice the postman running in my direction. He waves his arms and hollers, "Wait! Wait! I have a letter for you!" Out of breath, he runs over to the car, and jokingly puts it up to his forehead and exclaims, "Feels like money to me!" With that, he hands me the envelope and continues his delivery. I open it to discover a check from the hospital made out in my name for a large sum of money, a refund in the amount I paid for Zola's delivery, with no explanation, no letter – only the check.

On the drive to Lindenwold, I'm even more anxious to see Mary. If I had caved to my fear of not having money to pay for a new outfit, and refused her invitation for lunch, I wonder if this would have happened. I'm speechless with relief and happiness. I haven't seen her in weeks.

There's a faint smile on her face when I explain the incident with our mailman and the check, but she says nothing. The boys are abnormally well behaved today. They remember to say "thank you" for the special treats she gives each of them. Mary has prepared a wonderful lunch and to my great relief, the kids are well-mannered and help with the baby. Willie holds him when he gets restless. Afterward, we drive to Robert's new boutique where I try on the wool pant-suit. It's gorgeous. Now I have money to pay for it, with enough left over for expenses until I find work. Mary wants me to leave the kids with her when I go to New York next week. Several times she tells me to have a wonderful day, and not to worry about anything. She does, however, offer one suggestion, "Do not give out your telephone number to anyone."

I'm back in Manhattan where I belong

I'm thrilled to be back in Manhattan with a few hours to kill before my appointment. As I stroll along Lexington Avenue, I hear someone call out my name, "Jennifer! Hey, stop walking so fast – it's me, Barbara."

Barbara Loden is married to Elia Kazan who directed me in Arthur Miller's, *After the Fall* at the Lincoln Center. He chose me to replace her in the lead role of Maggie four days a week, to give his wife a much-needed break. There was immediate tension between us when first introduced. How we met later on in California is ironic to say the least.

Late one afternoon, when we were still living with Aunt Lowee in East LA, I was surprised when the Sperm Donor came home earlier than usual. He had bumped into Barbara at the Actor's Studio West, where she'd asked about me. He mentioned Mary along with my interest in a far eastern philosophy, but he couldn't remember the name of it. All he knew was that I had a teacher. She immediately asked for my telephone number.

When I heard her voice on the other end of the line, it was tentative at best given our strained relationship in New York. But she wasted no time asking about the philosophy I follow, and if I could arrange for her to meet Mary Blakemore. Not once did the issue of show business come up. I called Mary, who immediately asked me to bring her over. There was an urgency in her voice that didn't allow me to question why she wanted me to drive so far out of the way, when Barbara could easily have driven herself. I stopped everything, borrowed Aunt Lowee's car, and drove to her posh BelAir home where she was waiting outside as I drove up. She ran over to my car, still beautiful wearing a short white tennis outfit, revealing her long tanned legs. When she opened the door and sat down beside me, I recognized the expression on her face – like someone ready to jump off a cliff. As we drove along, neither of us knew the other well enough to discuss our personal lives, and I didn't know enough about the philosophy to have an intelligent discussion. We were on safe ground. It was a perfect start for a genuine friendship, leaving show business jealousy far behind.

As we walked down the hall to Mary's apartment, I decided to ask if she would give Barbara a private audience. She smiled at the two of us standing in the doorway, and motioned for her to come in. I walked back to the car to memorize a script for a new television show to begin in a week.

Three hours later, Barbara came out of Mary's apartment smiling, radiant and full of hope, not at all like the depressed person who went in. How well I understood. On the drive back to BelAir, neither of us felt the need to say anything. So often in the past, Mary would say that love is born in silence, and useless chatter dissipates spiritual progress. Suddenly she turned to me, almost whispering, "You know Jen, there's always people around me. They use me to get to him."

Later that evening, when I called Mary to express my gratitude for seeing her on such short notice, she made a point of asking me to call Barbara every day, and for us to keep in touch. We did while we were on the West Coast.

Eighteen months later, here we are having an impromptu lunch together in a small bistro on Lexington Avenue, catching up and renewing the promise we made before branching out in opposite directions. I get a real kick out of her non-stop monologue. Several times she expresses her gratitude to Mary for introducing her to this mystic philosophy, then laughs at her ex-psychiatrist who charged one hundred dollars an hour, as opposed to this path which is free of charge. On the same note she sent postage stamps to her teacher, Charan Singh Ji Maharaj in India, to cover the cost of correspondence. She's quick to point out that he returned the stamps along with his reply, then changes the subject, and begins to talk about the women's movement, film in particular.

After lunch we say our goodbyes, and once again promise to keep in touch, maybe in satsang next week if her schedule permits.

But for all her words, clearly her focus is riveted on filmmaking. Although my own life is deeply rooted in a spiritual journey, and being a single mother to three sons, the intensity of her ambition is a harsh reminder of my own – unsettling to say the least. After we go our separate ways, me to my agent, Barbara to her projects, I'm left with a deep sense of loss, that I'll never see her again. But I'm too excited over the prospect of reviving my career to entertain sadness. I hail a cab to Ben's office, and quickly shake off this feeling of despondency.

Manhattan epiphany

I'm awed by the changes in this sophisticated, newly decorated suite that houses some of the most powerful theatrical agents in New York. Once inside, I walk over to the receptionist to confirm my appointment. She looks at me and smiles, "Jen, have a seat. Ben's really glad you've come."

I feel an immediate sense of relief. I need to get back into the swing of things, the sooner the better. His office door opens, Ben walks over, smiling, arms outstretched, and gives me a big show biz hug, "Jen, thrilled to see you ... thought you dropped off the world."

In a way, it feels strange talking to him like this. I'm not the same person who left New York.

I laugh nervously in the attempt to explain, "Oh, just needed a little breather. I'm back now."

After the initial small talk he gets down to business. He wants to know if I'd like to read a script, that if I like it he'll send me on an interview today while I'm in the city. He goes on to say that he wants me to audition for the lead role in a new Broadway play. All the while Ben continues to talk, I remember Mary's remark about the new pantsuit I'm wearing today being great for my audition. When she made that remark, I had no audition. I jump at his offer and reply, "Great, let's have a look." I laugh at myself trying so hard to appear casual, almost blasé, when in reality I'm halfway to breathless at the thought of performing in a Broadway play once again.

I wade through the script, and quickly make note of one scene where the main character strips down to her waist. The language is x-rated, and the bedroom scene graphic with nothing left to the imagination. I argue with myself that I've never done anything like this before. Then again, times are changing, and if I want to return to show business I must change too, and quick. Still, I'm not sure I'll be comfortable if my kids see me in plays where I'm half-naked, and what of Mary? On the other hand – if I'm only acting a part, why be embarrassed for anyone to see it? I dismiss these thoughts as minor concerns. Just when I finish the script, Ben pops his head in the door and motions for me to come back into his office. Perfect timing. I'll be honest with him.

Before I have a chance to go into detail, he dismisses my concern as frivolous. He urges me to get all this nonsense out of my head and go on the interview, that we'll discuss it later, that there are many parts out there, and not to worry because the most important thing is to get back into the swing of things without wasting time adding, "OK Jen, give me your new telephone number."

Mary's words reverberate in bold psychedelic across my forehead, "*Do not give out your telephone number to anyone.*"

"What did you say?"

"I said, give me your telephone number."

"*My* telephone number?"

Growing somewhat impatient he replies," Yes, yours. Give it to me."

I stall in the hope of finding a synonym for telephone. "My telephone number?"

"Yes," his voice takes on a snappy tone. "Your telephone number! How can I send you on interviews if I can't call you?"

"Western Union?"

"Excuse me?"

"Western Union."

He just stares at me. Emboldened, I continue, "Send me a telegram."

As he begins to write down the producer's address for my audition, he suddenly looks at me like I have two feet of hair growing out my nose, adding, "Just call me from a telephone booth when your done."

This is one of those moments when, under ordinary circumstances, I'd want to drop through the floor. Instead, I assume the air of Cleopatra saying goodbye to slave trade, and leave him wondering if he just bumped heads with an asteroid.

On the way to my audition I begin to feel depressed when I should be happy. After all, isn't this what I want? But all I can think of is Barbara, and the coincidence of bumping into her like that. I can see myself in her, the burning ambition to prove myself even at the cost of my spiritual life; worse still, the denial of that sacrifice. She made it abundantly clear, her career took precedence over everything. I need to shake off these feelings.

I've lost none of my confidence as I walk into the theatre, a dimly lit house where both director and producer sit in wait for actors to nervously audition. The director remembers my performance in *The Dutchman* several years back, and he's quick to mention how much he enjoyed it. We chat a few minutes before I walk onstage to begin. Afterward, they seem impressed with my reading, and inquire as to my availability. If I'm offered this part, I'll refuse it. I have no intention of stripping down. My spirits should soar at the chance to get back into my groove, regardless of my negative opinion of this play. Instead, all I can think of are three little boys who wait for me in New Jersey, and how their lives will be torn apart if I continue to chase the ghost of my dreams. I feel nauseous.

As I walk through Midtown Theatre District, I'm suddenly faced with the harsh consequence of resuming my career in show business, while at the same time struggling to be a full-time single mom to three small children. What kind of fairytale world am I in not to understand the insanity of even attempting to lead a balanced spiritual life in an industry, whose foundation is based upon fanning the wildfire of ego? For the first time, I understand why Mary speaks so often on the issue of ego. What was I thinking? I'm standing on the corner of 42nd Street in Midtown Manhattan, tears streaming down my face, experiencing a total disconnect from the city I once courted.

It's over.

I never thought I would live to hear myself say it, but I can hardly wait to get back to New Jersey, pick up my babies and see Mary. Now I understand why she encouraged this trip to New York. I am the only one who can accept the terms of my new life, and let go of the old one. I remember her words, "Let's go."

The real work begins.

Standing on our own two feet

I'm so desperate to find work, I've even charted a plan for us to live in the car when the money runs out. I'll get the kids bathed and dressed for school in a gas station. If we have to – we will. That's all there is to it. The Sperm Donor never telephones to ask about his new son much less his other two, Rome and Willie. He never offers to help with doctor bills, or just living for that matter. I try hard not to let the boys know how critical things are. If I can make it through one day, surely the next will be better. This is what I hold onto. I would be lost without Mary. Sometimes in the middle of a day, there are moments when I feel her presence giving me the strength to go on. A year ago if anyone told me I'd be on welfare, I would have laughed and probably called them a liar, yet here I am today standing in the Acme check-out with my three kids and food stamps.

I'm so broke I can't make change for a dollar. Collecting welfare bothers me a lot; but I had no alternative as Mary paid a lawyer to facilitate child support. She advised me to follow through with his advice to apply for welfare. There is no other way the Sperm Donor will ever pay child support. Once in the system, New Jersey State will then go after the deadbeat dad in California. The lawyer explained, there is no shame in accepting aid until we're able to stand on our own two feet. Once the Sperm Donor pays child support, I'll request The Department of Family Services stop sending monthly checks.

I babysit every chance I get, which pays for a bag of groceries and little else. Twice this month, I've had to keep Willie home from school when I didn't have a quarter for a movie. He argues that school provides free milk for kids whose families can't afford it, but when I try to explain we don't take handouts, he says I'm unfair.

A New Beginning

Isn't it enough we're on welfare? I want my kids to grow up and depend on their own initiatives.

What job is there for a single mom with an empty refrigerator and three hungry, small children outside of selling blood? This week, we drove to Camden that should have a sign that reads, "Welcome to Hell's Half Acre." We drive through streets, that were once well kept residential neighborhoods, now burnt down, unlivable buildings. At the Camden Blood Bank, I sit Rome and Willie on two chairs I've placed in front of me. Zola squirms on my lap when they take my pint of blood. Romie whines for M & M's, and Willie's only concern is to get home in time to watch cartoons. As for me, fourteen dollars looks pretty good when you can't feed your kids. Afterward, my fourteen dollar windfall safely tucked in my jeans, we head for a gas station to buy two dollars worth of cheap gas for the clunker, then to a supermarket for two cartons of milk, a few vegetables, a bag of flour for gravy, and two bags of lentils. I can make forty lentil burgers out of one bag, and from the other – soup. I'm learning to stretch fourteen dollars like you can't believe. Ha! My next stop is the day-old bakery to pay one dollar for ten loaves of bread to freeze. We barely exist on twenty five dollars a month, but no one around here goes hungry.

Help is a telephone call away. I know this. All I need do is explain to Mary what dire straits we're in and the refrigerator will be filled to the brim this very day, but I can't make the call. Today, I telephoned to say I was sending her a card, and her answer, "Got enough money for a stamp?" She knows. I laugh and reply,

"Sure. I'm loaded with stamps." Her silence is proof enough that our circumstance is meant to be. At this juncture my life is about discovering how strong I am. How will I ever know if I'm not put to the test? Life has taken a hard turn.

As each day passes, I look more and more like Old Mother Hubbard, kids hanging on me with every step I take. This morning when I hear a firm tap on the front door, I open it to find our mailman with a big grin on his face. He holds two envelopes up to his forehead and says, "Feels like money to me." He hands me an envelope that contains the first check for child support from the Sperm Donor, the second envelope, our monthly stipend from welfare. At last, the long arm of New Jersey is grinding the wheels of justice. The Sperm Donor's monthly payment for three sons is hardly enough for rent –

let alone clothes, school, groceries or medical coverage but why complain? It's better than nothing.

Every month I'm on welfare, I can't wait to get off. I appreciate the help but I don't want the boys to grow up and think the world owes them a living. I'm not afraid of work and the kids are learning the same. This month's welfare check will be returned with a request to stop payment.

> *Dear Welfare,*
>
> *I am returning your check which came in the mail today. It arrived along with my first child support payment. In good conscience, I can no longer accept welfare. It isn't your job to support my family. I didn't sleep with the State of New Jersey. I slept with my husband, the Sperm Donor. The children are ours to care for – not yours. Had they been your kids, their last name would be New Jersey, as in Rome New Jersey, William New Jersey and Zola New Jersey. See what I mean?*
>
> *Please don't think I'm ungrateful for the much needed assistance these past months. Without it, we would have been forced to live in my car. Once again, I sincerely, and I really mean it, thank you – but don't look for me again.*

The same day I return the check, the telephone rings. It's the manager of our apartment complex who offers me the job I applied for two years ago. At the time, she remarked that I didn't look like a person who did menial labor.

"Oh no," I replied, "I'm used to this type work. I mow grass, paint and clean. I can do any job you have around here. These laundry rooms are so filthy, I'm here to apply for the job of cleaning them." I never heard from her again until now.

Almost apologetic, she says, "Look, I won't lie to you. It's hard work for little pay. This apartment complex has twenty four laundry rooms to be mopped, garbage cans emptied and scoured along with washers and dryers. Do this twice a week and I'll pay you one dollar per laundry room each time you clean them."

"I'll take it."

"Don't want to think it over?"

"How soon can we start?"

"We?"

A New Beginning

"I take my kids wherever I go."

"No problem. I'll pay you forty eight dollars at the end of each week."

"I'll start today."

I doubt I'll ever experience the same level of gratitude I feel at this moment, as though I just inherited a million dollars. When I telephone Mary, we laugh together. What would I do if she wasn't in my life? I've never known anyone who claimed to care about me, who didn't want something in return; her only concern is my spiritual life. At the moment my focus is limited to surviving one day at a time. My life is such that each day presents another hurdle to overcome, another struggle to barely eek by. Forty eight dollars looks like a million when the refrigerator is empty.

I'm unable to find work outside of cleaning laundromats. I look, I look, I look to no avail. Maybe this is meant to be but why? Every time an opportunity presents itself, a hurdle invariably stands in the way. This past week I got a cleaning job, but when I drove up to the stoplight my car broke down. Period. There was nothing wrong with my clunker. It stopped for no reason. A man helped me push it to the side of the road. When the kids and I walked back to the car that same evening, it started right up. This happens every time I try and find other jobs to supplement cleaning laundromats. We live right on the edge. One thing for sure, my thoughts are no longer centered on yesterday's dreams, but living each day as it comes. I'm so focused on that – hardly a moment to think about myself. Every day presents another lesson to learn, before going forward to the next.

I found three more jobs we can do together. We deliver newspapers, babysit and sell Fuller Brush door-to-door, or should I say *attempt* to sell. Mary says Willie is old enough to watch Zola while Romie and I walk up and down residential neighborhoods trying to sell brooms and mops. It's so hot outside, my feet burn from the hole in my shoe. Seems like we walk for miles on end, knocking on doors, trying to sell brooms and brushes without ever making a sale. Today, I made cardboard liners for my sneakers. There's no money for luxury items like new shoes. I almost sold a mop until the woman became distracted. At the exact moment I was about to close the deal, she looked past me to Romie yelling "giddyup" as he straddled her lawn ornament – a big red deer. No new sneakers for me.

I just answered another ad for housecleaners. The pay is fifteen dollars a day to clean a modest home. I jump at the chance. When I arrive for work, all I see is a mansion that requires a maid service. Still, it's a job that will pay for a week's groceries. I never turn down work no matter how menial or difficult. Knowing Romie's uncanny knack for getting into mischief, I always bring him with me. Today – so far, so good. He's content to sit at the kitchen table, watch cartoons and draw. Every now and then, I peek in to make sure he hasn't set the house on fire. We'll have lunch together after I finish cleaning upstairs.

When I walk into the kitchen, I'm horrified to see Romie trying to shove the woman's chocolate cake back in the refrigerator. He's eaten big chunks out of it, and left crumbs and little brown finger art everywhere. Within minutes the woman walks in, and seeing her cake on his face, his prints on the refrigerator door, begins to scream at me, "How dare you! How dare you let him eat my cake! I'll dock half your pay for this!" Romie's so scared he hides under the kitchen table, a hunk of cake still clutched in his hand. While I can't afford to lose my cool, I'd love to give her a slap she'd never forget. Instead, I politely inquire if I can make up the difference by doing her family ironing. Her reply is a firm, "Not in this lifetime."

I clean the kitchen and utter a few choice words to Romie, who by now is so stuffed he's fallen asleep under the table. I pull him out by the back of his jeans, lift him up in my arms, and wrap him in a blanket I brought from home. I carry him into the den, gently lay him on the couch, and cross my fingers he remains in dreamland until it's time to leave.

At the end of a very long day, a two-story house with six bedrooms, four bathrooms, one family room, one living room, and one extra large kitchen, the woman hands me seven dollars and fifty cents. Romie ate my paycheck.

My worse nightmare is what kids put in their mouths. The family dog licks himself, the kids kiss the dog, and the dog licks the kid on the mouth. They break every rule of hygiene, no matter how often I hammer home the needful.

Miracles delivering newspapers

Each morning at 3:00 a.m., I wake up the kids, wrap Zola in a blanket like a Chinese egg roll, and drive to Malaga where we pick up bundles of the *Atlantic City Press* before we begin our early morning, rural paper route. Willie and Rome fold, the baby sleeps, and I deliver. I've learned a lot about the human condition from serving newspapers. Usually I receive a twenty cent tip for delivering their paper every day, rain or shine. Last week I was so sick with a stomach virus and high fever, I had to call the district manager to say I couldn't serve my route that day. He told me to either deliver the paper or consider myself fired. What choice did I have? Every half hour, I stopped the car to throw up. What a mess. There are no options in my life. I do what's necessary for us to survive. "Hey you, Paper Lady," is my new name. Call me anything you want – just pay your bill on time. I can't afford to lose this job.

Our route ends in the projects, apartments originally built for low income housing – now little more than a rundown haven for druggies and pregnant women on welfare. With each new arrival, their monthly check increases. The only time to collect is the day it comes in. Last week, the old *Bulletin* man was beaten so badly he had to be hospitalized. He survived, but just barely. Junkies almost killed him for the forty dollars he had collected for the week. I'll drop the few customers I have in here. It's too dangerous. Anyway, they never pay the bill.

Early this morning, the sleet and snow begins to come down as we deliver newspapers in a rural area. By route's end, it's eight inches deep – ten in other places. I pull into the driveway of a burnt down farmhouse to turn around, when my clunker immediately gets stuck in the compacted ice and snow. I can see nothing but snow, no other homes, no one to help, just white for miles on end. The kids are asleep, huddled together under a mountain of blankets in the back seat. I need to get out of here. It's freezing cold.

I crawl under the car on my stomach, and try to dig the ice away from the tires with my hands. It doesn't work. I get back in the car and find a metal spoon in the glove compartment. Once again, I get under the car, and try to scrape the ice from the front tire treads to gain traction and back out of the driveway. By now my hands are so numb from the cold, my fingers hardly move. This must be the helplessness people experience when death comes, a circumstance so out of their hands, they have no control over the last, most important event of their lives. At this moment, I have no one to turn to, nothing concrete to see or touch. I get back in the car and sit with my face down on the steering wheel, when a tap on the window startles me. I look up to see a young man, slight of build, snow falling on his long dark hair, who is smiling and motions for me to open the window. He says, "Excuse me. I can't help but notice you need a hand. Tell you what, stay put in the driver's seat, and I'll push. Turn on the ignition, and once you get going, shift to first gear, then you'll be good to go. The car will start, and you can back out."

I am so desperate and cold I hardly notice how thin he is, but I'm so grateful for his help, I'll do what he says. No sooner does my car begin to rock back and forth, than my front tires gain traction. I quickly turn on the ignition, throw it into first gear, and my car starts. I stop and throw it in reverse, then back out of the driveway as instructed; but first I want to thank him ... he is nowhere in sight. For miles on end, I see nothing but snow, no homes far as the eye can see, just early morning sunrays reflecting off a country landscape, and the occasional blackbird perched on a tree limb. No matter what direction he walks in, I would be able to see him, there would be footprints ... there has to be. Yet, there are none. He is nowhere to be found. When I tell Mary what happened, she simply replies, "Didn't you ask for help?"

Yes, my prayer was answered. God took the form of a beautiful young man to rescue us.

The more I attend satsang, the greater my realization of how little I know, if that. It's easy to spout words, but to live a balanced spiritual life in the face of constant upheaval is quite another matter.

A New Beginning

My mind is like a wild boar who knocks down and destroys every attempt I make to walk closer to God. Even if by some miracle, I don't fall asleep in meditation, my mind is never focused. It forever runs out to buy a car that won't break down, or another paper route to pay the bills. All these thoughts and more, in the two and one half hours I should be sitting in focused meditation. Why am I so concerned with results? Why can't I just be grateful for the honor of sitting in prayer each morning? I see no spiritual progress on my end. I'm a total wretch. I fail every step of the way. If God doesn't find cause to judge me, why do I judge myself so harshly? Mary is tough on me. Actually, I think more so than anyone else. There are times when I feel as though I live under a microscope, that I must account for what I *don't do* far more than what *I do,* and heaven forbid I should have a negative thought. Let me have one bad thought, and she'll see to it that everyone within a two mile radius knows about it. There are times when I imagine myself saying to her, "Mary, why not use a megaphone? Why limit telling *just* New Jersey about me? Why not announce my faults to the entire world?" Then again, isn't this what I wanted? Didn't I pray for a true spiritual friend who would help me destroy my crippling ego? Back in LA when Mary asked me what I wanted, my answer was clear, "I want God in my life." Didn't I say, "Let's go?" I should have replied that I wanted *only* God in my life.

Meditating on a cake of ice

I'm so wiped out from taking care of three kids and working around the clock, that by the time I sit in meditation I fall asleep. Yet in every satsang, Mary warns us about the dangers of sleeping in meditation, of allowing the attention to drop below the eye center. I feel guilty about this, but what can I do? Last Saturday, she went so far as to say she would meditate on a block of ice rather than sleep through meditation.

Driving home from satsang this afternoon, a lightbulb goes off in my head. I quickly turn the car around and drive to an ice-house not far from where we live. Yep, I'm about to buy the largest block of ice they have on hand. No doubt I'll need a front-end loader to lift it from the trunk of my car to the bathroom shower for meditation tomorrow morning. Somehow the boys and I will manage. I can't wait until 3:00 a.m. Bring it on.

My butt is frozen stiff. I've been sitting on this block of Antarctica, my cheeks stuck to the ice for two nights in a row. I need a blow dryer to unthaw myself. True, I don't fall asleep but I don't meditate either. My mind goes ballistic sitting here cross-legged on this cake of ice. If the North Pole has followers of this path, meditation must be a slam dunk since they're already half frozen to death. When I explain my poor results to Mary, she can't stop laughing. Glad someone thinks I'm funny.

My life is changing so rapidly. No matter how hard I work to make ends meet, something always comes up that requires us to serve more paper routes. If I ever get to heaven and see anything that even resembles a newspaper, I'll turn around and leave. I'm on the lookout for another job to replace our big motor route, one that allows me to keep the boys with me. Seems like everything I make goes into car maintenance, mainly brake shoes.

Today Mary called and suggested I give a thought to making small felt birds with sequins and magnets on the back to decorate refrigerators. Done.

The kids and I are now in the business of hawking our felt bird magnets door to door for one dollar and fifty cents each. Twice a week, dressed in trousers, a clean shirt and tie, the boys carry a shoebox filled with colorful, beaded bird magnets to neighborhood doors while I wait on the sidewalk. I'm like Rose, in the Broadway musical *Gypsy*, yelling out, "Sing out Louise," but in my case it's, "Boys, don't forget your manners!"

Who can resist my little guys? I even wrote the script:

(A youngish housewife opens the front door. Three small boys stand at the door holding a shoebox filled with lovely felt bird magnets)

Smiling, the oldest son says, "Good afternoon Mam. We're selling bird magnets to pay for camp this summer. We sure would appreciate your buying one. Would you be interested in our, "Buy two-get-one-free sale?"

The youngest son looks pitiful, sniffling and coughing in his handkerchief, smiles and says, "Mam, we sure would appreciate your business."

The middle son smiles and says, "Thank you Mam, and have a great day."

(Their Mother has told them to be polite, and not dilly-dally at the front door. They turn around and walk back where she waits for them on the sidewalk.)

Some weeks we earn as much as one hundred dollars selling door to door. We need this extra work to offset the legal fees generated by the Sperm Donor. He's filed suit for divorce. Every time he takes me to court, I'm forced to take on another job to pay for lawyers. Where does it all end? I desperately need a new car, but that's not going to happen.

Last week my clunker conked out in a wooded area. The three of us walked a mile to the nearest gas station, the older boys on foot and me carrying Zola. Triple A said there's a limit to how many times they'll tow me, and I'm past it. Of course. I stopped cursing a long time ago, but there are times when it just feels right. Son of a bitch! Son of a bitch! Son of a bitch!

Mary just phoned. She emphatically says, "Jennifer, buy yourself another car. Today."

I have no credit. I have no collateral, yet here I am the proud owner of a used Jeep Commando, perfect for paper routes ... and another monthly payment.

Please pass the fucking butter!

Willie's late coming home from school every day this week. Today, I walk to the bus stop to meet him, and the driver tells me he isn't on the bus and hasn't been all week. I call one of his friends who explains, "Oh, he's at the bowling alley getting ready for the contest."

"Really? What contest might that be hun?" He doesn't know except that it's a contest. I thank him, hang up and immediately call the school who informs me that Willie's been absent for a week. Well how bout' that. Thanks for letting me know – I'm just the mother! An hour or so later, Mr. Nonchalant meanders through the front door with his empty lunch box, and tells me how much he learned in school today. I bide my time until lil ol' Willie tells me what he's really been up to. A contest indeed! He has no clue what's about to happen. I'm in the catbird seat here.

When he sits down for supper, he looks at me nonchalantly and says, "Mom, please pass the fucking butter."

I'm paralyzed from the mouth down hearing the f-word come out of his mouth. The kids have never heard me say "poo" much less drop the f-bomb.

"Excuse me. What did you just say?"

"I said, Mom, please pass the fucking butter."

Then Romie chimes in, "Mommy, I want fucking butter too."

Willie says, "Mommy, can I have two rolls with fucking butter?"

Zola inquires, "Mommy, what's fucking butter?"

Romie requests, "Mommy, I want two rolls with fucking butter too."

Zola accuses, "Mommy, Willie's taking all the fucking butter!"

I've heard enough! The words "fucking butter" echos in my ears like the Hallelujah Chorus. I get Willie's attention with a sharp, "William! Come with me young man!" We stand together in the bathroom. He looks very nervous when I say, "William, this is what fucking butter tastes like." I put a bar of soap in his mouth, and make him hold it there for a moment or so. After much whining, and a few soap bubbles, I calmly say, "Go back and tell your brothers that "fucking butter" doesn't taste like real butter. It tastes fucking bad!" He gets the point, and just as he turns to go, I add, "No television for the rest of the year for lying to your mother!"

He protests, but I cut him short as I'm unable to contain myself a minute longer. My voice takes on darker, more ominous tones when I shout at the top of my lungs, "You've been at the bowling alley all week!" His mouth flies open. "Yes little mister, I know all about it! I'm going to school with you tomorrow. Let's see what your teacher thinks about a young man who plays hooky, then lies to his mother. Oh, and a boy who teaches his little brothers the f-word!"

There's no glamour in being a single mom, and times like this, little reward. We work hard to just put food on the table. There's hardly time to sit back, and enjoy our kids grow up. A father should be around to teach his sons how to hit a baseball, how to pee and hit the toilet instead of the floor. He should be around to teach his boys how to grow into responsible good men. Still, the positives of our lives far outweigh the negatives. I'm trying to teach them the value of making right choices in life, and how Willie made a bad one when he played hooky from school.

Much to Willie's horror, the two of us walk hand in hand to his school. I'm appalled at what I see: kids running wild and teachers not in control of open classrooms. His teacher, a young woman who can't focus on anything I say due to the noise, seems clueless at best. To make matters worse, she manages to let me know that Willie's test scores are so high, the school wants to push him ahead two grades. Humm … something is not right here.

Right then and there, I decide to pull him out of public school. Much to her dismay, I request she hand over all his records. The minute they're in my hands, we leave and drive to a small Catholic school nearby, run by strict nuns. No frills, just hard-tail wooden desks, pencils, paper and a commitment to learn. They agree to accept Willie on one condition, that I hire a tutor to help pull his grades up. His test scores indicate he is six months behind the students at Saint Catherine. So much for pushing him ahead two grades.

A New Beginning

I need to earn more money for private schools and the never ending legal bills. I pay higher tuitions because we're non-Catholic. No matter, there's got to be a way. We haven't come this far to fall off the banana boat now. Fortunately, I pick up another job serving three thousand *Shopper's Guides* for weekly foot delivery.

I can't remember a time when I didn't wake up tired. When I was young, people thought I was beautiful. Those remarks always puzzled me, as I never saw beauty in myself ... still don't. All I see are wrinkles and paper routes. I'm so exhausted these days, that I actually fanaticize being wheeled into a private hospital room. The bed is covered with a patchwork quilt that a candy striper made just for me. I crawl under the covers, close my eyes and do nothing but sleep for months on end. But since I have no medical insurance, what I'd really do is worry about how many more paper routes we'd have to serve to pay for this vacation. Where do I hide? Nowhere.

There are times when I know for sure, I've missed out on some of the best years of my life enjoying my children grow up without the whip of hard work on our backs. However, one thing I don't miss is a man in my bed. If anyone wants to know what I consider the best part of marriage, I'll readily admit it's having someone take out the trash. Come to think of it, the Sperm Donor never did that either.

Mary just phoned. It's my birthday. She's treating me to an afternoon at the beauty parlor to have my hair cut, washed and set. It's been a long time since anyone fussed over me, the type fuss that makes a big deal out of birthdays. I've forgotten what it feels like.

I've made up my mind. Mary wants the kids to have a dog. Today I'm placing an order for one Collie puppy for pickup when the mother delivers in several months. When the woman tells me how much they cost, I exclaim, "Seven hundred dollars for one dog? What's it made of – gold?"

We now deliver flyers for concrete patio blocks to pay for our new arrival. It's worth every penny; my boys have something to look forward to. By summer's end, I receive the much anticipated call for the kids to come take their pick. They go straight to the runt of the litter, and take turns holding "Ike," so named for the latest addition to our family. Straightaway, our little trooper trots alongside the boys to help serve their paper route. Afterward, he'll join us at McDonald's for ice cream cones. I carry him to the back of the restaurant, hidden in the bottom of my oversized newspaper satchel. The kids muffle their excitement when I sneak him in this way. I can tell by the look on their faces, the employees know. Most look the other way and smile, as first Willie, then Romie, then Zola take turns holding our new puppy. Ike wears a McDonald's bib as he licks his first ice cream cone on planet earth.

If I've said it once, I've said it a thousand times, "Never, not ever, no never, never, never, never go inside houses when you collect for your paper route – even if it is in our neighborhood, and even if you do play with their kids." I hear so much on the news about children being abducted, that I've developed eyes in the back of my head. The rule is: be home by sundown. Period! If it's dark and and those boys aren't in the house, rest assured I'll drive up and down Locust Avenue, hand on horn to smoke'um out. It so irritates my neighbors, they open their front doors to see where the noise is coming from. Everyone around here knows from past experience, it's the paper lady with all the kids, who lives in the next to the last house on the block, the one with a basketball set-up on the curb. Yeah, it's her again. She's sitting on the horn looking for Rome and Zola. Who else?

It doesn't take long before I spot them sheepishly opening my neighbor's front door. They all but trip over their feet as they race down the steps to the car. I ignore them as they open the door, and hustle to the back seat. I'm bout' mama'd out. No one says a word. Yet.

Today, as we're delivering the weekly shopper in a large apartment complex, the manager runs up to me, waves a paper in my face and shouts, "Lady, if I find one more circular thrown in the dumpster, I'll report you to Shopper's Guide!"

My antenna goes up. That's Rome's route. Together, Ike and I find the section where he should be delivering circulars. Instead, he's sitting under a tree half asleep, a Marvel comic in one hand, M & M's in the other, when I startle him, "Rome, where are your papers?"

"Mom, you won't believe this."

"Try me."

"I was delivering my route when a large ..."

A New Beginning

I know where this is going, and decide to play along while he hangs himself. I complete the sentence for him, "spaceship?"

"Yes! Mom, it was a large intergalactic spaceship." He sees the expression on my face, and hastily adjusts his description, "Well … uh … more like a giant flying saucer that circled over my head, and made this weird sucking sound."

Hearing this, my vocal cords assume a more helpful tone, "Romie, did it sound like this?" I purse my lips together, and make a recognizable sucking sound, not unlike the familiar one heard when I inhaled a toke of marijuana in the old days.

"Mom …yes, it was just like that. Aliens beamed me up to the mothership!"

"Uh huh … and did you deliver your *Shopper's Guides* on the mothership?"

"Mom, they blindfolded me when they flew to outer space, but when they came back, I sorta remember them dropping me off under this tree where I am now. Don't be mad but they kept the *Shopper's Guides.*

"For the coupons?"

"Yes – but mainly to read."

If there was ever a time for me to repeat the five holy names, it's now.

A precedent setting case

Thanks to the Sperm Donor filing for custody of the boys, it's been two years of the New Jersey Department of Family Services investigating my character, my worthiness to be a mother, my capacity to support my family, not to speak of the judge who spoke privately to each of us, as well as a psychiatrist who grilled them, today is the big day. This morning at breakfast, I try my best to explain, that if the judge rules in his favor, Willie doesn't get to come home today. In the event it happens, I must hand him over along with his packed suitcase, to the Sperm Donor. I explain, we don't say goodbye since we live in each other's heart. I'm trying not to appear anxious, as the situation is upsetting enough. Romie begins to cry, and throws his arms around Willie's waist. Now they're both crying, as Zola hangs onto my legs. Divorce tears families apart.

During the long drive to the courthouse, I begin to wonder how I will feel when I see him. Will the last vestige of attraction rear its demented head when we stand next to each other in court? It's hard to imagine how a woman could feel anything for a man who so abuses his children through neglect, who forces a mother and three small boys to work ungodly hours cleaning laundromats, and serving newspaper routes to pay for the legal expenses he creates. What do I feel? Nothing. Time and hard work are the great pain erasers. The Sperm Donor well knows he can visit the kids anytime he wants, but he never does. Years pass without him seeing or even telephoning, but now he wants them. What's wrong with this picture?

Willie and I sit down in the courtroom, his packed suitcase on the floor next to my lawyer. Not easy. The Sperm Donor and I don't look at each other throughout the proceedings until the end, when the judge requests we stand before him. He looks directly at him and takes great lengths to explain, that while he understands his home in

A New Beginning

Los Angeles is larger than our small apartment, and certainly offer more financial security than I can, but after reviewing all the reports, while taking into consideration his personal interview with each of the boys, he finds it is inappropriate to break up "this little ball team," the name he coined us. He goes to great lengths to explain how we've bonded as a family. While it's true, circumstances force us to work hard for what little we have, this judge is of the opinion that hard work builds character and never hurt anyone.

The judge pauses a moment, then looks directly at me and continues, "You are a valiant woman. I applaud your courage in keeping this family together under adverse circumstances. Without incurring further legal debt, I now grant you full custody of the three children, Rome, William, and Zola. Case closed."

I'm so relieved, almost numb from worry over the possibility of giving up Willie had the judge ruled in his favor. If he wants to live with his father down the road, that's fine but not now, not when he's this young. I manage to be cordial to the Sperm Donor; I don't want to provoke more animosity, but here again I'm not the one who filed suit against me for the past three years. I gave him everything he asked for. I moved from California so he could be with her, and agreed to the divorce that gave him freedom to remarry. But I will never relinquish these children to him. I was told his decision is unique as there is no record in this state of a single mother, unrelated to a child with living birth parents, who has been granted custody over a living mother and father who claim to want him. I stand before the judge and thank him for his decision, adding the Sperm Donor has always been welcome to visit his children anytime he chooses, and still is.

I've been called a lot of things in my life but "valiant" is a new one. I'm embarrassed at the use of this word coming from the judge. I know who binds us together. Tonight, I'm counting three little heads in bed instead of two. Once they're asleep, I step outside to breathe in the fresh night air. I sit on the curb for the longest time, my face cupped in my hands, and cry for no apparent reason. I'm so tired.

My moment in the sun was too good to be true. The Sperm Donor doesn't want to visit the kids in New Jersey. He demands they visit him in California for monthlong stays. My reluctance to this request is based upon his past performance as a father, along with my fear that he won't keep close tabs on young boys unfamiliar with life in the fast lane. Here we go again – more paper routes to pay for never-ending legal bills.

The Court has ruled in his favor. The kids will fly to California for month long visits during summer vacation. Hopefully, they'll spend more time with Grandma Lowee.

By summer's end, I pick them up at the Philadelphia airport. They can't wait to tell me about their trip, particularly that fun time when the Sperm Donor treated Zola to a bag of coins for his all-day bus adventure, riding and transferring many times on the greater Los Angeles Transit System ... alone, or their trip to "a really big house where a nice man lived who had cool video games, and lots of girls almost naked." Romie volunteers, he thinks it's called the Playboy Mansion. It takes six months to get Hollywood, and a few choice words they picked up, out of their system.

Boot camp

The sum total of my life is work, work, and more work. All week, I look forward to Saturdays when I can sit quietly and listen to Mary discourse on the mystic way. Her straight forward explanation of the deepest of truths makes this philosophy easy to understand, then weave into my everyday life. Today, in the middle of her discourse on the dangers of unbridled ego, for no apparent reason she turns to me, and remarks that surely I won't object if she uses me as an illustration. Without waiting for an answer, she proceeds to spell out how I continue to be enthralled in my endless love affair with myself as an actress. I always know when she's headed in this direction, because a beeper goes off in my head warning me to stay cool, that getting uptight only makes it worse. Even though I understand being on the "hot seat" is part of the learning process to keep my ego in check, such moments are like being barbecued in a hot oven with every onlooker thinking, "Thank God it's her and not me." Times like this, I have to remind myself that I begged Mary to help me get rid of my ego. I had no idea what true spiritual help really means, and never did I dream it would be so painful. She never misses an opportunity to remind me that I'm free to leave anytime I want, that her door swings both ways. The choice of whether to leave or to stay is mine alone.

No matter where we go together, Mary will find someone to announce, "Meet Jennifer, my little Hollywood actress. Jennifer dear, tell Mrs. Oldsport what television shows you were on." Good Lord, here she goes again.

Mrs. Oldsport works at the bank. She is a short, egg-shaped woman reminiscent of an overweight partridge in mating season. All day, five days a week, she sits in wait at the drive-thru window. Today, she spots Mary's white Pontiac with me sitting beside her in the front seat, as she pulls up to her station. Her moon-shaped face lights up with anticipation of yet another embellished resume of my past credits. After a quick trip down memory lane, I plead with Mary, "Honestly, I wish you wouldn't go on like that to people. It's really embarassing."

Her standard reply, "Jennifer, I know what you wish, and when you lose that high opinion of yourself, I'll stop. Not until."

Tonight for some reason, I flash back to another grand mal mother of ego-busting incidents, when all of us are in Mary's family room listening to a discourse on the importance of meditation. Suddenly, she turns in my direction and abruptly announces, "You need to have all your teeth removed."

I quickly roll my tongue over my teeth to make sure they're still in my mouth, thinking, "Sweet Jesus, I hope she's not talking to me." I look around in the hope she has someone else in mind, but since the only person sitting next to me is Katherine, an eighty three year old senior with dentures, I know her remark is meant only for me. My vocal cords assume a higher octave and reply, "Mary, what do you mean?"

She quickly responds, "What don't you understand? Is it the word 'you'? Is it the word 'teeth' or is it the word 'removed'? Which word bothers you?"

They all do. I've just turned forty and the thought of losing my Hollywood investment in capped teeth bothers me a lot. Who wants to be toothless at forty? I can't believe what I'm hearing. "Mary, did you just say I should have all my teeth pulled?" There has to be an easier way to heaven. It's true, my years in show business created a gargantuan, irrepressible ego. It took me a long time to admit I even had one. If I hold out my arms, encircle the universe and all the galaxies, it will be small indeed compared to the size of my ego. Progress will surely be when I don't pass a mirror with the expectation of a vision winking back at me. It is this very ego that must go. I understand, but it doesn't make the process easier. Few realize how difficult this method of eliminating ego is on the teacher, far more than on the pupil. Vanity never goes down without a fight.

Sitting here, a million thoughts and doubts spinning through my head as Mary, unruffled by the jailbreak going on in my mind, continues, "Don't take my word for it. Get a second, third, even fourth opinion from a doctor."

Whenever she says, "Don't take my word for it," it's usually the kiss of death, as it infers my mind questions her, that I have doubts about the validity of what she says. After this last remark, she turns from me, and continues to explain the many illusions created by ego, how it's full of promises but offers nothing, how we come into this world naked, and leave the same way with worms feeding on our flesh. Ego has holes in it. That makes sense, but as soon as I hear the words "worms feeding on our flesh" her satsang flies right out the window. I can't focus on anything outside of dentures with tiny hands and feet swinging on chandeliers, and jumping out my pants each time I bend over.

Monday morning, I make appointments with four oral surgeons to ascertain whether or not to have my teeth extracted. Within a three week period, I've paid a visit to each doctor, and explained in great detail that even though I love my Hollywood teeth, I am considering having them all yanked out. When they enquire as to *why* I want this procedure done, I shrug my shoulders and reply, "I don't know – boredom I suppose." What can I say? All four doctors concur that while my gums *are* in bad condition, and *do* require treatment, my situation isn't so grim as to have every tooth in my head removed. They all chorus the same prognosis: gums need work ... don't pull teeth. Oh, happy day!

Emboldened with reports from the oral surgeons, I come to satsang and announce to Mary that all four doctors advised against having my teeth extracted. I have every expectation these reports will put the matter to rest once and for all. In one voice their consensus was to have my gums treated, far better than being toothless. She listens patiently as I continue to build my case. When I hand her the reports, she looks at me, smiles, then turns away and replies, "Jennifer do what you want. It's your decision."

Those eight words send chills up my spine. I leave satsang today on the horns of a major turning point of faith. It's true, Mary advised me to get second opinions, and while those very doctors advised *against* having my teeth extracted, the fact remains that for some reason, she holds her ground. Why am I so disturbed when I followed through with her suggestion? Who will I listen to? Should it be the rational voice of doctors, or what appears to be an irrational suggestion from Mary. It is a matter of faith. It's one thing to talk about it, and quite another to have my heels put to the fire.

The minute I walk through the door, I make an appointment with an oral surgeon in Philadelphia to have all my teeth extracted as soon as possible. The following Saturday when I come to satsang, I sort of expect a little pat on the back from her, as I'm more than willing to receive credit for this decision, but all she says is, "You're late Jennifer. Satsang began five minutes ago," without looking at me.

These aren't easy days, but I never lose faith in her judgment. I can never forget what my life was like before Mary. The mystics claim with one voice, that to slay the ego is the most difficult part of the journey, an impossible task without a teacher who is a true mystic. She is teaching me to recognize the nature of this insidious disease that attempts every step of the way, to gain a foothold in my psyche. The moment it starts, I begin my repetition. Simran works. This path may be free, but to become master of oneself is not.

Two weeks have passed since my Hollywood teeth were extracted. I still haven't spoken to Mary, although she made every arrangement for the kids to be looked after until I'm back on my feet. I'm missing her so. Over the years, never a day passed that I didn't speak to her. Now I never do. She is allowing me to learn a valuable lesson. God doesn't test my resolve, rather I am gifted the circumstances with which to test myself. Even knowing this, there are times when I feel so lost within, I hardly know what to say or do – yet I won't allow myself the weakness of running away from the one thing in my life that finally makes sense. Under difficult personal circumstances, Mary once said, "Lord, I know how strong you are, and you know how strong I am, but what I don't know is how strong *I* am."

After her husband passed away and she moved to California, Mary went through great struggles as she had no money, nothing to eat and nowhere to live except a park bench. Most would find this hard to believe, but early one evening she covered herself with newspapers to keep warm, and fell asleep on that park bench. In a dream, her teacher served her a fresh peeled avocado sitting upon a golden spoon. She awoke feeling refreshed, filled and satisfied after not eating for many days. During that same period, Mary was shunned by her spiritual teacher who refused to answer her letters. When the money ran out, she scouted for empty soda bottles to sell in order to buy stamps, and an envelope for the letter she had written to him on toilet tissue. She went through many such tests of endurance and faith to achieve her spiritual height. Apparently, there is no shortcut to divinity and no backdoor to heaven.

These hard tests come to teach me how to rise above my negative mind in the face of adversity, and to appreciate the gifts that inevitably follow once ego is crushed, and gives birth to humility. Like so many, I don't always understand nor do I appreciate, the form true spiritual aid comes in. Years ago when I said, "Let's go," little did I understand the implication of those two words. Now I know. Most can't stand up to the challenge, and leave. I well understand, because there are days when I fantasize being anywhere but here. However, there is never a time when I seriously consider leaving. Where would I go? Through deep meditation, Mary has changed my life forever. Knowing her compassion and gentleness of heart, my struggles are far more painful to her than to me. She never discusses her own poor health that grows worse by the day.

At last, I'm able to drive to the oral surgeon in Philadelphia for a check-up. The doctor is pleased and tells me, "You're healing up right nicely, but I have something to show you. Come with me." I get up from the dental chair, and follow him into an x-ray room. He asks me to face a large screen that displays x-rays of my mouth before teeth were extracted. Using a long ruler to point out the infected area he says, "Do you have any idea how lucky you are?"

I have no idea what he's talking about and reply, "I don't understand."

He continues, "What I mean to say is had your teeth *not* been extracted, this disease would have progressed into your body, and would ultimately have taken your life." When I mention the diagnosis from four doctors, he shakes his head and says, "They were wrong."

I cringe to think what would have happened to me, had I not followed through with her instruction. In Mary Blakemore, I have what I've always wanted – a teacher to guide me through every storm, one who understands the spiritual journey is fraught with landmines. Those who finally arrive, wear the crown of humility as they have made divinity the centerpiece of their lives. She is teaching me to develop an awareness that differentiates between those who cloud the ever expanding ego by advertising charitable works, and true self-effacing spirituality that prefers solitude to grandstanding.

The divine power that sustains all creation knows my every weakness. Every step of the way is a struggle.

A New Beginning

Moving on up

"Your attitude is your altitude. How high are you?"

Mary Blakemore

I shuck corn, snap peas and darn socks. I've even made several quilts sitting through Little League, street hockey, football, and Boy Scouts. Everyone within a ten mile radius can hear me call out, "Good save Zooey," before I'm back to the project at hand, multi-tasking while I watch the game. It's true that women can chew gum and walk at the same time, especially single moms. Not having enough money for anything outside of bare necessities, has taught me to be self-sufficient. I make my own clothes, summer shorts for the boys, and recycle hand-me-downs to look spiffy for the younger ones. Mary has taught me, there is nothing I cannot do given a positive attitude and love – her secret ingredient. The life she lives before me is the standard I struggle to weave into my everyday life. I fall every step of the way, but always pick myself up with even greater resolve to move forward, inward, and upward. Life under her mystic umbrella gives me the stamina to endure.

In 1971, Mary Blakemore, an elderly great grandmother who raised a large family, and Doug Brookins, a twenty six year old musician, and recording artist from Hollywood became business partners. How they began their fledgling business by renting an old chicken coop set back in a wooded area in Lindenwold, New Jersey, was a miracle in itself. They transformed it into a small workshop, where they began to make and sell advertising specialties. Over the years she tried to instill the same spirit in us, stressing that if we put love into all we do "we can't lose for winning." Another favorite topic was the subject of self-employment, that no matter how small, we should always remember that it's not important how much we have, but how well we do with *what* we have. With this in mind, I begin my own cottage business on a shoestring budget in my kitchen.

One night after supper, Zola makes the suggestion, "Mom, why don't you start your own business, and call it, Little Mother's Cupboard."

"Mom, wait up," Rome chimes in, "Call it, Little *Old* Mother's Cupboard since you're old, and sew at the kitchen table." That works. The old part goes down like gravel, but to these kids anyone over thirty is older than dirt. Anyway, what do they know? This evening my cottage industry begins in earnest. I work late into the night making samples of quilted potholders, and tea towels with matching stenciled apple designs. I'm on fire with ideas.

After several months of Mary's encouragement, I add stenciled doorhangers with bells that jingle at the bottom, along with handmade dolls to sell as tourist items in gift shops in Strasberg, PA. I even make dolls for Amish stores to resell. As business grows, I hire several homeworkers to assist with cutting and sewing. This allows me more time to design and assemble vintage-type vests and jackets made of velvets, brocades, and other fabric samples from an upscale furniture store nearby. Each time an appointment is scheduled with a gift shop buyer, I wear one of my patchwork jackets, as I know in advance they'll buy one right off the bat. But the item I am proudest of is my oversized skyline handbag.

One morning, I find a large box of neatly folded swatches of multi-colored, soft pastel leather on the back step of our carport. Whenever material is left over from orders Specialty House fulfilled, Mary gives me to use in my business. This expensive leather becomes the inspiration for my skyline handbags. I begin each by tie-dyeing the base fabric, both exterior and lining, before cutting out a skyline from the assortment of leather. After assembling, I attach it to the fabric, airbrush the outline, and name each bag in bold strokes. The first one I made, "A Starry night in Philly," sold two minutes after I took it from the display case. My jackets and handbags sell in boutiques faster than I can make them; the smaller items, in tourist resorts in the Poconos and Lancaster, PA. Through it all, I discover that it's all about attitude. What's taken me so long to learn this?

A New Beginning

The best way to get praise is to die!

Since the time we lived in Lindenwold, the rash on my legs has spread to the rest of my body. Whenever I ask the doctor what he makes of it, he always gives me the same stock answer, "Oh, just old age creeping up on you. Use lotion."

Of course his words "old age" certainly has an instant calming effect on me – like, are you serious? But today when he examines this rash, he suggests I take testosterone. Did he just tell me to take male hormones? Come on man.

My spot on answer is, "Thanks but no thanks Doc, don't I have enough cojones?"

On his end, there isn't a smidgen of laughter. I'm on the verge of asking him why he didn't choose the Antarctica over Alaska to do his missionary work. Had he chosen the former, he'd be looking at a guaranteed level of appreciation from people halfway to saving since they're near frozen to death already, as opposed to Alaska with better weather, retail malls, pizza, Mr. Goodbars, cashmere sweaters, and other good stuff. Glad I derailed this outburst as the nurse just popped in to whisper something in his ear. No doubt his little woman just called to say they're having recycled tuna for dinner, and to bring home a loaf of bread. Doctors! Grrrrrrr.

As I'm about to leave, the same nurse hands me a business card for a dermatologist he advises me to contact. For the past three years, I've come to him with the same rash, but only today, one week before he leaves for Alaska, he refers me to a specialist. Lucky for me it isn't serious or I'd be dead.

Dr. Chan takes one look at the rash on my legs, and orders a biopsy. Excuse me when I say her bedside manner is seriously underwhelming. I can just imagine her inspecting a slab of meat at the Acme the same way she lifts my legs up and down. I've always been healthy – why worry? On the other hand, a call from a doctor's office to come in for a biopsy result is time for concern.

As I wait in Dr. Chan's office, I know it isn't good news. She tells me the biopsy result confirms her suspicion that I have non-Hodgkin's terminal lymphoma, a rare form of skin cancer the medical field knows little of. I am stunned. More than that, I'm scared to death.

This doctor is cold, almost blunt in her assessment of this disease. In the same manner I would say, "Please pass the mustard," she explains that until a few years ago people died quickly, even now there is no cure. My time is short. After her last remark all I can hear is my fear of death. Her lips move but I cannot hear sound ... *I'm dying ... how long.* As Dr. Chan continues, I feel my legs giving out from under me, and I begin to hyperventilate ... *got to get out of here.* Under normal circumstances I would telephone Mary, but she's so ill, I just cannot. Before leaving, Dr. Chan refers me to a famous research scientist in this rare deadly skin disorder.

Dr. Eric Vonderheid teaches at Hannaman Hospital in Philadelphia, where patients travel the world over to be treated for this disease. When I first met him, he appeared more as Mister McGoo searching for a misplaced paper, while at the same time complaining about the bad lighting during my checkup. He went so far as to ask the interns if they knew where his glasses were. Whereas Dr. Chan is cold, indifferent and self-promoting, Dr. Vonderheid is calm and compassionate. His research on this deadly form of skin cancer is world renowned. He offers reassurance that since little is known about this disease, hope springs eternal. He never speaks of "how long I have" but the possibility of a cure. My tension lessens; little by little, he puts me at ease. I'm not so crazed with fear as I've been. For the next three weeks, I'll be on the receiving end of many tests to determine if my body can withstand the treatment he recommends. I still haven't told Mary. No need. She insists I call her immediately after my appointment today in Philadelphia with Dr. Vonderheid. She knows something is wrong.

Zola is home from college. I've never been happier, or more relieved to see him than just now. This of course flies in the face of my "kitchen table philosophy" of not wanting my children to think of me as a needy, aging mother dependent upon her sons to look after her. I've always wanted them to find their own way, and stand on their own two feet without such an encumbrance. It's not my nature to depend on others, yet here I am leaning on my youngest son. Today, he'll drive me to Marlton for the first in many treatments to be administered three days a week for the next four months, in the hope of putting this disease in remission. I like the doctor. I'm beginning to feel less deathward bound.

After my first treatment, Zola and I stop at Denny's for coffee and a bite to eat – the usual, a grilled cheese and French fries. I've little appetite, but he's hungry and can order whatever he wants. I'm not myself these days. I know it but there's nothing I can do about it. For the first time in my life, I'm confronted with the reality of my own mortality, the overwhelming fact of leaving a life I'm not prepared to give up. Never have I been more aware of the short time I have left on earth, and my inability to let go of this crippling fear of death. My youngest son looks at me in bewilderment. He reaches over the table, takes my hand in his own and says, "Mom, this is the first time I've ever seen you afraid."

It is no small task to face my limited store of breaths, wondering what the last one will feel like. Death isn't a pleasant subject. You know, the all pervasive, "It's something that happens to everyone else but never to me." During our drive home and throughout the night, his words resound in my ears like a recording I can't turn off; until I remember something Mary said many years ago just after our arduous drive across country. I was standing in her small kitchen at Coachman Manor Apartments when she made the remark, that throughout those two and one half months before Zola was born, she never once sensed the presence of fear in me. I was surprised to hear her say that; for if not then, why now? Where is the path I have embraced or at least thought I had? Where is God in all this?

After many weeks of sleepless fear gripping nights, my life has suddenly taken a turn for the better – like my first awareness of spring when robins flutter about building their nests in preparation for a better future, when barren limbs on the plum tree outside my bedroom window becomes a clubhouse for small chatty birds, and yellow forsythia, harbinger of better days to come.

By the hand of grace and clarity of thought, I have my first great epiphany: all things that come my way are for my spiritual betterment. That being the case, why aren't I grateful for this turn of events, rather than miserable in the fear of death? Over the years, Mary taught that life is no more than a classroom where lessons are learned, and with each lesson learned comes a blessing. Through this new awareness I begin to understand that every moment of my life, from childhood to the present, has assisted in turning me upward bound, my struggles no more than lanterns along the way. Although I have always felt alone, I've never *been* alone. So often at critical junctures throughout my life, I have experienced the presence of someone watching over me. Nothing is happenstance. I've always lived my life by turning to this world for solutions, and putting man's opinions, my own included, before all else … like a game of Russian Roulette. The divine remedy lies in attitude: to let go of my crippling fear of death, and let God direct the show. Above all, to be grateful for the outcome regardless of what it is. It's all or nothing. The stakes are high in the game of love.

Emboldened with my new understanding, I begin to look at the struggles of my childhood, and how ambition almost destroyed me in show business. I survived a loveless marriage, then raised three children as a single mother, along with all the heartbreaks in between. Am I prepared to spend the rest of my life terrorized by this disease nipping at my heels? The very thought is unacceptable. I am not prepared to pay the price for such a compromise. While it is true that I have *it*, it is also true that *it* will never have me – unless I allow it. Should fear exist in my heart, then let it be the fear of displeasing a loving God. I bow before my teacher again and again for preparing me to face the many assaults life doles out, never more difficult than now, and may one such as I continue my journey without delay. Above all, let me never use illness or age as an excuse not to hold true to my vows. Should a negative thought rap on my door, grant me the fortitude to kick it away like a can of beans rolling down a hill.

Part IV

My New Life

Remembering you

When I searched deeply into the prism of heart's rainbow, I found you

My kids have gone their separate ways. Today, when there's no need to rush home and make dinner, feed the dog or do anything else for that matter, I can take my time returning from a business trip in Lancaster, PA. In the past, Mary discouraged me from traveling late at night but old habits die hard.

I'm desperate for a cup of coffee to keep me awake during the long drive back to New Jersey. I spot a McDonalds, and go in the drive-thru to save time. No sooner do I pull up, than I hear a sing-song voice come out of the order machine, "May I take your order?"

"One small coffee please."

The voice further inquires, "Are you aware senior citizens receive a discount?"

I'm sure this woman has me confused with someone else, after all the drive-thru is quite a hop from the take-out window. No doubt the camera made a mistake. If she sees me up close, she'll know I'm not a senior. I bite my tongue and reply in a lilting voice, "I'll come inside to place the order. Sorry to be a bother." I park my car, lock it, and head into McDonalds for the single purpose of giving this woman a good look. She'll realize her mistake, that in no way do I come close to resembling a senior citizen. There she is. I walk briskly up to the counter, flash my broadest smile and say with precisely the same inflection as the original request, "Remember me? 'One small coffee please?'"

Once again, as though life will stop on planet earth if she doesn't hawk the senior discount, she snaps, "Like I said, senior citizens pay less."

My discount coffee in hand, I walk out of McDonalds feeling like Eve turned sixty. This is a first. No one has ever referred to me as old. Come on. All right so I am sixty, but I still bolt up steps two at a time. OK, so there was the bathing incident a few months back. An Avon candle someone passed on as a Christmas gift, softly flickered on the bathroom counter as I was enjoying a luxurious soak, when for no apparent reason, I glanced down and noticed my middle section had suddenly taken on a life of its own. It wasn't the flat stomach I'd sported for years, or even yesterday. No. This one had rolls on it like Mount Vesuvius ready to erupt. To make matters worse it was giving me the proverbial bird.

I think about the absurdity of things like, "Why don't I have wrinkles under my age-defying armpits instead of my face?" Age, that silent marauder, that cuckold sporting a Diane Vreeland mask squatting at the end of my bathtub, reminds me that I've passed fifty nine – like I fear aging. I'm always the one who gives the bird to mental spooks who try and pull me down, but today isn't my best day. I feel miserable. I really do, same as if I reached into my pocket for a LifeSaver and pulled out a dog turd. What's wrong with me? I can't get myself together. Seems like only yesterday, I daydreamed in my rigged up tree house in Aunt Lowee's backyard; the many times I drove the boys back and forth to Little League. When my turn came around to make hot dogs, I laughed out loud each time I made a veggie dog when they asked for seconds. Where has my life gone?

I'm sitting in a parking lot watching the Amish horse and buggies pass by, their black silhouettes press upon a breathtaking sundown against a rural backdrop, complete with a reminder from Ronald McDonald that all things must come to an end. I watch the seagulls scrounge for food, pecking away at discarded trash here and there. Perhaps this is what I've done with my life. Maybe I'm like those birds who live on the periphery but never take flight. I think about my incredible life, survival only made possible by the many years I spent in Mary's company.

I've reached a point where the dreams I began life's journey with, have vanished. They have slowly acquiesced to deeper, more introspective visions. Is it possible only one year ago today, Mary passed away? The life so familiar to me came to an abrupt halt the morning of July 15, 1998. For one year she tried to prepare me for her departure, but I couldn't accept being without her. She was my friend and spiritual mentor for over thirty years; and what a wonderful, if not turbulent close relationship I enjoyed. In my wallet I still keep a note she wrote, that clearly stated I was a tough nut to crack. She never gave up on me, although many times I came close to giving up on myself. Mary was always loving, always fair, and surely to God, always right ... and the toughest of all taskmasters. I can't stop thinking of her, of how quickly time has passed since the day we first met. These thoughts herald an avalanche of loneliness that rushs to the core of my being.

When she passed away I hardly shed a tear. But here I am, one year later having a complete meltdown, crying in a McDonald's parking lot; not audible in ways people in the van parked next to me are forced to roll up their windows, more like private tears. I've contained my grief as though recognition of it somehow validates her death. Mary was the only person I ever felt safe enough with to confide in. She always listened. Where most kept their distance for fear of being reprimanded, I ran to her with the same fears, often with laughter, many times with sadness, but always *to* her rather than away from her. My good fortune was knowing that if I was too weak to rid myself of ego, I'd better stick with someone who could, and would. I'm not easy to be around these days. Perhaps this is what dying is like, the isolation of leaving the world alone – the same way I came in.

How can I get on with my life without her; can't sit here forever, can't drive home in this condition. I need another coffee.

For no reason my thoughts go to Mary's business partner, Doug Brookins. From the start we never hit it off and the few times I spent in his company, I could easily have done without. Yet today, I can't get him out of my mind. Years ago, I heard a recording of him singing and playing guitar, and was struck by his beautiful voice – at the time not realizing it was his; even more surprised to find out he was a professional singer on many popular television shows of the sixties, as well as the youngest member of *The New Christy Minstrels* for a time. He gave up a lucrative career after Mary wrote to him in Hollywood, and asked if he was interested in starting a small business with her in New Jersey. He was twenty six years old, talented, good looking, with agents and recording contracts sniffing at his door. He gave up his career, his family and all he held dear, to move east and accept her offer. In 1971, they pooled their joint savings of five thousand dollars between them, and the golden years of Specialty House of Creation began. All they needed was a place to hang their hat.

After months of looking for a small rental space to open their fledgling company, she answered a local ad. The landlady immediately led her to a dilapidated chicken coop located in the back of the adjoining property. Most people would have been horrified at the prospect of working in an old chicken shack complete with droppings. They would have left immediately, but not Mary who saw a golden opportunity to house their new company. Grateful for a nice place to work once cleaned and painted, she rented it for twenty dollers a month. She saw the finished product in each of us. Clearly, Specialty House of Creation, often referred to as SHC, was no exception. It was designed to be a different type business, one where seekers could practice the teachings of this path in an environment conducive to spiritual life, as they moved in the world in a normal balanced way.

Mary and Doug wasted no time transforming an old chicken coop into a proper business setting. They cleaned, painted, wired for electricity, installed a toilet, shower and sink. For the convenience of everyone there, a small kitchenette was built. It had a two-burner hot plate and a refrigerator which sat atop freshly poured concrete floors. Many odds and ends demanded attention in order to secure a certificate of occupancy. When the township completed the inspection, a certificate was issued. In no time at all, Specialty House of Creation at 121 Holly Street, Lindenwold, New Jersey, was open for business.

What I remember most, was Mary never separated our daily lives from the spiritual, a hallmark of those golden years. To her, everything was spiritual without boundaries; she made it abundantly clear our lives couldn't be both. They were either spiritual or worldly, no in between. I laugh when I think back on the first day Specialty House of Creation opened for business. I had scraped up just enough money to hire a babysitter for the week. Mary was adamant that our workday begin at seven sharp. I arrived at 6:45 a.m. and sat on a makeshift doorstep, and waited for the others to arrive. I felt honored just being there.

That first morning, she pointed to a light green smock hanging on a clothes rack in the corner. She bought it for me so I wouldn't get my clothes dirty when working. I was one of the original employees at Specialty House of Creation, but three little boys who needed a full-time mother made working there impossible. As I look back on those early years, it's hard to understand how Mary and Doug barely eeked out a living. They made no profit for nearly fifteen years, even though they supported nine followers of this path who worked there. One could argue the point that in order to feed so many profit had to be made, but in the early years that wasn't the case. Never a day passed, Mary didn't send food to the shop. She fed everyone. There is an old saying, "You can't make a silk purse out of a sow's ear," yet that is precisely what happened to me, along with so many others who worked for SHC back then. Talents no one knew existed began to manifest in the form of sales, and other creative endeavors. I had earned a living as an actress. Outside of that what talents did I have? What talents did any of us have that we were aware of? We were young and of the opinion the universe hung on our every breath. Yet the Specialty House salesman, who couldn't speak an intelligent sentence, began to receive orders for their handmade merchandise, keyrings, belts, etc.

It was during this time, I began designing gift items and handbags for small boutiques and gift shops to augment the day-to-day expense of raising and educating children. Now that my boys were older, Mary was determined I secure other work outside of paper routes and cleaning laundromats. Little by little, my cottage business replaced them, and what a relief it was. She was a fountainhead of creativity and shared it with me. Not a week passed that she didn't come up with another idea for my handbags and jackets. Clearly, Mary Blakemore was as much a part of life's miracle as breath itself. Those were the golden years at Specialty House of Creation, a way of life that unfolded in a natural way under her mystic umbrella.

With the growth of the gaming industry, SHC moved to a larger facility in Elmer, NJ. Two years later, Doug and Mary purchased five acres of prime real estate for the men who worked at the "shop." It was conveniently located just up the road from Specialty House. One afternoon, Mary and I drove up to take a look at their new two-story home. It was beautiful. In addition, they set up those same men with generous long-term retirement accounts to build on for their future. There was never a time they didn't share their success by rewarding the employees with large bonuses. That same afternoon she confided, that Doug had never taken profit from their business until recently when the accountant strongly advised against this practice. He was told to either draw a salary or give it to the United States Government as a charitable contribution. Mary laughed at that statement, and referred to him as "Ol' Doug."

An explosion of corporate business began to come their way. Suddenly they went from hand-painted ad specialty items, and barely breaking even in a renovated chicken coop, to big business with casinos and major corporations. Doug and Mary shared their wealth by helping others.

As her health grew progressively worse, it seemed the rest of our lives were tested to the extreme. All of this coincided with a corporate giant reneging on a multimillion dollar purchase order. Given the circumstances and Mary's deteriorating health, Doug felt he had no recourse but to accept the explanation of his sales manager who presented the corporation's specific demands. Doug referred to them as, "Further discounts payable on the sly," adding, "I've never done business like that. Why would I start now?"

This didn't seem plausible at the time, in light of good business relationships enjoyed for nearly three years. Nevertheless, the question persisted in Doug's mind, "Why now suddenly, and not then?" Although he could have sued for breach of contract as he held legally binding purchase orders, he also knew they possessed inexhaustible resources that would keep him in litigation for years to come – no doubt, until he was an old man.

Doug could no longer oversee the daily business activity, as Mary's failing health demanded his full attention twenty four hours a day. Finally, in 1992, he had no recourse but to put his trust in leaving the operations of their company in the hands of three old employees. Truth be told, the day he left was the beginning of the end of Specialty House of Creation, a great company designed to meet the spiritual needs of it's employees. Their goal was never about profit, but the blessings of success did come.

Even today, doubts remain as to what really happened. Why would two additional corporations producing similar products in the same time period, suddenly stop doing business with a loyal and dedicated supplier? When I asked Doug about this, he replied, "This is all a lot of water under an aging bridge."

In the summer of 1998, I found out Doug never mentioned to Mary the loss of their three largest accounts, and the devastating effect it had on the company. He didn't tell her that most of the employees had left. Those difficult times meted out severe tests of faith on everyone's part; of loyalty and support for one another, above all, tangible proof of steadfast devotion to the teachings in the face of disaster. It was a perfect learning field for the practical application of mystic philosophy in our everyday lives, during the good times as well as the bad.

Someday people may ask, "What was so special about Specialty House of Creation?"

"Mary and Doug," I will reply, "They were the sparkle."

In the event the spiritual component is removed, all that will remain is a business, same as any other commercial enterprise; the luster of those golden years little more than a passing thought. But I was there in the beginning. Never will I forget those magical years when a divine emissary used her one pointed love to bring out the best in everyone.

I need coffee.

Laughter is the Best Recipe

I'm still at McDonalds having my third cup of coffee. The cars next to me have changed six times since I parked in this one spot. That's good – strangers make good friends; they aren't inquisitive, and their presence is company of sorts. After Mary passed away, I couldn't afford the luxury of memories. But today, sitting in this parking lot, remembering is all I can afford.

Why cooking comes to mind I'll never know because it was always my nemesis. It wasn't a priority as I was too busy trying to support my family. My aspirations went no further than to be a good short-order cook grinding out meals, and praying to God they didn't fall on the floor when served. Mary, on the other hand, loved to cook. At six years old, she fried potatoes for five brothers by standing on a wooden orange crate.

Once I stood next to her as she rolled pie dough, an experience similar to watching ballet from the best seat in the house. In the early days she cooked for everyone who worked at *SHC*, and invented more new dishes than one could imagine. Her motto "slow and steady wins the race," was precisely how she cooked – slow and steady, never measuring. putting a little of this here, a dash of that there until bingo, out of the oven came another masterpiece. She made pies, cookies, cakes, dips, soups, and meatless vegetarian casseroles to tantalize the palate. Mary made no bones about what made her cooking so tasty. She said, and I firmly believe it to be true, her secret was the main ingredient – love.

More often than not she used cooking as a means to explain the simplicity of the mystic way of life. She taught that if we cook with love, the food we prepare would automatically be successful; better yet, it would taste good. Mary topped off that remark with, "Jenny, you can't lose for winning."

She hammered home, that to cook without love was a surefire means to make someone ill. I loved the sound of her voice when she called me "Jenny" and laughter when I announced the similarity of this path to a Chinese eggroll – me the stuffing, and Mary the wrap holding me together. My self-deprecating humor was never more appreciated than when she laughed. Sitting here like this, all the wonderful times I spent with her are coming back so fast, I can't cry for laughing – like the evening I attempted to make her rice pudding recipe, and gave a taste to a friend standing in the kitchen. He remarked that should I drop a spoonful on his toe, he'd walk away with a fracture. Well really. It took years for me to discover that cooking was never about food. It was about love – the secret ingredient that made everything she prepared so delicious.

Sitting in this McDonald's parking lot, I laugh out loud thinking back on her one pointed attempt to teach me to cook. My lessons began a couple of weeks after we arrived in New Jersey. One evening as I stood over the stove drowning broccoli in a ten gallon pot of water, the telephone rang. No formality needed; I knew it was Mary when I heard, "What's cooking Jenny?"

I was convinced a candid reply would ignite her penchant for the culinary, that a truthful answer to "What's cooking?" wouldn't bode well for me; instead, it would lead to a fifteen minute dissertation on the necessity of preparing good hot meals from scratch every night for the boys. Those three words "good hot meals" implied the absence of canned food.

Finally, after I tap danced a few moments, out came my insightful answer, "Stuff – you know, veggies … stuff like that."

She laughed, then quickly replied, "Drowning broccoli again are we?" Without waiting for another mindless quip on my end, she insisted the boys would love her "No Nonsense Memphis Chili" recipe, that I should write it down, better yet make it for dinner tomorrow night, adding as a postscript, "Don't forget to sprinkle Fritos on top. They'll love it."

I hastily jotted down her recipe on a napkin, and pressed it between plumbing and septic systems in the Gloucester County yellow pages.

It took little effort for Doug to persuade Mary to assist in writing a cookbook on vegetarian cuisine. It would be a welcome distraction from her deteriorating health and hospitals. Many of her greatest dishes were prepared on the fly. His challenge was to find those recipes, that over the years she had jotted down on the backs of envelopes used as bookmarks tucked away in boxes of memorabilia, or written in the margin of a favorite book. But she easily recalled the ingredients, and added to each recipe a humorous story about all of us. None were spared.

Doug came up with an idea to publish a gourmet vegetarian recipe book, along with short anecdotal stories on the adventures of Mary's group. The stories are all true, given a creative twist here and there. Several went the way of the delete button when it spun over the page limit.

One such story describes an incident that occurred several days after she moved to the new property, where both home and business were joined together on three acres of wooded setting on Jesse Bridge Road. True to form, Mary dug right in. She painted, cleaned windows, raked dead leaves and debris from the backyard. I had come over that same day to help out, when suddenly I heard her call my name from the other side of the yard. I quickly walked over to find her standing beside a large heavy metal grate she had discovered under a pile of moldy leaves. She wanted the men at the shop to carry it to the wooded area across the property, and irritated that no one was there to help. Ignoring the grate's excessive weight, she turned to me and said, "No one is ever in tune. Come on Jenny, we'll do it."

It was so heavy, I couldn't budge my end one inch, much less carry it to the woods. Without saying a word Mary knew what I was thinking, that it would take ten weightlifters and then some, to carry this heavy piece of metal such a distance. She looked at me and remarked offhandedly, "Do your simran. Come on, let's get this done. I've got a pie in the oven." The two of us carried that iron grate the equivalent of a city block but I never felt its true weight. Afterward, she looked at me and laughed, "Now let's have some pie."

Many such inspired incidences occurred throughout my life with Mary. Although the discussion of miracles on the mystic path is frowned upon, they do happen for those with eyes to see and ears to hear.

Next came artwork, the wonderful caricatures of Doug and Mary along with the rest of us. They worked against time until it finally came together, short stories edited, artwork completed, and recipes good to go. All that remained was a title for this labor of love. Despite her illness, she never lost the ability to laugh no matter whose trainwreck crashed head-on into her life. Predictably, she smiled and said, "Laughter keeps the devil away."

It's one thing to laugh at others, and quite another to laugh at ourselves. She taught that adversity is the greatest of all teachers, and hidden in struggle are the great life lessons for they highlight our weaknesses. Mary taught, it's far better to learn when the opportunity presents itself, for it may never come again.

The *Laughter is the Best Recipe* manuscript was completed with her approval two weeks prior to her passing.

I glance down at my watch thinking it's past midnight, yet only a few hours have passed. I've been sitting in a McDonald's parking lot remembering my life with Mary … now it's time to go home. I've had so much coffee, I just might float back to New Jersey.

Letting Go

I hang my dreams on crescent moon, her silence bathed in swaddling glow

There is loneliness in me beyond expression. Two years have slipped away since Mary's passing. I still come over each morning to mop the front porch, pull weeds or do any chore that requires attention, same as when she was here. Each morning I swept the back patio. If there was no glare from the sun, I might catch a glimpse of the face I had grown so to love, as she rested on the couch in the family room.

Early on, I learned right quickly that if my attitude wasn't a good one, she would take away whatever small job she had given me to do. The drill was always the same: I'd wait a week or so while she cooled off before I drove back once again to park my car on the road, and pull weeds from the front yard out of her sight – or so I thought. This was Mary's way of teaching me what a blessed gift it was being allowed to serve others, no matter how small. Seva, an Indian word meaning "selfless service," was one she rarely used where our group was concerned. She taught that we of ourselves are incapable of doing anything, that the only doer is God. Even if he put our names up in lights, we should know whose hand put it there, and remember who owns the lights. Her greatest gift was loving me enough to help crush my arrogant mind in order that my soul could breathe free.

Before going to work on the morning of July 15, I came over to bring Doug her laundered bedsheets, and noticed her favorite red roses were still in bloom. Several hours later, I received the call that Mary was gone. That was Wednesday. The following Friday I looked at the same rosebush but only one red rose remained, yet out of the same stem grew its twin of opposite color – a snow-white rose. I still have it pressed between the pages of a book she gave me. There is a Southern tradition, that children who have lost their mother should wear a white rose on Mother's Day to signify her passing, and a red rose if she lives.

My New Life

This morning as I'm sweeping the back patio, I hear someone raise the kitchen window. When I look up, I see Doug Brookins smiling at me. To my surprise he wants me to come up for coffee, but I quickly make an excuse, and continue to sweep. For the next few days, each morning he pops his head out the kitchen window and invites me up for coffee, and same as the day before, I make an excuse and say "no." On the fourth morning, I notice someone left the garage door open. In the past, whenever I visited Mary I entered through that same door she always left open for me. In like manner, today I intuitively know I'm expected to walk upstairs to the kitchen – same as always. When I reach the top of the staircase, I notice he's sitting at the kitchen table having coffee. When Doug sees me, he stands up and offers to make my breakfast. I smile at the thought of him waiting on me, but decline. Over my objections he insists that at the very least, I join him for coffee. I can hardly say no when he's already poured it.

The next morning, once again the garage door is left open. Same as yesterday I walk up the steps, but this time he's sitting at the table. Without getting up, he smiles and asks casually, "Know how to make cinnamon toast?"

Did he say what I thought he said? Come on. Do I know how to make cinnamon toast? It's true my cooking slogan is more or less, when the smoke alarm goes off that's when dinner's ready, but come on. I stifle an acerbic retort, and make an even greater effort not to display my irritation at his insensitive remark – in view of the fact that I've raised three kids, and the last I heard none of them died of starvation. After a pregnant interlude he cuts to the chase. Smiling, he politely asks if I would make him a cup of coffee. Of course I will, although I'm waiting for him to ask if I know how to boil water. This "getting to know you" period continues for several weeks.

Several weeks pass. Morning coffee with Doug has become my habit. He begins to feel more like an old friend, someone I can trust. Despite myself, I'm beginning to like him; his sense of humor, in particular, isn't far from my own. This morning he suddenly props his elbows on the table, rests his chin on his hands, and looks intently at me for a moment and says, "I don't like your earrings."

Somewhat taken back, and yes, I'm surprised at his audacity, I slowly take them off and reply. "Then I won't wear them." Still he continues, "And I don't like that dress you're wearing."

I look into his eyes and say, "Is it the dress or me in it?"

Without hesitation he answers, "Both."

"I don't like the tie you have on," and before he can interrupt I add, "I don't like your shirt either."

By now he's amused at the way things are going. The fever blister on my lip is making me more uncomfortable than I already am. When I run my tongue over the side of my mouth, he gives me a sympathetic look and says, "Shall I carve you a new pair of teeth from hard rock maple?" Good Lord, what did he say? Did I hear him right? Totally unaffected by the horrified look on my face, he continues, "What's the matter Jennifer? Don't think I can do it?"

I'm beginning to feel like someone who just had a frontal lobotomy without knowing it. I have no intention of giving him the upper hand so I flash my sweetest smile and reply, "I'm sure you can Doug. Carve me a set, and knock out a tooth in the front while you're at it." He all but belly laughs at my reply, but before he has a chance to say anything else I add, "Oh, and one more thing."

"What? Forget something?"

"Get a new barber. The back of your hair looks like Pee Wee Herman."

"Come on." Slightly irritated, he reaches back to feel his haircut, and begins to explain, "I cut it myself."

To his last remark I sincerely reply, "Looks it."

In the past I hardly looked at him, but I'm beginning to notice how handsome he is, not that it matters but he is. I always thought of him as a faceless sourpuss, and why would I want to know him much less look at him? I never knew him at all. I like his sense of humor and goodness of heart. Now when I look at Doug, I think of Mary. We are old friends getting to know each other all over again; our relationship of so many past lives is beginning to unfold. He looks at me a moment, then pointedly asks the same question Mary put to me when I first came to this path, "What do you want?"

To his question, I nonchalantly reply that I would like to help in whatever he does. Smiling, he offers me a job at Specialty House.

I like working with all my old friends, some I've known since the early days when we sat until the wee hours listening to Mary give satsang at the Sweetheart Tree, but something is wrong and I can't quite put my finger on it, only to say things have changed. Call it sparkle, call it whatever, but when I come to work each day it's the same as if I opened my front door, and found vacant rooms with no furniture and all the windows covered. The most obvious difference is the manner in which business is now conducted. These changes occured when Mary was ill, and Doug unable to oversee daily operations; the accounting system for one, and spending more than was taken in for another. Those he left in charge seem to be running things by the seat of their pants. There is no order, no leadership, and no harmony among themselves. In short, Doug returned to a Specialty House of Creation in chaos, debt and disarray.

Mary was a stickler for cleanliness. She taught the exterior of our lives reflects the same attention given to the interior spiritual condition. They are one in the same. If anyone tried to separate the two, her reply was standard, "Cleanliness is next to Godliness."

If they were in the middle of a large leather goods order, she still insisted Doug stop production to clean up. He argued, "Mary, we're on a deadline. There's no time for housecleaning!" She responded with silence, picked up a broom and began sweeping the floor. Everyone followed suit. In no time the dust from the manufactured leather goods was cleaned up to her satisfaction.

Doug's return to Specialty House is regarded more as an intrusion upon their lives than the warm homecoming it should have been. Understandably, this hurts the most and cuts the deepest. In satsang he speaks only of reconciliation and renewed cooperation. Same as Mary before him, he teaches the principles of weaving the ancient truths of the mystics into our daily lives, of the oneness of creation, and never missing life's opportunities to apply the practical nature of this philosophy. To illustrate, he relates an incident that occurred one summer when he noticed a striking ebony butterfly unable to find water in the noonday heat. He brought it a capful, then another, then another until finally he placed it on the ground where it continued to quench its thirst. Later that evening when he mentioned the incident to Mary she replied, "I'm sure the Lord enjoyed it."

Life without her has put me in a mood I can't shake.

The years following her death in 1998 are a definitive turning point for everyone in Mary's group, in different ways. On my end, every moment is a struggle to get through another day without letting anyone know how depressed I am. The initial grief I experienced after her passing has become an abysmal state I neither recognize nor understand, a well so deep I find it difficult to save myself. My mind is like a pendulum swinging one way one minute, the other way the next. I can't go on like this, feeling so lost without her. On the upside I'm beginning to understand the pitfalls of allowing this negative state of mind to have full sway. It's clear to me now my depression is no more than a bad habit, a holiday for a weak mind who finds it easier to sustain a depressed train of thought than to break it. My God, what's the point? Why follow a spiritual path if I don't have the courage to face myself? What it all boils down to is blame. Who can I blame? Mary always said, "When you point your finger at someone, you have three more pointed back at you."

Who is the architect of my miserable state of mind? Only me. If I had been truthful to myself, I would have put up a better fight. I would have said, "Old girl, depression isn't positive and it certainly isn't spiritual." Why did I cave in? I should have burdened my rebellious mind with meditation, rather than stroking it with depression. Why is it so difficult to take a hard look at myself?

My mistake was to entertain negative thoughts. Each day I piled more and more on until finally, I couldn't think clearly. My usual sense of humor was replaced by mood swings, and meditation non-existent. I'd like to kick myself for being so stupid but it's not the time for guilt trips, and more wasted moments beating up on myself. The job at hand is to stop this depressive madness in its tracks. The more I think about the mountain I've created, the more helpless I become in chopping it down. What exactly can I do? If I have no control over the hour of my birth, over the hour of my death, over breathing, what *do* I have control over? What?

This night I beg forgiveness that should my prayer be granted, I will set the record straight. I lost my way. I make no excuses for myself. The mystic way of life is one of surrender to the Beloved, of love and forgiveness, of generosity of heart never made more evident than the passing of a loved one – of letting go. I have enjoyed the company of great mystics far too long not to understand that a positive attitude is paramount to spiritual progress. It is the barometer of spiritual height, or the lack thereof. Is it possible the solution to my depression is as easy a fix as one simple attitude adjustment on my part?

My New Life

It has been a sleepless night reliving the past thirty years with Mary Blakemore … from the early days of our six day trek across America to gifting me the strength to raise three children as a single mother. She taught me to face life boldly by making each circumstance a gift, rather than an obstacle to hide behind.

One evening so long ago when the heat was still oppressive and lingered on as Indian summers do, all of us sat cross-legged on the floor in Mary's family room in rapt attention as we listened to her speak on the oneness of creation. No sooner did she open the front door to let in fresh air, than one dry leaf blew inside where we sat. Someone picked it up to toss back outside when she stopped him and said, "Why are you doing that? Don't you think God capable of assuming the form of a leaf to be with his kids? He just wants to be with you this evening. "

I can no longer turn to her physical self for comfort. The time has come to embrace my life with all she taught me over the past thirty years, the only meaningful way to express gratitude. Grief, my heart's companion for so long a time, has been lifted. I let go. When she took me by the hand and led me through this journey called life, I was a mere babe. Oh Mary, how lucky for me there was a you. The world would be lost without mystic sons and daughters who always walk amongst us.

Tharon Ann

The Anurag Sagar
(Ocean of Love)

"God is within us and we can only realize him within."
Baba Kehar Singh Ji Maharaj

My brain wants relief from thinking. I wonder more about myself than the creation. Here I am, miles down life's road feeling like a slug bopping along on its last hot night out on the town. There's no drug powerful enough to remove the melancholy that wafts into my consciousness whenever I think of the divine emissaries who have watched over me. I'm always in the upload mode, assimilating rather than being. I still feel like racing to the top of the mountain and back down again without exhaustion, until of course that perfect moment when I get up each morning, look in the mirror, and wonder whose face stares back at me – one with more lines than a Texas backroads map. What has become of my life? I dream of being as nature running counterpoint to life after daybreak; a feeling so intense, I mourn the snow which selfishly neglected to arrive this year. Maybe pining for winter is no more complex than missing that one dash into Starbucks for a cup of chia under the pretext of bad weather. Perhaps it's as simple as that.

This morning when I got up for 3:00 a.m. meditation, more aptly my three hours of would-be prayer, all I thought of was traveling to India instead of sitting quietly. From there I segued into, "Should I have chow mein for dinner, or go for the gold with enchilada left overs?" Meanwhile the sun came up, and what happened to meditation? I wrote a novel, I traveled to India, I baked an apple pie but did I have one focused moment of true meditation? Oh my ...

I finally receive a copy of the *Anurag Sagar*, a book I've wanted to read for years. Turns out, an excellent translation is available through a little known Radha Soami Satsang Dera Tarn Taran, India. The original text by Kabir Sahib Ji, a fifteenth century mystic, is now translated as well as explained by the Patron of this Dera, Baba Kehar Singh Ji Maharaj. What triggered my desire was a passage I read in *With the Three Masters*, a remark Maharaj Sawan Singh Ji made to his driver, Seth Vasdev, "Without studying the *Anurag Sagar,* one cannot fully understand the difference between Kal and Dayal Ma, nor can one fully grasp the teachings of Sant Mat; that unless this book is read, the mystic path can never be understood." His statement goes to the core of understanding mysticism, of good and evil, life and death.

I cannot put this book down. I read it front to back, refuel with a second cup of coffee before reading it front to back again. This translation and explanation of the *Anurag Sagar* written five hundred years ago, is both profound and disconcerting, unlike anything I have ever read. It is the definitive story of creation, a succinct explanation of how this world evolved. I've waited a lifetime to receive a straight forward answer to the one question that has puzzled me since childhood. In his exposition of the *Anurag Sagar*, Baba Ji clearly explains the reason for soul being separated from its origin. In the past whenever I asked Mary this question, one she could easily have answered, her response was predictable, "Go within and find out for yourself." If I pressed her, she would smile and calmly reply, "That's for me to know and you to find out."

The *Anurag Sagar* begins with questions asked by Dharam Dass, the main disciple of Kabir Sahib Ji, regarding the creation of the universe. The teacher answers him in great detail with a complete description of creation. At the end of each chapter, my ritual is the same: I put the book down, and walk into the kitchen to make myself a stiff cup of coffee before going outside. It's freezing cold, not at all like other winters in New Jersey, the seasons segue one into the other without my knowing it. I sit here bundled up in Mary's wool shawl, watching vagrant snowflakes drift from the rooftop onto my eyebrows, and look up in wonder at icicles still forming on the limbs of trees after the snowfall earlier this evening.

Tonight there are millions of stars in the night sky, like Himself blinking in laughter at my efforts to assimilate the vast mysteries of the galaxies. Some things just are. They are part and parcel of the divine romance only lovers know, a subject not to be decimated by the intellectual mind in its feeble attempt to understand; the same mind that has never let up in my entire life its persistent effort to undermine my search for God. How can such a mind understand the divine? I can't look at a blade of grass without acknowledging the existence of divinity in every atom and grain of sand. All that is part and parcel of creation has a purpose, a balance. What of human beings? Outside of eating, drinking and procreating, what is my purpose? God knows who I am but *I* still don't know.

This night, a blanket of stars rests upon my body as I lay my head on earth's pillow in gratefulness to my teacher for lifting my consciousness. I pray that whatever small dreams I still entertain, be as inlets vanishing into oceans rather than split-rail fences separating a neighbor's property. I dream of India and making chapatis with beautiful honey-skinned women. Once again, this faraway land invades my thoughts. What is it that haunts me so?

Mary never missed a year traveling eight thousand miles to the Punjab, a state in Northern India which takes its name from the Persian translated to mean, "The land of five rivers," a lush area coveted and fought over by empires for millennia. At an advanced age she continued to spend three months out of every year at Dera Beas with her spiritual teacher Charan Singh Ji Maharaj; and always returned to share wonderful stories of sadhs and great mystics – enough to encourage us to make this trip at least once in our lifetime. My concern was leaving three young children for so long. It was always a comfort to hear her say, "Don't worry Jenny, when the time comes I'll take you to Dera myself."

But today, India seems a long way off. I'm eager to know more about this Baba. I've read all his published books in English, only to discover the mystic philosophy he teaches is precisely the same path I follow.

My New Life

Meeting Baba Ji

Baba Ji has planned a world tour of his satsang centers for the summer of 2004, with the intent to visit followers in each country, the United States included. I am beside myself with anticipation.

We've been granted permission to meet with Baba Ji this evening. On the way to Burlington, New Jersey, I have the same feeling of happiness as when I drove over to see Mary each morning, as though my heart would burst at any given moment. It's almost too good to be true, that within minutes I will sit in the company of a mystic of the highest order. What could I ever have done to deserve the type company I've enjoyed from the moment I came to this path. Some would say it is karma. From my perspective there's no karma good enough to merit the company of mystics. I call it grace.

We're invited into a modest apartment where we're served a cup of chia by a gracious Indian couple, both followers of Baba Kehar Singh Ji Maharaj. They go out of their way to make us comfortable as we sit in wait for our audience with him. After ten or so minutes, we're led into a small room where he receives guests. The moment I step through the door, I am so mesmerized by the radiance emanating from him, I can hardly speak. We're invited to sit on the floor in front of him. Baba Ji is elderly yet he sits with a straight back, his feet rest under a small table placed before him. I notice my right foot is within inches of his, requiring great restraint on my end not to touch his toe with my own. Dressed in white leggings, white kurta, blue vest and a white turban, his ample snow-white beard glistens against honey-colored skin. His dark eyes scan each face as he blesses us in ways human language cannot describe. I've covered my head with Mary's white lace scarf, and continue gazing into his eyes to receive his darshan, an Indian word meaning the blessings received when a mystic glances lovingly at someone. Mary was also a great mystic, yet in all the years I spent with her, she never referred to herself as anything but a follower of this path. Such is the humility of true mystics.

Baba Ji greets us in a warm friendly manner. He immediately puts us at ease with his unique sense of humor. Although there is a translator, he understands what is said to him. Clearly he speaks more English that he lets on. At one point when his words aren't properly translated to their exact meaning, he corrects the translator. Most of his remarks are directed at Doug. He advises him never to get involved in the politics of a spiritual path. I find this interesting because Mary avoided the same pitfalls; the more a mystic path began to resemble organized religion, the less she approved. Mary preferred informal gatherings where satsang was given in relaxed, intimate settings where people felt comfortable enough to ask questions, and receive direct answers. What wonderful times.

There is an interesting exchange between Baba Ji and Doug. For one born with so many words, I am speechless. Being in such close proximity to a mystic cannot be described; an experience rather than a dialogue. At the end of our audience, he stands to give each of us prashad; in this case, rice in small packets. It is considered an enormous blessing to receive prashad directly from the hand of a mystic. Truth is, whatever a mystic gives is a blessing. No sooner do I hold out my hand to receive it than Baba Ji looks directly at me and says, "No ... not the way to receive prashad ... here, I'll show you ... like this." He takes both my hands in his own, firmly puts them together then, with palms facing upward, he places the rice packet in my cupped hands. He explains to me, "This is the proper way to receive prashad." I feel as though I'm in the company of an old friend, same as when I first met Mary.

Baba Ji has accepted Doug's invitation to be his guest when he returns to the United States.

The day we've looked forward to has finally arrived. Baba Ji will give satsang today in a large open room at Specialty House of Creation. For the past two months we've prepared for his visit by sending out invitations to his followers. A small stage has been set up for him to give satsang, chairs and mats for those in attendance, and a small daycare center to accommodate families with children.

Earlier we were told he would arrive at twelve noon – Indian time loosely translated to mean, Baba Ji will arrive when he gets here. The room is filled to capacity with many of his followers who've come from New York, upstate New Jersey, Pennsylvania, Virginia and Maryland. Everyone is eager for a glimpse of him, including those initiated into this philosophy by other mystics. There are few places left to sit. The Indian women dressed in colorful Punjabi attire, sit cross-legged on floor mats; women to the right, men to the left Indian style. What a morning ... still no sign of Baba Ji.

No sooner do we step outside to wait than the car carrying Baba Ji and his traveling party, turns into the long driveway and slowly pulls up directly in front of us by the side entrance. There is a second before he steps out of the car when my lungs aren't portal enough to contain my breath – a timeless moment beyond the capacity of human language to describe its fullness. His august presence ushers in complete silence. Only seconds before this same room buzzed with chitchat. Now that he is here, quiet prevails.

Baba Ji slowly walks up to the stage and sits down. He is followed by the Pathi, a singer of shabds or poetic songs of love and devotion which highlight his discourse along the way. In Punjabi, this is referred to as "Gurbani," literally translated to mean, "Message of the Teacher." For several minutes he glances into the audience, his face moving from one side of the room to the other as he gives darshan to each individual before beginning the discourse in his native Punjabi language, with an interpreter to give the English translation as instructed.

Throughout his discourse, he emphasizes the importance of attending satsang, and of going within through the practice of daily meditation. This process, to quote St. Paul in 1 Corinthians 15:31 of the Bible, is clearly defined as "I die daily." This may be viewed as startling to some, brought up as I was in the Christian tradition. I never understood what those three words actually meant. However, after a lifetime of deep personal research, I have discovered similarities rather than differences in the truths they share. These ancient wisdoms are the very foundation of spirituality, the genesis of religion and philosophy long before their mystic teachings were cast aside, and over the ages lost forever in the dogma of institutions.

His discourse, "See With Your Own Eyes," is taken from a shabd by Kabir Sahib Ji, the author of *Anurag Sagar*, in which Baba Ji explains, our body is a large mansion containing secrets. The first part of this shabd explains the hidden mysteries resident in the human body from our feet up to our eyes. The second half of the discourse offers an explanation of the spiritual treasures hidden within, from the eyes up to the top of the head. I love his simple, direct approach. He speaks in ways that people with no education to the most erudite can easily grasp.

Since time began mystic teachers have come to this earth. Never aloof, they appear more as close friends or family relations. True mystics never charge money or boast of miraculous powers. Always self-supporting, they never accept donations for their own livelihood, only for the benefit of others. They look the same as we do, and even talk like us. Mystics come in all professions, ethnic backgrounds and gender. Some take birth in poverty while others are born into wealth. There are mystics who prefer a celibate life while others are married with children; some have very large followings, others with small, hands-on relationships with their initiates. My bond with Mary Blakemore was parent to a child. She always laughed when she said to us, "You never know who you're sitting next to – better watch your words."

After he answers questions and gives prashad to each person waiting in line, Baba Ji leaves to relax in the pool area while lunch is prepared. Before I walk next door and ask Baba Ji to bless what will be eaten by the sangat, I spread a white cloth over the tray that holds various samples of the foods to be served.

When he sits down at the table and his lunch placed before him, I start to leave but he motions for me to sit with him while he eats – an unexpected blessing. His translator makes wonderful "prantas" filled with chopped onions and potatoes, one of his favorite foods when served hot from the stove. After lunch I offer a hand towel and a large bowl of warm water in which to wash his hands before he takes afternoon rest. Baba Ji will stay the night in Doug's new cottage.

Later in the afternoon he enjoys sitting by the poolside. All who attended satsang earlier in the day have gone home; we have him all to ourselves. After a bit, I look up to notice the sun has set without my knowing it. Everyone has left the pool area except Baba Ji resting in a lounge chair, and me sitting on the ground beside him. He smiles broadly and reaches down to pull me up, "Here, take my hand. You help me walk up the driveway, and I'll help you within."

The many beautiful shabds Baba Ji has composed are sung throughout India. Knowing his love for music, tonight Doug will play his guitar and sing "Amazing Grace." Hand in hand we begin our walk up the long driveway, his steps deliberate and of steady gait. I hold onto his hand, and plead with time to grant me a few more moments alone with him.

As we walk along he mentions how sick he was the day before – so much so, the doctors urged him to rest rather than give satsang today. He pauses a moment before he begins to describe a dream he had in the hospital, one that brought back wonderful memories of the first time Baba Ji as a young man, first met Mary in India.

On that particular day Mary accompanied her teacher, Charan Singh Ji Maharaj, then Patron of Radha Soami Dera Beas, along with two other advanced devotees, Mrs. Sant Ram and Mata from Jumma. He was to give satsang at Radha Soami Dera Tarn Taran in celebration of the life of Baba Jaimal Singh Ji. In those days, it was the habit of Patrons of both spiritual communities to discourse at the other's Dera, as both were built by order of Baba Jaimal Singh Ji. It was a time when they were a spiritual family, same as brothers who visited back and forth on a regular basis. On that particular day, young Baba Kehar Singh Ji was scheduled to give a preliminary discourse. Afterward the two Indian ladies sitting with Mary, summoned him over to be introduced to her and said, "Come and meet Madam Mary from America."

Baba Ji continues, "When Mary asked those ladies about me, they told her I was the son of Baba Pratap Singh Ji, then Patron of Dera Tarn Taran. Mary signaled for me to come near her. She and Mata from Jumma put their hands on my head, and said these very words, 'One day you will become head of this Dera.'" He went on to say, those words spoken by Mary proved to be true so many years later on May 12, 1988, when he became Patron of Dera Tarn Taran.

Clearly, our friendship with Baba Ji is Mary's gift to us, a divine request granted from one great mystic to the other. Baba Ji holds my hand as we slowly make our way up the driveway. He continues to share his wonderful memories of Mary with one who feels her absence every waking moment.

Baba Ji allows time for a final visit before his departure. He waves goodbye from the car, and gives each of us the greatest prashad of all – his darshan. He is on his way to Canada, France, England, and other countries on his worldwide tour.

Born Anew

I dream endlessly of traveling to India for Baba Ji's darshan. Even when I try and focus on business at hand, my thoughts always return to him. I feel strangely different these days, in that my life has changed. All the seeds Mary planted within me are just now, after so long a time, beginning to sprout.

On Doug's end so much has happened with his company, he no longer feels comfortable working at the business he and Mary built from scratch, that coupled with living on the same property, and for good reason. All they struggled to achieve began to unravel during the years he was her caregiver. Their partnership, sealed with a handshake, lasted over thirty four years. After her death, Doug returned to his company, but he couldn't pull it back to the same high standards as before he left … no matter how hard he tried.

Even now, no one at Specialty House seems to grasp the severity of the overwhelming problems at hand. Not a day passes an issue doesn't arise to remind Doug that it's time to move on. No greater sorrow than to have those we hold dearest to our heart, in the end, throw it away.

After so many years of protecting Mary's dream of Specialty House of Creation, a successful company and home for spiritual seekers, he has made the decision to sell the property. In addition, the buyer made an offer to purchase his business as well. In 2007 he accepted the proposal. I wish I could say I'll miss being here when we leave – but I won't.

What a job! It's taken months, but everything is finally packed up. Today we move into the new home, and is it gorgeous. He purchased a fifteen acre working ranch overlooking a hayfield, complete with wildlife, herds of whitetail deer, wild turkeys, geese, horses, rabbits, birds and a woodpecker that never shuts up. This is a new beginning for both of us, almost too good to be true.

I live on one end of the house and Doug on the other. It never occurs to me that people continue to gossip about our relationship. If we're more than just friends, wouldn't I be the first to know? Come on. Whenever I put a question to Mary she didn't feel like answering, her reply was always the same, "That's for me to know and you to find out."

Suffice it to say, Doug and I are best friends with no strings attached. Although we never discuss my reason for being here, I cook, clean, do the laundry, look after his calendar, and serve him morning coffee. Of course. I also feed the many species of birds around here. If there's time left in the course of a day, I write and enjoy the solitude of country living.

Our new lifestyle seems natural. We both gave up our careers in show business for a spiritual life, and each of us came to Mary at a young age. We have volatile natures when provoked, although his temperament is usually quiet and soft-spoken, words rarely used to describe me. In truth, we've settled into the flow of an old relationship without giving it a thought.

In the past whenever a man asked me out I always refused, and with good reason. I paid my dues and then some, leaving in its wake a lack of interest, and too busy to entertain thoughts of them. The romantic dreams of a young woman vanished years ago; the Sperm Donor took care of that. Still, the gossip continues. One afternoon as I worked in the garden, Doug walked across the yard and said, "See that fellow standing by the driveway?"

Without looking up I answered, "What about him?"

He paused for a second, then smiled, "He thinks you and I are a couple."

I laughed, "Hope you set him straight. Did you?"

He just smiled and walked away. At the time I thought his remark a bit odd, but I quickly forgot.

About the same time I began writing this book, something miraculous happened that triggered a personal awakening, one sorely needed, and long overdue. Sleep was never a problem until I used a powerful drug prescribed in the treatment of cancer, that made me nauseous, and affected my ability to fall asleep. After weeks of no rest, I was advised to take a low dosage, five mg., of Valium at bedtime. I used it for no other purpose, and never during the day, but as time went on my body craved higher doses.

My New Life

Several years later, there were nights when I was too tired to stay awake, yet I couldn't fall asleep. All I could do was sit barefoot on the side of the bed and stare at the floor, until finally I reached over and took four Valiums out of the bottle. I wanted to take them, I needed them, but something stopped me from doing so. In that moment I realized my addiction, that whatever I took that night to ward off sleep deprivation, wouldn't be strong enough two weeks down the road; add to that, the dangerous side effects I was beginning to experience. I walked into the bathroom, flushed one month's supply and resolved never to take another, same as when I quit drinking and smoking so many years ago. I was determined to stop this habit the old fashioned way – I just stopped.

What happened afterwards was a mystery to me. The withdrawal from Valium quickly turned into an unexpected "coming to grips with" and facing all the negatives I had buried throughout my life. Some refer to such things as ghosts of the past. Not me. I prefer to call them repressed perceptions and feelings that reside deep within the subconscious of every human being, whether ignored or acknowledged. It was Mary Blakemore who taught the decision was mine as to what road I would take in life, and what type future I would carve out for myself.

In the months to come my personality changed at home. I was impossible to live with, negative, always finding fault, and viewed everything around me with jaundiced eyes – Doug in particular. Yet without him, I could never have survived this dark period; not just the crash withdrawals, but the negatives I had successfully buried over time. Resentment, hate, anger, guilt, jealousy, all came rushing to the fore. But in order to get rid of something, I first had to face it. I began to experience thoughts and feelings of someone who felt cheated out of life. As the days progressed, I grew more and more accusing until finally Doug put his arm around my shoulder, and confided that if I could find the strength to endure this ordeal, not just the withdrawals, but facing my personal demons, I would be free to experience all I ever wanted. The irony of it all was that to look at us we were the same as before; our daily life went on as usual. Not one of our friends had an inkling of the nightmare going on inside me, and in the totality of the experience, not even I knew. It was too real for me to be an objective bystander. My life had suddenly turned into a personal hell only Doug understood.

After six long hellish months locked in a prison of my own making, and struggling with personal issues I never wanted to face, a person I only dreamed of becoming finally emerged; one who could laugh and say "why not?" rather than mind's eternal lament "why me?" My life, most of which I had long forgotten, gradually unfolded throughout this experience, as did the voice in my first book. I stopped writing *about* a person I couldn't remember, to telling my story in the immediate first person as it happened every step of the way. *Tharon Ann* began as self-discovery, rather than a memoir to be read and shared with others.

It is a beautiful spring afternoon; not really different from yesterday, but certainly better than so many in my past that appeared more as winter. I am finding my way; no doubt why I feel so buoyant these days. It's strange to be in the twilight of my life, and feel more as a light-hearted, exurberant young girl looking forward to whatever lies ahead. My new life has begun to unfold without effort, leaving in its wake those yesterdays I no longer require. A part of me has gone up in smoke as I run to greet the one I began life with.

This afternoon, we'll drive to the architect's office to pick up blueprints that Doug commissioned for the development of a small community where Mary's group can live together in retirement, even grow our own food. Last night, he mentioned the possibility of a gift shop where our creative skills could be sold to supplement incomes.

I'm leery of this move.

He is the lamb. I am the tiger.

My New Life

Will you marry me?

If my life took a drastic turn for the better the day I met Mary Blakemore, the same may be said for that first morning Doug left the garage door open for me to come up and have coffee with him. Strange as it seems, I am experiencing a transformation of consciousness that changes moment by moment. Even though I enjoy my life, I still have the same loneliness of my birth – like a person starving to death, who stands outside a bakery window looking in. The baker is aware of my condition yet he won't open the door. I once mentioned this to Mary. She smiled and explained that my loneliness was the precursor to a spiritual awakening, and someday I would understand. Someday? Good Lord, how old do I have to be? If not for the company I keep, I wouldn't have lasted past thirty in this upside down world.

It is a balmy spring evening. Doug and I are sitting on the couch eating popcorn and watching television, when he abruptly stands up, looks at me and says, "I'm turning in. See you tomorrow."

I'm used to his ways and think nothing of it. I accept him the way he is, and why wouldn't I? He accepts all my idiosyncrasies. Truth is, I'm glad he's turning in early; now I can finally switch to a channel I like. Instead, I sit here just long enough to fall asleep and wake up for 3:00 a.m. meditation. I walk to the kitchen sink, splash cold water on my face, and don't bother to comb my hair or make a cup of coffee. No sooner do I sit down than I hear him call out my name, "Jennifer, will you come in here?"

Is he serious? It's three in the morning. He calls my name again, this time in a softer, less demanding voice, "Jennifer, will you please come here? It's important."

What can be so important at three in the morning? I try not to sound impatient, but he isn't sick and it *is* 3:00 a.m.

"Is it so urgent that ... " I stop before finishing the sentence to put on a sweater. Without waiting for him to call me a third time, I walk into his bedroom and notice he opened the bay window to let in fresh night air. He has a slight smile on his face as he leans forward in his chair ... yet he doesn't say a word. He just looks at me standing in the doorway, my hair disheveled, no make-up, the last of yesterday's mascara casting a shadow under my lower eyelashes, and still wearing the jogging pants and sweat shirt I fell asleep in. I venture to ask him again, "What Doug? What do you want?"

"Will you marry me?"

Did I hear him right? I'm so stunned by his proposal I can hardly speak. He's asking me to do what I vowed never to do again – marry. I finally answer him the only way I know, "Jennifer ... my name is Jennifer ... Jennifer, will you marry me."

My answer makes him laugh. Once again he repeats his proposal, "Jennifer ... will you marry me?"

"OK."

Hearing this, he raises his eyebrows, laughs and repeats my answer, "OK? Just OK?"

I know what he wants to hear. I reply nonchalantly, "Sure. OK, I will." For want of something, anything, to fill this unexpected moment, I ask, "Should I make coffee?"

Doug and I have been together for many lives, but here we are together again, picking up where we left off from some other time, some other place, paying off the last vestige of karma between us. As we sit in the kitchen having coffee in the wee hours before the sun comes up, he reaches across the table, brushes a strand of hair away from my face and says, "I wasn't sure what you would say."

We sit like this for the longest time, our relationship budding forth as effortlessly as night segues into the miracle of dawn.

We agree. It's out of the question for us to get married without first asking Baba Ji for his blessing. We call a Punjabi friend who agrees to broker a three-way international telephone call to India, and speak directly with Baba Ji to explain the nature of it all. Doug and I are in agreement that if he refuses to give his permission, we won't get married. Now all we can do is wait ... until the telephone rings.

At last, our three-way conversation between our translator in Burtonsville, Maryland, Baba Ji in Dera Tarn Taran, India and the two of us in Elmer, New Jersey is about to begin, our fate to be determined within seconds.

We immediately hear his wonderful gravelly voice on the other end of the line exclaim in English, "Yes! Yes! No permission needed. It is ordained by the Almighty that Mr. Doug and Miss Jennifer marry. Satisfy the laws of your country and marry in a civil ceremony. When I come to America, I'll perform your ring ceremony." However, Baba Ji's final remark to us is akin to catastrophic insurance in the event either of us gets cold feet. He knows both our mercurial natures, and adds, "If Mr. Doug and Miss Jennifer don't marry in this life, they will have to come back and take another birth in order to get married!"

Such is our destiny: in this life Mr. Doug and Miss Jennifer will be husband and wife.

Doug took care of the marriage license, along with arrangements for a minister to preside over a quiet ceremony in our home this afternoon. On the big day I'm wearing a white two-piece suit with gardenias in my hair and, this could only happen to me, rummaging in the laundry room for a safety pin. Doug on the other hand is calm, collected, and dressed in a sedate, navy pinstripe suit. He waits in the living room, and grows more and more impatient as I'm taking forever to get dressed. Truth is, I'm a bit discombobulated. Even though we've known each other a very long time, I suddenly feel like a sixteen year old girl who hardly knows what to do with herself, compounded by the fact that I can't find a safety pin to replace the button that just popped off my slacks, that, and my new high heels don't fit from going barefoot all the time, that, and sneezing every five minutes. Maybe I'm allergic to gardenias, otherwise why am I sneezing? I never sneeze.

Suddenly the doorbell rings. Still barefoot, I muffle a sneeze and open the laundry room door ever so slightly. For a few moments I quietly absorb the beauty of our home, now transformed into a wonderland of lights. While I was getting dressed, Doug placed candles everywhere, each one a stamp of approval for our marriage. Even this pales when compared to my groom who is talking to the minister. I've never seen him more handsome. No bride ever had a more beautiful husband than I have in him. Whatever jitters I had, have left by the same door they entered.

After we exhange simple gold wedding bands, the ceremony over and the minister gone, Doug takes both my hands in his, looks deep into my eyes and says, "Well, I guess we should be grateful we're not on respirators."

Such is our beginning – loving, laughing and moving in the new order of things. We are married on May 12, 2008. I am now Jennifer Brookins. Baba Ji will seal this union by performing our ring ceremony in a short while. Nothing else matters. In the weeks to come, we adapt to our new relationship like ducks to water. I loved him first as a friend, so in truth little has changed. Attitudes perhaps, the open expression of affection – maybe, but the ties that bind are deeper than I realized.

Something wonderful is in the air, not just the exterior of my life but within. Oh, the old me still has an acerbic retort when provoked. God only knows it's here, my silent companion who reminds me of the distance I still must travel on this path, but I'm happy. I'm content in my own skin. It's taken a lifetime for me to be able to say those three words without wincing: I like myself. Given my life experience, if this balanced state of mind can happen to someone as ordinary as me, it can happen to anyone.

On this special day, our ring ceremony is performed before many who have come once again for the privilege of receiving Baba Ji's darshan. We stand before him knowing that as he slips the wedding rings on our fingers, our destiny is being fulfilled with his blessing. Afterward as Baba Ji gives us prashad, he casually remarks to Doug, "You're two years late," making reference to an incident several years back when he asked one of his followers if Doug and I were married.

The fellow replied, "No, Baba Ji, they are not married."

Baba Ji replied, "They *are* married!"

Once again, the fellow replied, "No, Baba Ji, they are *not* married. They are just friends!"

Baba Ji countered, "They *are* married!" And before the poor fellow could reply again, Baba Ji dismissed any further discussion by saying, "Oh, what do you know."

This summer my dreams have come true during Baba Ji's visit. He is a guest in our home. After satsang, he rests on the back patio while his lunch is prepared. When I open the sliding glass door to offer him a glass of water, he looks up and motions for me to come outside. I don't want to intrude on his privacy, but he adamantly insists I join him. When I start to sit down on the chair in front of him, he holds out his arms to me. As I bend down to hug him, instead I find myself sitting on his lap while he pats my back as a father would a small child. Imagine.

This evening, many have come a long distance for the privilege of visiting with Baba Ji. After dinner, he walks into our living room, and sits down on the leather chair covered with a white cloth. For a few moments his eyes scan the room as he gives each of us darshan, and immediately puts everyone at ease. Afterward, he begins to answer each question put to him, and acknowledges the faces that belong to the same people who asked the same questions when he was here last. He forgets nothing and no one. He smiles patiently, and gives each one their due. Baba Ji seems to be enjoying himself when unexpectedly he removes a paper from his vest-pocket, and begins to read a poem. He speaks in English, and recites the lyrics to a shabd he wrote in celebration of our marriage. It's hard to believe we are the recipients of such attention.

All my misconceptions about love have vanished. I begin life anew.

Come to India

All my life, I dreamed of meeting God face to face, of sitting on his lap as would a small child. I dreamed of a God who would speak to me, and answer my questions; a loving God who cared equally for all his children, a God I had access to. How do we fall deeply in love? I am no authority on the subject, except to say it is a state of not knowing when it begins or where it ends. I have no say in matters of the heart.

I am beside myself with joy. Baba Ji has invited us to be his guests at Dera Tarn Taran, Punjab for his birthday celebration on December 26. Since I was a young girl I dreamed of traveling to India, yet I never had the opportunity. When I was thirty five years old, Mary promised to take me. So many years later her prophesy has come full circle, but little did I know how it would be fulfilled. Doug will take me to India in Mary's place. At long last I am going. I didn't realize until now, the Indian word "Dera" also means home.

I'll write about India, my travels, and of Baba Ji and his Dera.

I lay my body down upon a spring late in its arrival, somewhat frazzled from the wear and tear of life's journey. Yet on this beauteous day, I find myself unshackled from the languid thaw of wintry snow, and shadowy underworld of my yesterdays so devoid of nightingales. Now they do fly from my heart as readily as breathing. Barefoot did I come into this world, and barefoot am I now in this best of all seasons.

Epilogue

Mary E. Blakemore

Mary Blakemore led a householder's life before she was initiated in 1958 by Charan Singh Ji Maharaj of Dera Beas, India. She dedicated her life to this path of soul science, to helping others understand, that they are spiritual beings having a human experience, rather than human beings having a spiritual experience. Two weeks after her initiation into this mystic path, Charan Singh Ji advised her to immediately travel to Florida and give satsang to seventy five seekers who requested initiation. In her many years of service to him, Mary worked tirelessly, supported herself and helped others to find their way. Charan Singh Ji once said to her, "Mary is there anything you want? Is there anything you need?"

Mary responded, "The only thing I want, Maharaji, is that when I leave this world you will say, 'Well done, my good and faithful servant.'"

He replied, "Mary, that was said about you a long, long time ago."

For most of us, the path to God realization is a very long journey, but for Mary, it was simply a matter of lighting the wick. Over the years, a multitude of seekers found their way to these teachings through her. She was the conduit through which I was accepted for initiation by Maharaj Charan Singh Ji on November 24, 1968, and doubly blessed to be mentored by one of his greatest devotees for over thirty years. To this day, she remains an enigma ... a mystery, an object of controversy to those more interested in the political network of spirituality than its content.

Mary Blakemore extended her life by five years. She willingly took great suffering upon her own body to help clear away the burden of heavy karmas from those who found shelter in her company. She passed away on July 15, 1998 at the age of ninety two years.

Aunt Lowee

Aunt Lowee became a devoted follower of this same philosophy several years after I left Los Angeles. She loved to sit quietly in meditation, and continued to throw her "Annual Doll and Bear Tea Party" to the delight of friends and neighbors. At an advanced age, she became an iconic painter and continued to attend satsang regularly until she became too old to drive.

Barbara Loden

Barbara Loden won a Tony award in 1964 for her performance of Maggie, in the hit Broadway play *After the Fall.* She also wrote, produced, directed, edited and performed in the independent film, *Wanda,* which won The International Critics prize at the Venice Film Festival. She died of cancer in 1980 at the age of forty eight.

"Laughter is the Best Recipe"

Laughter is the Best Recipe by Doug Brookins, is a gourmet vegetarian cookbook extraordinaire which contains Mary Blakemore's unique vegetarian recipes along with short, anecdotal, true and humorous send ups, about many of those in her group. Each recipe is preceded by a singular story which makes for a fun and unusual book for the neophyte vegetarian cook.

Baba Kehar Singh Ji Maharaj

Radha Soami Dera Baba Bagga Singh is a spiritual community, located on Railway Road, District, Tarn Taran, Punjab, India. The present Patron, Baba Kehar Singh Ji Maharaj has built spiritual centers throughout India where he discourses on the teachings of Sant Mat. In addition, he travels extensively abroad, discoursing and blessing many with the gift of Initiation into the Mystic Path of Surat

Shabd Yoga. Dera Tarn Taran is a non-profit and charitable organization. Radha means, "Soul," and Soami means, "Lord" – Lord of the Soul.

Charan Singh Ji Maharaj

Charan Singh Ji Maharaj was the Patron of Radha Soami Satsang Beas, Dera Baba Jaimal Singh, District Amritsar, Punjab, India. He was succeeded by the current Patron, Baba Gurinder Singh Ji Maharaj, who travels throughout the world discoursing and blessing many with the gift of Initiation into the Mystic Path of Surat Shabd Yoga. As with Dera Tarn Taran, Dera Beas is also non-profit and charitable. Both Deras teach the same philosophy, but are independent of each other.

Acknowledgements

Doug Brookins

I could never have written this book without you.

Rome, Zola and William

It is my hope that you rediscover in this memoir, the remembrance of the many wonderful times you had growing up in the arms of a single mother who may have been tough, but always loving and always tried her best.

Apollo

Child of the universe and holder of more PhDs than any human being should acquire in a lifetime, in this your quintessential advanced age, I salute your cosmic intelligence for the many hours you spent lecturing me on my abnormal love of semicolons, topsy-turvy dyslectic grammar, and overall weird stream of consciousness style of writing. My dear, of course I listened to you. I just didn't do it. Go figure. A contrary mind is the hallmark of the aged.

Tess

I'm not using your real name and here's why: in the event, *Tharon Ann* gets trashed, we can still find work as short-order cooks in a vegetarian restaurant ... somewhere. It could happen. I thank you for your spartan endurance, and for reading this book many times through, front to back, until finally you voiced out loud (with two witnesses present) that you would rather commit yourself than have another go at it. You were always encouraging, even though once I became so frustrated, I chucked the manuscript out the window, its pages covering the hayfield out back.

Fina, Annette, and Denise, my favorite hair stylists at Hair Tech, in Bridgeton, NJ

Thanks for allowing me the privacy of sitting under the hair dryer for a simple wash and set for two hours straight, once a week, from beginning to end of this book. Now that we've moved, I do my own hair. Quite frankly, and you know I wouldn't say this if it wasn't the truth, it usually turns out looking like the fright-wig of Princeton. The owner should give each of you a big raise. You're the best!

The morning crew at Starbucks, in Somers Point, New Jersey

Thanks for letting me sit at the very back table, the one with a leg in dire need of repair, but with an excellent wall outlet to plug in my netbook. I sat in that spot for many weeks to wrap up the last two chapters of *Tharon Ann*. I'm sure you don't remember me, but I'm the ol' lady who nursed a single chia latte for 3 1/2 hours. Who knew.

The conductor on the train from Delhi to Amritsar

Thank you for allowing me to change seats after the armrest flew up, conked me on the head four times, and came close to knocking me

My New Life

unconscious attempting as I was, to begin the sequel for this book. Next trip around, I might just back-pack it from Delhi to Tarn Taran. Why not?

Just one more thing ...

When I began writing this book, I had no idea from chapter to chapter what was next, much less how it would end, as I had forgotten so much of my life in its subtle details. It began simply as an exercise to joggle remembrance; but as I plugged along memory began to express itself and I wrote ... an effort of four years plus to completion.

If you enjoyed reading Tharon Ann, and in some way relate to my journey, I would love to hear from you at *JenniferBrookins.com*.

Tharon Ann is self-published, and my responsibility to make known to the public. It is not enough to write the book, (although God only knows it should be) it must be marketed. It would be so helpful if you would please take a few minutes and post a review, and rating on *Amazon.com*. Also appreciated, if you would tell your friends about Tharon Ann, as well as share on social media. If you follow me *@JBrookinsAuthor on Twitter*, I'll follow you back – ditto *Facebook*.

Should you like to see *photographs* not shown in Tharon Ann, and read additional humorous stories about those of us in Mary's group in the early days, you will definitely enjoy reading *Laughter is the Best Recipe,* gourmet vegetarian recipes for the neophyte cook.

PS: The recipes are tasty and healthy!

Thanks so much,
Jennifer Brookins

Made in the USA
Middletown, DE
31 May 2015